ATLAS OF CHRISTIAN HISTORY

Atlas of Christian History

by Tim Dowley

Cartographer Nick Rowland FRGS

Fortress Press
Minneapolis

ATLAS OF CHRISTIAN HISTORY

Cover design: Alisha Lofgren

Library of Congress Cataloging-in-Publication Data
Print ISBN: 978-1-4514-9970-4
eBook ISBN: 978-1-5064-1688-5

The paper used in this publication meets the minimum
requirements of American National Standard for
Information Sciences — Permanence of Paper for
Printed Library Materials, ANSI Z329.48-1984.

Manufactured in China

16 17 18 19 20   9 8 7 6 5 4 3 2 1

Photograph acknowledgments
p. 16: © Alessandro 0770, Dreamstime.com
p. 28: © Tomas Marek, Dreamstime.com
p. 34: © Alexey Bykov, Dreamstime.com
p. 42: © Rsazonov, Dreamstime.com
p. 58: © Ancher, Dreamstime.com
p. 62: © Paul Prescott, Dreamstime.com
p. 64: © Mrplum, Dreamstime.com
p. 70: © Baucys, Dreamstime.com
p.86: © Hecke01, Dreamstime.com
p. 99: © Takahiro Sanui, Dreamstime.com
p. 114: © Byelikova, Dreamstime.com
p. 118: Tim Dowley Associates Ltd
p. 122: © Colin Young, Dreamstime.com
p. 126: © Ajay Bhaskar | Dreamstime.com
p. 130: © Lee Snider | Dreamstime.com
p. 140: © Kevin Duke | Dreamstime.com
p. 150: © Giuseppe Fucile | Dreamstime.com

What are all histories but God manifesting himself?

OLIVER CROMWELL (1599–1658)

Contents

List of maps

This atlas has been designed to examine the origins, beginnings, growth, and worldwide spread and development of Christianity. With such a vast subject, the selection of topics has been of necessity somewhat limited. However, it is hoped all major topics and geographical areas have received attention. The European Reformations have been relatively underemphasized as this atlas is a companion to the *Atlas of the European Reformations*, which gives extensive attention to this topic. An exhaustive chronology has also been included to provide a useful timeline against which to understand events and developments.

All research and writing has been undertaken by Dr Tim Dowley. The cartography is the work of Cambridge-based Nick Rowland. Page layout and design has been carried out by Trevor Bounford of Bounford.com, while the index and gazetteer have been compiled by Christopher Pipe of Watermark. The academic consultant is Dr Aaron Denlinger, Professor of Church History and Historical Theology at Reformation Bible College in Sanford, Florida.

Dulwich, December 2015

Nearly 2,000 years ago, Jesus of Nazareth was put to death on a cross in an obscure corner of the Roman Empire. Today, the worldwide Christian faith has grown as never before, particularly in Africa, South-East Asia, and South America.

Christianity rapidly spread beyond its original geographical region of Roman-occupied Palestine to the entire Mediterranean area, as described in the Acts of the Apostles in the New Testament. Three centres of the Christian church rapidly emerged in the eastern Mediterranean. The church became a significant presence in its original heartlands, with Jerusalem a leading centre. Asia Minor (modern Turkey) was already an important area of Christian expansion, which continued, with the great imperial city of Constantinople (modern Istanbul) becoming a particularly influential centre. Further growth took place in the south, with the Egyptian city of Alexandria emerging as a Christian stronghold.

With this expansion, significant debates opened up. While the New Testament deals with the relationship between Christianity and Judaism, the expansion of Christianity into Greek-speaking regions led to discussions about how Christianity related to Greek philosophy. Christian writers tried to demonstrate, for example, that Christianity fulfilled the great themes of Plato's philosophy.

Early Christian expansion also faced obstacles. The 'imperial cult' – which saw worship of the Roman emperor as a test of loyalty to the empire – was strong in the eastern Mediterranean, and many Christians were penalized for worshipping only Christ. The expansion of Christianity regularly triggered off persecutions – for example, the Decian persecution of 249–51, which was particularly vicious in North Africa.

State religion

Christianity was given official recognition by the Roman state in 313, by the Emperor Constantine, and soon after became the official religion of the Roman Empire. This period of Christian history was marked by controversies over the identity of Jesus Christ and the Christian doctrine of God. A series of councils attempted to resolve these differences, and ensure the unity of the Christian church within the Empire. The most important of these was the Council of Chalcedon (451), which set out the Christian interpretation of the identity of Jesus as 'true God and true man'.

The fall of the Roman Empire – traditionally dated to 476 – led to widespread insecurity within the Western Church. In the East, the church continued to flourish, as the Eastern Empire, based at Constantinople, was largely unaffected by the attacks from northern European invaders that eventually terminated Roman power in the West. The removal of Rome as a stabilizing influence gave a new role to the church in the West – particularly to its monasteries. The founding of the first Benedictine monastery at Monte Cassino c. 525 is a landmark in this process. The increasingly important political role of the pope also began to emerge during this period.

The major disruptions within the Roman Empire in the 5th century led to a growing rift between the Western and Eastern Churches. Increasing tension over political as much as theological issues led to the Great Schism of 1054, by which date the Eastern Church had extended its influence as far north as Moscow.

Middle Ages

In Western Europe, Christianity underwent a major renewal between 1000 and 1500 – the 'Middle Ages'. The political and social influence of the church was consolidated, and the personal authority of the pope to intervene in political disputes reached new heights.

Theological thinking known as 'scholasticism' developed, with 13th-century writers such as Thomas Aquinas and Duns Scotus achieving great theological sophistication. But Scholasticism came to be increasingly questioned. From the 14th century, the European Renaissance stressed the importance of returning to the roots of Christendom. The linked humanist movement believed it was essential to study Scripture in its original languages, creating pressure for new Bible translations.

The rise of Islam in the 7th century had a major negative impact on Christianity in North Africa and the Middle East, and seemed about to expand yet further in 1453, when Muslim armies captured Constantinople. By the early 16th century, Islam was poised to enter Austria – though military defeats in fact limited its influence to the Balkans.

Reformations

The 16th century saw major upheavals within Western Christianity – the European Reformations. Alarmed at what they saw as the disparity between apostolic and medieval visions of Christianity, men such as Martin Luther and Huldrych Zwingli pressed for reform. Although the need for reform was widely conceded within the church, reforming communities now appeared outside the mainline church. By the time of John Calvin and his reformation of Geneva, Protestantism had emerged as a distinct type of Christianity, posing a major threat to the Roman Catholic Church.

In the late 1540s, the Catholic Church itself commenced a major process of reformation and renewal, often known as the 'Catholic Reformation' – formerly the 'Counter-Reformation'. The discovery of the Americas led to new interest in spreading the gospel abroad. The Society of Jesus, the 'Jesuits', founded by Ignatius Loyola in 1540, took the lead within the Catholic Church, sending missionaries to the Americas, India, China, and Japan. Christianity also expanded through substantial emigration from Europe to North America, beginning in the late 16th century.

In the 18th century Evangelical Revivals that started in Germany spread to Britain and North America, partly in reaction to the speculation of Deism, and to the deadness of Protestant orthodoxy. John Wesley, George Whitefield, and Jonathan Edwards were leaders in this movement, the repercussions of which were eventually felt throughout the world.

Growing hostility towards the church in France contributed to causes of the French Revolution (1789) and to a new spirit of anti-clericalism. The French Revolution saw Christianity temporarily displaced from French society, and revolutionary movements throughout Europe sought to repeat the success of their French counterparts, creating serious difficulties for the Catholic Church, especially in Italy.

Missions

There was a surge of Protestant missionary activity from Britain during the last years of the 18th century. The Baptist Missionary Society, London Missionary Society, and Church Missionary Society all played major roles in planting Christianity in Africa, India, and Oceania. American missionary societies also established Christianity in several regions of the world, notably Korea.

The churches of late 19th-century Europe and the United States encountered new problems caused by the Industrial Revolution, particularly the rapid rise in the numbers of workers in the newly industrialized cities of Britain, France, and Germany.

The publication of Charles Darwin's landmark works divided Christians between those who accepted his views and those who rejected them. Geology, and the wider application of scientific methods to society, also created new tensions. During the 1840s, the German philosopher Ludwig Feuerbach (1804–72) argued that the idea of God was merely a projection of the human mind.

20th Century

At the turn of the 20th century, many Christians believed the kingdom of God – or at least a better world – was at hand. Two world wars, and 50 years' fearing a third one, buried all hopes of human perfectibility. The Russian Revolution (1917) led to the world's first atheist state, while dictatorships in Italy, Germany, and Russia challenged Christianity in the inter-war period.

World War II had a devastating impact upon Christianity, with the intentional direction of war against civilians, and the indifference of most leaders in the Christian West to the sufferings of the Jews. The defeat of Nazi Germany in 1945 led to Eastern Europe coming under Soviet influence, and the state adoption of anti-religious policies. After the fall of the Berlin Wall (1989), Christianity experienced a renaissance in these countries.

The Pentecostal movement, begun in 1901 in the USA, held that Christians could experience the supernatural power displayed by the apostles, and spread rapidly worldwide, becoming the fastest growing Christian movement. It was particularly popular in the Third World, notably in Latin America and among the African Independent churches. Today Christianity is primarily a faith of the developing – rather than developed – world.

Part 1

The Early Christians

It is incredible to see the ardour with which the people of that religion help each other in their wants. They spare nothing. Their first legislator has put into their hearts that they are all brethren

LUCIAN (AD 125–180),
ON THE EARLY CHRISTIANS

The Mission of the Twelve

There are many – not necessarily reliable – traditions and legends about the missions of the twelve apostles, who travelled widely carrying the message of the risen Christ, suffering and often meeting violent deaths for their faith. One story claims that the apostles cast lots to decide who should go where.

Peter is variously said to have preached in Antioch, Pontus, Galatia, Cappadocia, and Rome; his brother Andrew to have preached to the Scythians (modern Georgia) and Thracians (modern Bulgaria), evangelized Byzantium, and to have been crucified at Patrae, Achaia (Greece). 'Doubting' Thomas Didymus supposedly preached to the Parthians, Medes, Persians, Hyrcanians, Bactrians, and Margians, and even reached India, where the Mar Thoma Christians regard him as their founder. Philip – though arguably Philip the Evangelist (see Acts 8), not the Apostle – possibly preached in Carthage, North Africa, and Phrygia (modern Turkey).

Matthew – 'Levi' – is said to have written his gospel in Antioch, and preached in Persia, Parthia, and Ethiopia. Bartholomew – also known as Nathanael – apparently journeyed to India with Thomas, taking Matthew's Gospel, as well as to Armenia, Ethiopia, and Southern Arabia. James, son of Alphaeus, may have evangelized in Syria; while Simon the Zealot is said to have preached in Persia. James, son of Zebedee, preached in Judea – and, according to legend, in Spain. His brother John was banished to the Aegean island of Patmos, and alone of the Twelve is said to have died a natural death, in Ephesus. (An early tradition has it that he escaped unharmed after having been thrown into boiling oil in Rome.) Judas – also called Lebbaeus and Thaddaeus – preached in Edessa, Armenia, and Mesopotamia, and died at Berytus. Matthias – chosen by lot to replace Judas Iscariot – according to tradition travelled to Syria with Andrew.

THE APOSTLES AND TRADITION

NORTH SEA

BRITAIN
Glastonbury

ATLANTIC OCEAN

Joseph of Arimathea
One tradition has Joseph visiting Glastonbury, England

Paul believed to have been beheaded. Peter believed to have been crucified upside

James the Greater

Rome

Luke

SPAIN

MEDITER

AFRICA

map 1

Extent of Roman Empire c. AD 117

Miles
0   250   500   750

Kilometers
0   250   500   750

RUSSIA

Philip
Supposed to have been cruelly
killed by Roman proconsul in
Asia Minor

Andrew

SCYTHIA

Bartholomew
Various traditions
about his death

w believed to
een crucified

BLACK SEA

CASPIAN SEA

MACEDONIA

**Derbent
(Albanopolis)**

PHRYGIA

CAPPADOCIA

ARMENIA

Smyrna

Hierapolis

Jude

Matthias

ae

GREECE

ASIA MINOR

Philip

ISLAND OF PATMOS

SYRIA

Bartholomew

Thaddeus (Lebaeus)

PARTHIA

Ephesus

N   SEA

Jerusalem

Simon the Zealot
Tradition says he was
killed in Persia for refusing
to sacrifice to the sun god

ASSYRIA

Matthias
(who replaced Judas Iscariot)
Said to have been
burned to death
in Syria or Armenia

PERSIA

John
d of old age after
exiled to the island
Patmos during
ersecution of the
peror Domitian

EGYPT

Mark

RED SEA

INDIA

Jerusalem
es, brother of **John** executed
y Herod Agrippa c. 44 AD

Thomas
Said to have been killed
when pierced by the spears
of four soldiers

INDIAN OCEAN

Near Jerusalem
James, the brother of Jesus.
Josephus claimed he was stoned
then clubbed to death c. 70 AD

Matthew
Some traditions claim
he was stabbed to death
in Ethiopia

ETHIOPIA

Thomas

MALABAR COAST

Madras

The Christian faith began in Palestine, regarded by the Jews as their 'Promised Land', but ruled by foreign powers for much of its history because of its favourable strategic location. Egypt and Assyria had fought over it for centuries, then Babylon conquered Assyria, and with it Palestine. The Persians allowed some Jews to return from exile to Palestine, before the Greeks under Alexander the Great conquered the land around 300 BC. There followed rule by the Seleucid dynasty and semi-autonomy under the Hasmonean dynasty before Rome captured Jerusalem in 63 BC. Palestine remained under Roman rule at the time of the birth of Jesus.

First century Judaism

Jesus, the apostles, and the earliest converts to Christianity were all Jews, and their teachings were presented in a Jewish context. The Judaism of Jesus' time was characterized by strict monotheism, a gradual shift from temple ritual to an emphasis on personal ethics, restlessness under foreign occupation and oppression, a strong sense of community, and widespread expectation of a coming messiah.

By the time of Christ, several different Jewish groups had formed holding varying views on religious authority, theology, and the Roman occupation. They included a conservative elite called Sadducees ('righteous ones'), the pious Pharisees ('separated ones'), the ascetic Essene sect of Qumran, and revolutionary Zealots.

The Christian faith entered a world of great religious diversity. First-century Roman Palestine featured not only Judaism, but also the political religion of the Roman state, the Roman imperial cult, the personal religion of the mystery cults, and various schools of Greek philosophy.

Christianity spreads

After his death, Jesus' followers in Jerusalem formed a community of believers that soon spread, first to Samaria, then to Phoenicia, Gaza, and Egypt, and later to the Syrian cities of Antioch and Damascus, and to Cyprus, as the message was carried by itinerant preachers and missionaries. At first all believers were Jews, but they were soon joined by Gentiles; they were called variously followers of 'the Way', 'Christians', and 'Nazarenes'.

In AD 62 the death of James, leader of the Jerusalem believers, led some to leave the city, weakening its Jewish Christian community. During the First Jewish-Roman War (or Great Revolt, AD 66–73), Rome destroyed Herod's Temple and sacked Jerusalem. According to the Romano-Jewish historian Josephus (ad 37–100), most inhabitants were killed, committed suicide, or fled. The destruction of the Temple ended the priesthood and sacrifice system, and was a lasting catastrophe for Judaism.

The Christian community may have left Jerusalem just before the siege, taking refuge at Pella, beyond the Jordan, though some believers later returned. Christian communities founded by the apostles near the Mediterranean coast survived, as did those at Capernaum and Rimmon, in Galilee, and Cochaba, in Gaulanitis.

After the failure of the Bar Kokhba Revolt (or Second Jewish Revolt, AD 132–35), the highest Jewish court, Sanhedrin, moved to Jamnia (Javneh), Galilee. Many Jews were killed, expelled, or sold into slavery after the two rebellions against Rome; this, combined with the conversion of pagans, Samaritans, and Jews, gradually resulted in a Christian majority in Palestine.

Christianity separated from Judaism gradually over several generations, the destruction of the Temple and disaster of the two Jewish Wars accelerating this mutual estrangement.

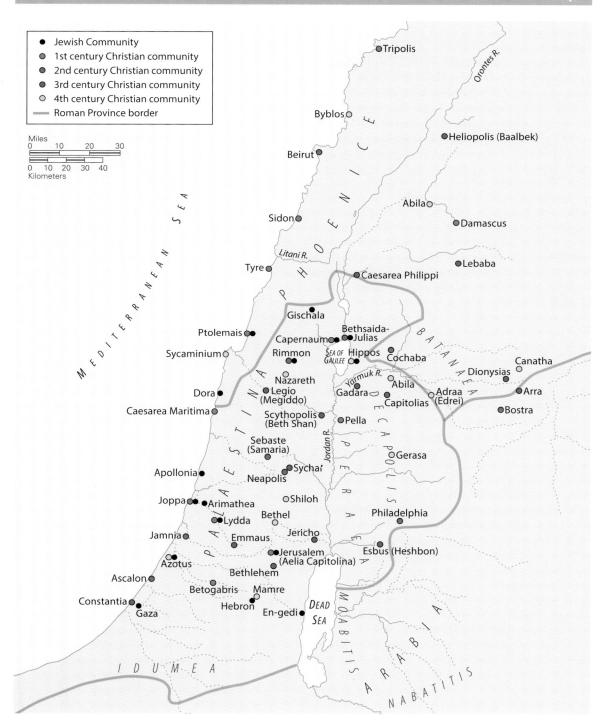

Legend:
- Jewish Community
- 1st century Christian community
- 2nd century Christian community
- 3rd century Christian community
- 4th century Christian community
- Roman Province border

Miles
0   10   20   30

0   10   20   30   40
Kilometers

MEDITERRANEAN SEA

PHOENICE

Orontes R.

Tripolis

Byblos

Heliopolis (Baalbek)

Beirut

Abila

Damascus

Sidon

Litani R.

Lebaba

Tyre

Caesarea Philippi

BATANAEA

Gischala

Bethsaida-Julias

Ptolemais

Capernaum

Rimmon

SEA OF GALILEE

Hippos

Cochaba

Canatha

Sycaminium

Nazareth

Yarmuk R.

Abila

Dionysias

Dora

Legio (Megiddo)

Gadara

Capitolias

Adraa (Edrei)

Arra

Caesarea Maritima

Scythopolis (Beth Shan)

Pella

Bostra

Jordan R.

P

Sebaste (Samaria)

E

DECAPOLIS

R

Apollonia

Sychar

Gerasa

Joppa

Neapolis

E

Arimathea

Shiloh

A

Lydda

Bethel

Philadelphia

Jamnia

Emmaus

Jericho

PALESTINA

Jerusalem (Aelia Capitolina)

Esbus (Heshbon)

Azotus

Bethlehem

Ascalon

Betogabris

Mamre

Constantia

Hebron

En-gedi

Gaza

DEAD SEA

MOABITIS

IDUMEA

ARABIA

NABATITIS

Paul and his fellow Jewish apostles carried the Christian message to regions beyond Palestine. With the express purpose of evangelizing Gentiles, they travelled extensively in Asia Minor and Greece, visiting synagogues in the Jewish Diaspora – where their teaching often provoked opposition – but also speaking with Gentiles in the marketplaces. They left behind small, uncertain groups of Jewish and Gentile Christians whose faith was built up by subsequent visits and by letters such as those we know in the New Testament.

By the end of the first century, Christianity was still confined virtually to the eastern Roman Empire, possibly concentrated in Asia Minor – where Jewish communities were long established and had created around them many semi-proselytized 'God-fearing' Gentiles. There were also believing communities in Italy in Rome itself, Puteoli, around the Bay of Naples, and possibly also in Spain. The only church known outside the Empire was at Edessa, beyond the River Euphrates.

Names of towns and cities with Christians are given in the New Testament – for instance the seven churches of Revelation chapters 1–3 – and in contemporary correspondence. The Christian Father Ignatius of Antioch (c. AD 35/50–98/117) writes of churches at Magnesia and Tralles, and later writers mention Alexandria, home of one of Paul's several helpers, Apollos.

The first significant persecution of Christians, under the Emperor Nero (r. 54–68), was short-lived and concentrated in Rome but did not hinder the growth of the church.

DISTRIBUTION OF CHRISTIANITY BY AD 100

Tergeste
Po R.
Ravenna
Genoa
ILL (DA
ADRIATIC SEA
CORSICA
ITALIA
Rome
Puteoli
SARDINIA
Pompeii
TYRRHENIAN SEA
SICILIA
M E D I T E
Carthage
MALTA Melite
TRIPOLITANIA

- ● City with Christian community by AD 100
- ● City with large Jewish community
- ▨ Areas with Jewish communities
- — Border of Roman Empire
- *MYSIA* Roman province or region

map 3

DACIA

sa

M
A)

MOESIA

Serdica

Danube R.

BOSPORUS

BLACK SEA

MACEDONIA

THRACE

Thessalonica

Philippi

Beroea

Apollonia

Byzantium

BITHYNIA AND PONTUS

Amisus

Prusa

Ancyra

Halys R.

Nicopolis

MYSIA

Troas

PHRYGIA

CAPPADOCIA

ACHAIA

AEGEAN
SEA

Pergamum

Thyatira

Sardis

Smyrna

Philadelphia

ISLAND
OF PATMOS

Ephesus

Laodicea

Antioch
in Pisidia

GALATIA

Lake
Tuz

Caesarea
Mazaca

Athens

Hierapolis

Iconium

Corinth
Cenchrea

Magnesia

Tralles

Colosse

Lystra

Aegina

Miletus

Derbe

CILICIA

Edessa

Attalia

Perge

Tarsus

Euphrates R.

Myra

Seleucia

Antioch

CRETA

SYRIA

A

N

E

A

N

S

E

A

Salamis

Paphos

Tripolis

Damascus

Sidon

Tyre

Ptolemais

Capernaum

Cyrene

Caesarea

Pella

Joppa

Samaria

Berenice

Lydda

Jerusalem

CYRENAICA

Alexandria

Pelusium

Gaza

NABATEA

Memphis

Babylon

AEGYPTUS

Nile R.

Miles
0   100   200
0   100   200 300
Kilometers

The second century, particularly the period following the Bar Kokhba revolt, saw a decisive split between Christianity and Judaism. The destruction of Jerusalem and its Temple, the exile of the Jews from Judea after the revolt, and the appointment of a Gentile – Mark (or Mahalia) – rather than a Jew as Bishop of Jerusalem all helped widen the breach. By this time the majority of Christians were of Gentile origin.

During the second century Christian communities spread west and north, as far as Gaul and Germany. Also many groups were established in North Africa, laying the foundations for a strong church there in the third century. In Egypt, Christianity began to extend beyond the great city of Alexandria into surrounding rural areas. Further Christian communities were founded in Mesopotamia, and in Asia Minor the church spread both north and east.

Christians were largely left in peace, unmolested by the authorities, during the period of the Antonine emperors – Nerva, Trajan, Hadrian, Antoninus Pius, Marcus Aurelius, Lucius Verus, and Commodus (AD 96 –192) – which greatly helped the growth of Christianity throughout the empire.

By the end of the third century the complexion of the Christian world looked quite different. With the westward expansion of the church, as far as Roman Britain, Rome – as well as Alexandria and Antioch – had become an important centre.

DISTRIBUTION OF CHRISTIANITY BY AD 300

NOR SE

BRITANNIA

BE

Durocorto

ATLANTIC OCEAN

GALL

177: Centre of Christian persecution

Burdigala

AQUITA

HISPANIA

Toletum

Cordoba

Hispalis

BAETICA

Elvira

Malaca

Tingitanum

Tipa

MAURETANIA

Miles
0 100 200 300 400 500

0 100 300 500 700
Kilometers

map 4

- Town/city with Christian community by AD 300
- Strong Christian community by AD 300
- Border of Roman Empire in AD 300
- *MYSIA* Roman province or region

Colonia Agrippina

Rhine R.

GERMANIA INFERIOR

usta
orum

Danube R.

Lauriacum

Carnuntum

RAETIA

NORICUM

astodunum

Aguntum

PANNONIA

312: Edict of Milan
grants religious
freedom

Poetovio

dunum

Aquileia

nna

Mediolanum
(Milan)

Mursa

Singidunum

DACIA

ITALIA

ARBONENSIS

Salonae

DALMATIA

ssilia

MOESIA

BLACK SEA

Rome

MACEDONIA

THRACIA

Chalcedon

Sinope

Puteoli

Philippi

Byzantium
(Constantinople)

303: Great Persecution
launched here

BITHYNIA

Amisus

Neocaesarea

Neapolis

Thessalonica

Nicomedia

PONTUS

ARMENIA

Carales

Beroea

Troas

MYSIA

Nicaea

Ancyra

GALATIA

Nyssa

Caesarea

MEDITERRANEAN

Nicopolis

Assos

Pergamum

ASIA

LYCAONIA

CAPPADOCIA

Melitene

303-12:
ns severely
ecuted

Chalcis

Athens

Sardes

Smyrna

Philadelphia

Antioch

Nazianzus

Samosata

Carthage

Corinth

Ephesus

Laodicea

Lystra

Iconium

CILICIA

Edessa

SICILIA

Cenchrea

Miletus

Derbe

Tarsus

Rhegium

Cirta

Sicca
Veneraria

Syracuse

Perga

Myra

Salamis

Antioch

Palmyra

Thagaste

RHODES

Dura Europos

3-12:
ns severely
ecuted

CRETA

Gortyna

CYPRUS

Emesa

SYRIA

Sidon

Damascus

Cyrene

250, 311: Centre of
Christian persecutions

Caesarea

Pella

Leptis Magna

Berenice

CYRENAICA

Alexandria

Joppa

Sebaste

Lydda

Jerusalem

Azotus

Bethlehem

by 300: Possibly 50% of
population Christian

Memphis

AEGYPTUS

ARABIA

LIBYA

FRICA

Oxyrhyncus

Hermopolis

Nile R.

*RED
SEA*

Nag Hammadi

Constantine the Great

In AD 312 Constantine the Great (274–337) won the decisive battle of the Milvian Bridge, outside Rome, having invoked the 'God of the Christians' and having put the new Christian '*chi-rho*' symbol on his shield. This victory put him on a path to supreme power.

The Empire was collapsing: despotism, endless wars, and civil strife had already destroyed its traditional values. For at least a century the emperors had been either rough barbarians or corrupt tyrants, sustained by the legions. As the political, economic, and military situation deteriorated, invasions by barbarian tribes from both the north and east became increasingly successful.

Between 306 and 323 Constantine strove to halt this decline and to rally Christian support in his struggle for power. Although still tolerant of the old faiths, his grant of toleration for Christianity at Milan in 313 inaugurated a new era for the long-persecuted Christians, who were now for the first time allowed to worship in public and to build churches. When Constantine moved his capital to Byzantium – renaming it Constantinople – he even erected a number of new churches at public expense.

Despite Constantine's hope that Christianity would serve as an integrating force, theological disputes continued to divide. One important split was that by the Donatists in Carthage, stubbornly standing for ritual holiness and total separation of church and state, which caused a major Christian schism.

NOR
SE

BRITANNIA

Londinium

ATLANTIC
OCEAN

GAL

314: Constant
Council of /
mainly to ac
Donatist sc

HISPANIA
Toletum

+ Cordoba

MAURETANIA

Miles
0   100   200   300   400   500

0   100   300   500   700
Kilometers

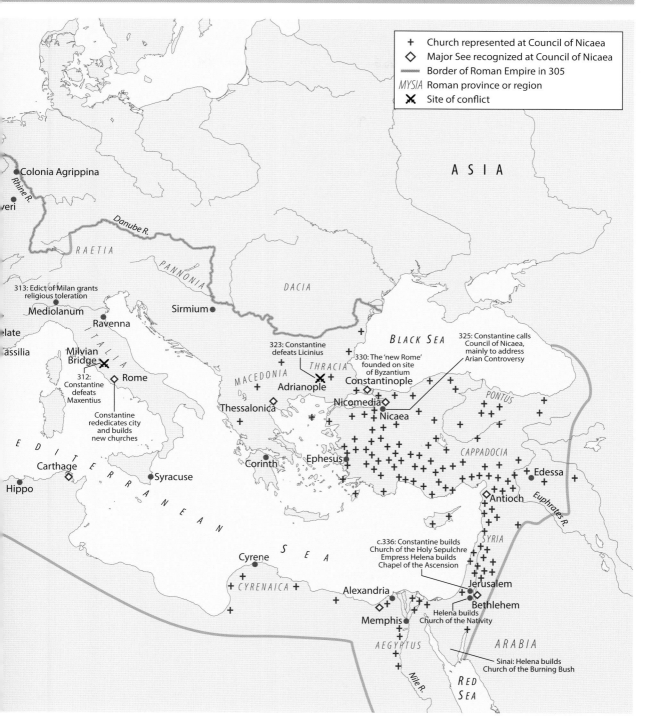

Legend:
- ✚ Church represented at Council of Nicaea
- ◇ Major See recognized at Council of Nicaea
- ▬ Border of Roman Empire in 305
- *MYSIA* Roman province or region
- ✖ Site of conflict

A S I A

Colonia Agrippina

Rhine R.

...veri

Danube R.

RAETIA

PANNONIA

DACIA

313: Edict of Milan grants
religious toleration

Mediolanum

Sirmium

...late

Ravenna

...ssilia

BLACK SEA

325: Constantine calls
Council of Nicaea,
mainly to address
Arian Controversy

Milvian
Bridge ✖

ITALIA

◇ Rome

312:
Constantine
defeats
Maxentius

Constantine
rededicates city
and builds
new churches

323: Constantine
defeats Licinius

330: The 'new Rome'
founded on site
of Byzantium

MACEDONIA

THRACIA

Adrianople

Constantinople

Thessalonica ◇

Nicomedia

PONTUS

Nicaea ◇

*M
E
D
I
T
E
R
R
A
N
E
A
N*

Corinth

Ephesus

CAPPADOCIA

Carthage ◇

Syracuse

Edessa ●

Euphrates R.

Hippo ●

Antioch ◇

S E A

*c.336: Constantine builds
Church of the Holy Sepulchre
Empress Helena builds
Chapel of the Ascension*

SYRIA

Cyrene ●

✚ *CYRENAICA* ✚

Alexandria

Jerusalem ◇

Bethlehem ●

Helena builds
Church of the Nativity

Memphis ◇

ARABIA

AEGYPTUS

Sinai: Helena builds
Church of the Burning Bush

Nile R.

*RED
SEA*

Part 2

The Church under Siege

The church, by its connection
with Christian princes,
gained in power and riches,
but lost in virtues.

JEROME (347–420)

MAXIMIANVS.

The Arian Challenge

Around 318 a particularly divisive dispute flared between Arius (c. 250–c. 336), a presbyter in Alexandria, and the Patriarch Alexander (r. 313–26). Arius was teaching that, if the Son of God had been crucified, he suffered – as the supreme deity cannot do. He argued that Jesus Christ was therefore not eternal, but made by the Father to do his creative work. By dividing off the Son from God the Father, Arius undermined Christ's status as God's revelation and as the saviour of humankind.

The controversy led Constantine to call a major synod of several hundred bishops to Nicaea, Asia Minor, in 325, including representatives of many Greek provinces, but also two presbyters representing Si(y)lvester, Bishop of Rome (r. 314–35). The Emperor Constantine presided in person at the opening session of this First Council of Nicaea, the earliest worldwide ('ecumenical') council. Its agreed creed rejected Arius' hypotheses and affirmed that Son and Father are 'of one substance' (*homoousios*, consubstantial).

Arguments over this wording led to fifty years' further controversy. While Western bishops largely upheld Nicea, confident that the creed maintained the Son's equality with the Father while maintaining a proper distinction between persons, many Eastern bishops worried that it collapsed Father and Son together into a single entity (modalism). Athanasius, Bishop of Alexandria (r. 328 –73), was chief theological champion of what finally became orthodox teaching on the deity of God the Son, as defined in the Creed of Nicaea, revised at the Council of Constantinople (381), and decreed by the Emperor Theodosius I (r. 378–95). This marked the end of Arianism within the Empire. But the barbarian Gothic, Visigothic, Frankish, and Vandal kingdoms all adopted Arianism in opposition to Rome and Constantinople.

THE SPREAD OF ARIANISM

NOR
S

British/Irish monk Pelagius opposes teachings of Augustine in Africa; 417 excommunicated

Seine R.

ATLANTIC OCEAN

▲ Burdigala

Ebro R.

Carthago Nova ▲

Miles
0   100   200   300   400   500
0 100   300   500   700
Kilometers

map 6

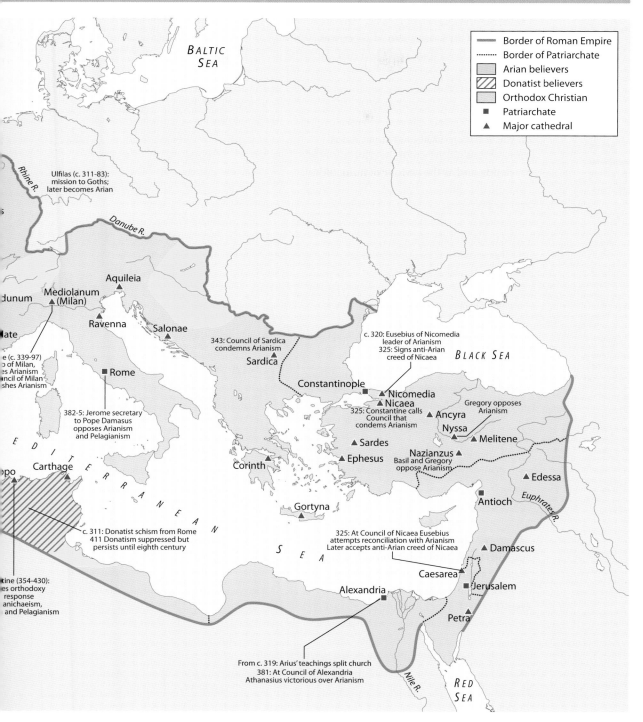

BALTIC SEA

Rhine R.

Ulfilas (c. 311-83): mission to Goths; later becomes Arian

Danube R.

Aquileia

Mediolanum (Milan)

...dunum

Ravenna

...late

Salonae

343: Council of Sardica condemns Arianism

c. 320: Eusebius of Nicomedia leader of Arianism
325: Signs anti-Arian creed of Nicaea

BLACK SEA

...e (c. 339-97)
...o of Milan,
...es Arianism
...ncil of Milan
...shes Arianism

Sardica

Constantinople

Nicomedia

Rome

Nicaea

Gregory opposes Arianism

382-5: Jerome secretary to Pope Damasus opposes Arianism and Pelagianism

325: Constantine calls Council that condems Arianism

Ancyra

Nyssa

Melitene

M E D I T E R R A N E A N

Sardes

Nazianzus

...po

Carthage

Ephesus

Corinth

Basil and Gregory oppose Arianism

Edessa

Euphrates R.

Antioch

c. 311: Donatist schism from Rome
411 Donatism suppressed but persists until eighth century

Gortyna

325: At Council of Nicaea Eusebius attempts reconciliation with Arianism
Later accepts anti-Arian creed of Nicaea

Damascus

...tine (354-430):
...es orthodoxy
...response
...anichaeism,
...and Pelagianism

S E A

Caesarea

Jerusalem

Alexandria

Petra

From c. 319: Arius' teachings split church
381: At Council of Alexandria Athanasius victorious over Arianism

Nile R.

RED SEA

Legend:
— Border of Roman Empire
···· Border of Patriarchate
▨ Arian believers
▧ Donatist believers
▨ Orthodox Christian
■ Patriarchate
▲ Major cathedral

THE ARIAN CHALLENGE   31

Monophysite Christianity

From the outset, Christians were people with certain beliefs – especially about Jesus Christ – seen as fundamental to the existence of the church. The fourth, fifth, and sixth centuries were marked by lengthy controversies – particularly in the Eastern Church – about how Christ, the Son of God, was himself God (the doctrine of the Trinity); and how he was both man and God (the doctrine of the person of Christ, or Christology).

This was a period of great importance in the formation of orthodox Christian theology. Deliberations in councils were often influenced by power struggles between the Bishop of Rome and the Emperor, by the rival claims of the five major patriarchates, and by the need of the imperial administration to maintain unity against the threats of the Persian Empire, the empire of Attila, and the barbarian kingdoms pressing in from the north.

This was an age of domination by emperors, of abrasive personalities, and of rancorous conflict between leading bishops. Technical terms with no biblical origin were made key words in statements of belief. Usage of such words contributed to misunderstandings and misrepresentations between the Latin-speaking West and the Greek-speaking East – and even between different sections within the Greek Church. Such disputes contributed to major divisions in the Christian world.

Numerous councils of bishops were held during this period. Four of the most important – Nicaea (325), Constantinople (381), Ephesus (431), and Chalcedon (451) – came to be regarded as ecumenical councils, binding on the whole church, although some parts of the Eastern church rejected decisions made at Ephesus and/or Chalcedon.

Nestorius

While the fourth century church often dealt with questions about the Trinity (in the Arian debates), in the fifth century disputes erupted over equally difficult questions about the nature of Christ. How could Christ be both human and divine, without the divine swallowing up the human? A theologian named Nestorius (d. c. 451) arguably attributed distinct personhood to each nature; while the third ecumenical council, in Ephesus, maintained the integrity of each nature and the singularity of Christ's person.

In AD 449 a theologian named Eutyches (c. 380–c. 456) was teaching that before the incarnation Christ had two natures; after the incarnation, the divine swallowed up the human, so that there was only one nature. Such a view gained support at a further church council at Ephesus in the same year, a gathering that Pope Leo I (r. 440–61) denounced as a 'synod of robbers' (*latrocinium*).

Chalcedon

The fourth ecumenical council, at Chalcedon (451), brought together more bishops than any previous synod – roughly 600, almost all from the Eastern half of the Empire. This council succeeded in resolving the Christological controversy among many of the Greek and Latin congregations with a formula still widely accepted among Orthodox, Roman Catholic, and Protestant churches. The (mainly Greek) bishops endorsed Leo's position: that Christ is one person with two natures – one human, one divine – each distinct, but both united in the one person. The crucial words are (in translation): 'one and the same... Son, Lord, Only-begotten, to be acknowledged in two natures without confusion, without change, without division, or without separation'. This creed was as important for the views it rejected as heretical (for instance Adoptionist,

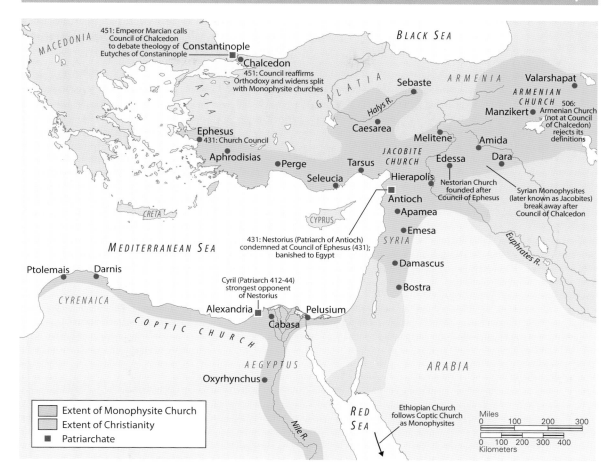

451: Emperor Marcian calls Council of Chalcedon to debate theology of Eutyches of Constaninople

451: Council reaffirms Orthodoxy and widens split with Monophysite churches

506: Armenian Church (not at Council of Chalcedon) rejects its definitions

431: Church Council

Nestorian Church founded after Council of Ephesus

Syrian Monophysites (later known as Jacobites) break away after Council of Chalcedon

431: Nestorius (Patriarch of Antioch) condemned at Council of Ephesus (431); banished to Egypt

Cyril (Patriarch 412-44) strongest opponent of Nestorius

Ethiopian Church follows Coptic Church as Monophysites

Extent of Monophysite Church
Extent of Christianity
Patriarchate

Miles 0 100 200 300
Kilometers 0 100 200 300 400

Gnostic, Arian, Nestorian, and Monophysite) as for its statement of what had come to be widely believed as orthodox. With such carefully worded statements of belief, the church now felt enabled to resist opponents who ridiculed such apparent complexities as the doctrine of the Trinity.

In Egypt and other parts of the Near East 'one-nature' (Monophysite, or Miaphysite) Christians, who rejected the consensus of Chalcedon, were the ancestors of modern Coptic Christians.

In 428 Nestorius (c. 381–c. 451), a native of Syria and student at Antioch, was invited by the Eastern Emperor to become Patriarch of Constantinople. Both a popular preacher and reformer – and opponent of Arianism – Nestorius campaigned to defend the full humanity of Jesus, but in doing do seemed to suggest there are two separate Persons in the Incarnate Christ, one divine and the other human. The Council of Ephesus (431) reasserted the unity of the Second Person of the Trinity – at once human and divine – and condemned and banished Nestorius. He died in Upper Egypt around 451. However other Eastern bishops refused to submit to the council's decision and proceeded to form a 'Nestorian' Church, based in Persia.

Monophysites

This dispute also represented a clash of theological traditions between Antioch – represented by Nestorius – and Alexandria – chiefly represented by Cyril, Patriarch of Alexandria (r. 412 –44). In 451 the Council of Chalcedon condemned the belief, which Cyril seemed to hold, that in Christ there was only one nature, insisting there were two natures – one divine and one human – existing (contrary to Nestorianism) in only one person. Those who believed there was only one nature came to be called 'Monophysites' (from the Greek for 'one nature'). The party that upheld the council's definition of two natures – and whose beliefs were favoured by the Byzantine Emperor – is called Chalcedonian, or Melkite.

Nestorianism

An old tradition claims that King Abgar V of Edessa corresponded with Jesus, was healed by one of his followers, and was a very early Christian convert. Whatever the truth,

4th century Coptic monastery of St Antony, Egypt.

Abgar IX (179–214) did actually convert, bringing his subjects with him in the first mass conversion of Gentiles. Between 435 and 489 the Nestorians based themselves in a school in Edessa, east of the Euphrates. But when the head of that school, Narses (or Narsai, ?399– c. 503), was forced to flee to Nisibis around 471, Nestorian Christians came to be identified with Persia, the Persian church becoming officially Nestorian in 486. A school developed at Nisibis, and the see of the Nestorian Patriarch (*Catholikos*) was located first at Seleucia-Ctesiphon, the capital of the Empire, and then at Baghdad, around 775.

The Nestorians suffered under the early Sassanids, for whom Zoroastrianism was the favoured religion. After the Muslim conquest of Persia in 651, the Nestorians were alternatingly tolerated and persecuted. Over the centuries they lost ground to Islam, though a diaspora of Nestorian refugees helped spread their beliefs into new areas.

The Nestorian Church survived by turning east. By the 6th century, Nestorian missionaries were active in Arabia, India, and Turkestan, and had followed the Silk Road as far as east as China. In Chang'an, the contemporary Chinese capital, stands a Nestorian Stone – with an inscription in Chinese and Syriac – originally set up in 781 to commemorate the arrival of Nestorian missionaries in China 150 years earlier. However in 987 a monk reported that the church in China had entirely vanished.

Top section of a stele of AD 781 celebrating 150 years of Monophysite Christianity in China. This 'Nestorian Stone', or 'Chang'an Stone', is now housed in the Beilin Museum, and has inscriptions in both Chinese and Syriac.

Monophysitism

Monophysite (or Miaphysite) Christians formed another alternative hierarchy to those following the Chalcedonian definition. In the mid-sixth century Jacob Baradeus, Bishop of Edessa (r. 543–78), created Monophysite bishoprics throughout the East. The Syrian Jacobites (named after Baradeus) and the Copts of Egypt and Ethiopia formed themselves into autonomous Monophysite churches. Armenia also became Monophysite in this period, mainly to achieve independence from the Empire and Constantinople.

Cut off from the Empire like the Nestorians, Jacobite missionaries travelled along the caravan routes, especially into northern and central Arabia. Both Nestorians and Monophysites suffered when the Mongols arrived in the 13th century, and their numbers fell further in the 17th century, after one group united with the papacy.

THE SPREAD OF THE NESTORIAN AND MONOPHYSITE CHURCHES

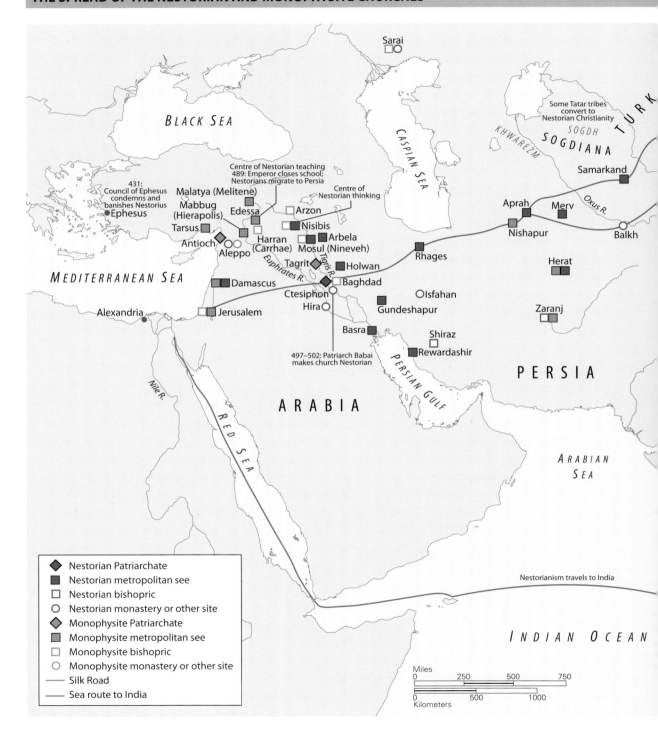

Sarai

BLACK SEA

CASPIAN SEA

Some Tatar tribes
convert to
Nestorian Christianity

KHWAREZM · SOGDIANA · SOGDH · TURK

Samarkand

431:
Council of Ephesus
condemns and
banishes Nestorius
● Ephesus

Centre of Nestorian teaching
489: Emperor closes school;
Nestorians migrate to Persia

Centre of
Nestorian thinking

Malatya (Melitene)

Mabbug
(Hierapolis)

Edessa

Arzon

Tarsus

Nisibis

Aprah

Merv

Oxus R.

Nishapur

Balkh

Antioch

Aleppo

Harran
(Carrhae)

Arbela

Mosul (Nineveh)

Rhages

Euphrates R.

Tagrit

Holwan

Herat

MEDITERRANEAN SEA

Tigris R.

Baghdad

Damascus

Ctesiphon

○ Isfahan

Hira

Gundeshapur

Zaranj

Alexandria

Jerusalem

Basra

Shiraz

497–502: Patriarch Babai
makes church Nestorian

Rewardashir

PERSIA

Nile R.

ARABIA

PERSIAN GULF

RED SEA

ARABIAN
SEA

Nestorianism travels to India

INDIAN OCEAN

◆ Nestorian Patriarchate
■ Nestorian metropolitan see
□ Nestorian bishopric
○ Nestorian monastery or other site
◆ Monophysite Patriarchate
▩ Monophysite metropolitan see
□ Monophysite bishopric
○ Monophysite monastery or other site
— Silk Road
— Sea route to India

Miles
0   250   500   750

0   500   1000
Kilometers

map 8

N A I M A N S

Karakorum

MONGOLIA

MANCHURIA

Hami

Almalyk

ekath

K E R E I T S

Olon-Sume-in Tor

Kalgan

Liaoyang

Kashgar

Beijing

N S

U I G H U R S

Khotan

Indus R.

TIBET

Yellow R.

YELLOW SEA

Luoyang

Chang'an
Nestorian Stone
set up in 781

Ganges R.

CHINA

845: Emperor Wu-Tsung dissolves
Nestorian monasteries

Quanzhou

Canton

INDIA

liana

BAY

OF

BENGAL

SOUTH
CHINA
SEA

Meliapur

ard

Kadamattan

chin

uilon

ndrum

CEYLON
(Taprobane/Sri Lanka)

From the third century onwards, Goths were raiding the Danube frontier of the Roman Empire. In the fourth century the Visigoths advanced west of the River Dniester and the Ostrogoths east of the Dniester. In about 350 the Goth Wulfila (Ulfilas, c. 311–83) converted most of his people to Arian Christianity. Many of the Germanic tribes, such as the Vandals, who subsequently came into contact with the Goths, similarly adopted Arianism. After 376 the Huns forced both the Visigoths and Ostrogoths southwards and westwards.

By the time of the Emperor Theodosius I (347–95) tensions between the Eastern and Western halves of the Empire had become overt and under his sons the Empire was divided permanently. The emperor allowed Visigoths to settle in the Balkans, but burdened them with such huge taxes that they eventually rebelled and – shockingly – sacked the city of Rome itself in 410.

In the century that followed, further massive tribal population migrations threw Western Europe into political turmoil. Any hopes of continuity and stability centred on the Bishops of Rome, such as Leo I 'the Great' (r. 440–61), who by skilful diplomacy extended the power of Rome throughout the West and resisted the Huns, in 452 persuading them to withdraw beyond the Danube. Following the death of their leader Attila in 453, the menace of the Huns diminished, although other barbarian peoples continued to assert territorial claims.

Between 493 and 553 the Arian Ostrogoths invaded and controlled Italy, posing an serious threat to the Catholic church there. But Lombard invaders from Germany in turn overcame the Ostrogoths, forming their own kingdom in 584. The Visigoths sustained a powerful kingdom in Spain and southern Gaul, as did the Vandals in North Africa.

Meanwhile the Frankish chief Clovis I (c. 466–c. 511) had taken advantage of the declining Roman Empire to unite northern Gaul under his leadership in 494, adopting Catholic Christianity and overseeing the mass conversion of his people. His successors founded the Merovingian dynasty that ruled the Frankish Kingdom until the Carolingian dynasty emerged in the eighth century.

Gregory the Great

Pope Gregory I, 'the Great' (r. 590–604), an outstanding leader of the western half of the Empire, laid the foundations of the Medieval papacy. An accomplished administrator of the extensive church lands and skilful political leader, he resisted the claims of both the emperor and the Patriarch of Constantinople, made a separate peace treaty with the invading Lombards, and eliminated the power of the Byzantine exarch at Ravenna. He also attempted to convert the pagan tribes of England and Germany, launching the Latin missions to Britain led by Augustine of Canterbury (596) and Paulinus (601). Anglo-Saxon invasions of Britain had pushed back the Celtic church, leaving the path clear for Roman Christianity to take a new hold in England.

These shifts signalled the beginnings of the gradual transformation of Christianity from a Mediterranean into a European religion. Yet, despite a scattering of leaders of ability, Christianity generally declined between 500 and 950, divided internally and suffering from external political instability.

Legend:
- ■ Patriarchate
- ■ Archbishopric
- + Bishopric
- + Bishopric founded in C6
- Catholic
- Arian
- Pagan
- Pagans converted to Catholicism

NORTH SEA

BALTIC SEA

JUTES

CELTIC LANDS

Bangor
Clonard
Ardmore

ANGLES AND SAXONS

SAXONS

London
Canterbury

Tournai
Cologne

Laon
Rheims

Seine R.

KINGDOM OF THE FRANKS

Rhine R.

ALLEMANNI

Danube R.

BAVARIANS

AVARS

BRITTANY

Loire R.

Nevers
Tours
Mâcon
Châlon

Maurienne

Rhône R.

LOMBARD KINGDOM

ILLYRICUM

Ravenna

ATLANTIC OCEAN

Alès
Carpentras
Uzès
Toulouse
Carcassonne
Agde
Arles
Toulon
Elne

BASQUES

Rome

APULIA

Dumio
Braga

VISIGOTHIC KINGDOM

Coria
Toledo

Tagus R.

BRUTTIUM

ROMAN EMPIRE

MEDITERRANEAN SEA

Niebla
Cordoba
Seville

Carthage

SICILY
Agrigentum
Syracuse

Annaba
NUMIDIA

Miles
0　100　200　300

0　100　200　　400
Kilometers

The First Monks

Most religions include people who take their beliefs more literally, more seriously, or more exactly than the rest. Sometimes this means rejecting things that other people consider normal and good – for example marriage and sex. Sometimes it's a matter of increased piety – more praying, at more inconvenient times. And sometimes it means withdrawing from society to a solitary life, devoted to cultivating the soul, or to a community life, apart from the world but with others of similar persuasion.

There had always been such a strand within Judaism. In the time of Jesus, John the Baptist was a solitary ascetic, living on a restricted diet in the Judean wilderness and preaching a stern message of repentance. Probably the best-known religious community of this period is that which settled at Qumran, on the north-west shore of the Dead Sea.

A thread of asceticism can also be traced through some early Christian groups in the centuries immediately following. James, first leader of the Jerusalem church, was noted for his frequent fasting and prayer. Some early Syriac-speaking churches seem to have restricted baptism to those who were celibate. And asceticism was common among some early fringe Christian movements, such as the Montanists and the followers of Marcion of Sinope (c. 85–c. 160).

The call to asceticism

After the official toleration and recognition of Christianity in the time of Constantine, the church began to attract many new members – but standards of ethical and spiritual practice fell as less now seemed to be demanded of adherents. Believers who sought a purer form of Christianity began to withdraw from the existing churches – and from society itself.

THE SPREAD OF MONASTICISM

Columba (521–97) founds monasteries and evangelizes north Britain

NORTH SEA

Iona (563)
Whithorn (Candida Casa) c. 397
Lindisfarne (635)
Jarrow
Wearmouth
Clonard (520)
Bardsey
Bangor Iscoed (514)
Canterbury (596)
Llantwit (C6)

372: Martin of Tours founds monastery

St Brieuc (C6)
Aleth (C6)
Marmoutier
Auxerr
Ile de Noirmoutier
Tours
Ligugé
Poitiers
Cite
Ly

ATLANTIC OCEAN

Nile R.
C5: 9 monks take Syrian monasticism to Ethiopia
RED SEA
ETHIOPIA
Axum
Lalibela
to same scale and projection as main map

map 10

Nola (394) Monastic community + date of foundation
- Monasteries following early Egyptian model
- Monasteries following British and Celtic tradition
- Monasteries following Rule of Benedict
- Sites of other monastic communities
← Spread of Egyptian monasticism
← Spread of Benedictine monasticism
← Spread of British and Celtic monasticism
  Area following Egyptian monasticism
  Area following Benedictine monasticism
  Area following British and Celtic monasticism
  Border of Roman Empire

BALTIC SEA

•Fulda
ernach

•St Gall (612)
ude
St Maurice
•Vercelli (360)
Bobbio•
•Lérins (410)
eilles
c. 415:
Cassian founds
ey of St Victor
gyptian model

614: Columbanus
sets up monastery
in Celtic tradition

480: Benedict, founder of
Benedictine Order,
born here

c. 529: Benedict founds
first monasteries of
Benedictine Order

•Nursia
•Subiaco
Rome (570)•
•Monte Cassino
•Nola (394)
c. 529: Benedict
founds monastery

•Vivarium
c. 539: Cassiodorus
establishes 'Vivarium'
Gives way to
Rule of St Benedict

ppo
gius
390)

agaste (388)

MEDITERRANEAN SEA

Mt Athos
(C9)

Meteora

Chalcedon
Constantinople (400)

Mt Olympus

Mt Latmos

Myra

BLACK SEA

Macrina (c. 327–79)
founds small community

•Annesi •Neocaesarea
Sebastea•

Caesarea (360)
Basil the Great (330–79)
organizer of Greek/Byzantine
monasticism

Seleucia
Salamis•
(335)

•Chalcis

Betw. 370/378 Basil
founds monastery
on Mount of Olives
432 Melania the Younger
founds convent on
Mount of Olives

Jerusalem
•Canopus
Alexandria•
Wadi Natrun (320–30)• •Nitria
Scetis (330)•
•Pispir
Gaza
Bethlehem
•Mar Saba

c. 478 Sabas (St Saba)
founds Byzantine
monastery

Antony (c.256–356)
pioneers desert
monasticism

After 320: Pachomius
founds many monasteries
and convents

Candidum•

Mt
Sinai

Tabennisi

RED
SEA

Nile R.

see inset

Late C4: Jerome founds
2 monasteries
c. 460: Theodosius the Cenobiarch
founds Monastery of Theodosius

548–65:
St Catherine's Monastery
built by order of Justinian I

Miles
0 100 200 300 400 500

0 100   300   500   700
Kilometers

The monastic life came to be seen as the ideal for the most devout.

From private asceticism, some began to pursue the life of the hermit, dedicated to God. Antony (or Anthony the Great, c. 256–356), a young Egyptian, is the earliest celebrated Christian hermit (though some doubt whether he was the innovator and pioneer he is claimed to be – even whether he was an historical figure). He is said to have spent 15 years as a hermit, living among tombs in the desert, before moving to the middle of the desert to escape human society and cultivate a closer relationship with God. Finally Antony set up a community of monks at Mount Colzim, near the Red Sea.

Many similar hermits withdrew to the deserts of Syria and Egypt, in temporary or permanent retreat from society, and in search of a more spiritual form of life. Living alone or in small groups, they dedicated their time to prayer and meditation, often also attempting feats of spiritual and physical endurance, such as fasting or sleep deprivation.

Communal monasticism

The first communal Christian monastery we know of was set up around 320 by Pachomius (c. 287–346), who founded an ascetic community at Tabennisi, by the River Nile. Rejecting extreme rigour, Pachomius laid down regular routines for meals and worship. Further communities followed, and, although the first were for men only, Pachomius later also superintended communities for women. He created an important pattern for monasticism: a community of monks, sometimes living in a single building, and following a set rule. Initially, a looser arrangement tended to prevail, where the group of monks spent most of their time alone in individual huts, but gathered for communal meals and prayer.

By the end of the fourth century, the monastic life had spread from Egypt throughout the Christian world, both town and country. There were by this time at least 300 monastic houses in the city of Constantinople, and others in such remote spots as St Catherine's, Mount Sinai; rock-cut caves in Cappadocia; and the Holy Mountain of Athos, Greece.

Eastern model

Basil the Great (330–79) who was made Bishop of Caesarea, Cappadocia, in 364, founded a community that introduced important new features. He ruled that monks and hermits should be better integrated with the local church; that the local bishop should have authority over a monastery; and that communal rather than solitary prayer should take priority within the monastery. Basil also wanted to ensure that monasteries served society: his own community offered medical help, poor relief, and education to those living nearby. Basil's model for monastic life was summed up in two 'rules' that Eastern Orthodox monks still observe today.

Western monks

Martin of Tours (d. 397) pioneered monasticism in Western Europe. The monastery he set up at Marmoutier, France, became noted for its austerity and holiness, and acted as a catalyst for the spread of Christianity into France. Further monasteries were founded: on the island of Lérins, near Cannes, by a monk named Honoratus around 410; and in 415 at Marseilles by John Cassian (d. c. 433), who wrote widely on monasticism.

Another innovator, the Roman statesman Cassiodorus (c. 485–c. 585), founded a monastery at Vivarium, in Calabria, southern Italy, which introduced the study and copying of ancient manuscripts, an activity that became associated with Christian monasteries and helped save much of classical culture.

Benedict

Benedict of Nursia (c. 480–c. 547) – so-called 'Father of Western Monasticism' – created the definitive 'rule' for monasteries in Western Europe. Little is known about him, and there is some doubt whether (like Antony) he actually existed. Benedict is supposed to have been born in Nursia, Umbria, and studied in Rome. After living as a hermit in Subiaco, southern Italy, he is said to have set up what became the influential monastery of Monte Cassino in 528. Benedict's 'Rule' was written there, but only after his death, when a copy reached Pope Gregory I, did it become widely known.

Benedict's monastic rule is of huge significance. It divides a monk's life into two essential activities – prayer and work (in Latin, orare et laborare) – and required vows of poverty, chastity, and obedience. Benedict also stipulated that the monastery should provide care for the weak and the sick, and hospitality to strangers. Daily life in a Benedictine monastery was built around a set pattern of seven prayer services: Matins (or Lauds), Prime, Terce, Sect, Nones, Vespers, and Compline.

Gradually the Rule of Benedict supplanted all other rules for monasteries in Western Europe. Benedictines established monasteries throughout the West, supporting education and promoting culture. Even today, most monasteries observe the Rule of Benedict largely as it was originally set out.

Ireland

Beyond the orbit of Rome, a different form of monasticism sprang up in Ireland, where it took on a similar pattern to Egyptian monastic communities. Irish monks became known for their devotion to Christ, mystical spirituality, scholarship, asceticism, restlessness, and evangelistic zeal. The Irish monasteries became known for their libraries and richly illuminated (illustrated) manuscripts, with their distinctive, intricate Celtic designs. But while monks elsewhere were required by the Rule of Benedict to stay put in one geographical location, the Irish monks exhibited a strong wanderlust known as *peregrinatio*: a self-imposed exile and wandering for the love of God.

Justinian I

After Constantine I moved the capital of the empire to Constantinople (formerly Byzantium) in AD 330, Rome and the rest of Italy came increasingly under the influence and control of the Bishop of Rome. The Latin Catholic Church of the Roman West and the Eastern Orthodox Church of the East increasingly took on separate identities as the political division of the Roman Empire into East and West became permanent.

Although for many years the emperor in the East continued to claim authority over the West, the last to retain any real control beyond the Byzantine East was Justinian I (r. 527–65). Italy, western North Africa, and southern Spain were controlled by Germanic tribes when he became Byzantine Emperor; but by the end of his reign he had conquered all these lands and instituted an 'Exarchate' government over Italy at Ravenna, on the Adriatic coast. Defeat of the Arian leadership of the Vandals in North Africa and the Ostrogoths in Italy helped strengthen Catholicism in the West.

Justinian took an active interest in the church, allowing little deviation outside what he considered orthodox belief and practice. He was intolerant of other Christian traditions and beliefs, which led to divisions within the Eastern Empire – a debilitating effect that contributed to the lowering of the resistance of Christians to the arrival of Islam in the following century. Justinian is credited with building a number of new churches, as well as the reconstruction of the great Hagia Sophia in Constantinople after it had been burnt down during riots, and the development St Catherine's Monastery at Mount Sinai, Egypt.

THE EMPIRE OF JUSTINIAN I

SCOTS

NORTH SEA

ANGLO-SAXONS

ATLANTIC OCEAN

BRETONS

Seine R.

FRANKISH KING

Lugdur (Lyor

Arl

Narbonne

SUEVIC KINGDOM

Toletum

VISIGOTHIC KINGDOM

[Granada/ S.Spain] 550: Justinian reconquers

Corduba

Cartagena

BERBERS

Miles
0   100   200   300

0   100   200   300   400
Kilometers

map 11

DANES

BALTS

SAXONS

THURINGIANS

Elbe R.

Oder R.

SLAVS
c. 517: crossed Danube to form
short-lived kingdom in Slovenia
Frequent attacks on Balkans

AVARS
567: Attack Balkans

Dnieper R.

Dniester R.

Danube R.

BULGARS

HUNS

LOMBARDS
568: Invaded
northern Italy

OSTROGOTHIC KINGDOM

Milan

Aquileia

GEPIDAE
c. 567: Destroyed by
Lombards and Avars

DALMATIA

Capital of Byzantine Italy
538-48: Church of San Vitale
Ravenna

Viminacium

Danube R.

ALANS

Busta Gallorum
552: Ostrogoth
Totila defeated

Salonae

Ratiaria

Justiniana
Prima

Serdica

Beroea

Marcianopolis

BLACK SEA

Scodra

THRACIA

537: Church of
St Sophia

Amisus

Rome
Pope John III

ITALIA

MACEDONIA

Philippopolis

Adrianople

Constantinople

Nicomedia

Gangra

Neocaesarea

Dyrrachium

Thessalonica

Nicaea

Ancyra

Amasia

Sebastea

Larissa

GALATIA

CAPPADOCIA

Nicopolis

Sardes

Synnada

Iconium

Caesarea

Melitene

Amida

Corinth

Ephesus

*EASTERN
ROMAN EMPIRE*

Tarsus

Anazarbus

Edessa

D
I
T
E
R
R
A
N
E
A
N

S
E
A

Rhodes

Myra

Seleucia

Antioch

Hierapolis

*VANDAL
KINGDOM*

Gortyna

Salamis

Apamea

SYRIA

Palmyra

Leptis Magna

Ptolemais

Tauchira

Tyre

Diocaesarea

Caesarea

Damascus

Bostra

Alexandria

Jerusalem

Petra

ARABS

TRIPOLITANIA

EGYPT

*RED
SEA*

Legend:
- Roman Empire before Justinian
- Roman Empire at death of Justinian 565
- Frankish Kingdom at death of Clothar I 561
- Political borders
- ◆ Patriarchal sees
- ■ Metropolitinate/Archbishopric
- ✗ Site of conflict

The Rise of Islam

Muhammad was born in Mecca in AD 570. In 610, he claimed the angel Gabriel had told him that he had been chosen to turn people from the prevalent paganism, polytheism, immorality, and materialism to worship the one true God – Allah – whose prophet he was. However, when Muhammad gained only 40 followers in a hostile Mecca, he and his friend Abu Bakr fled to Medina in 622 – an event celebrated as the *Hegira* (*hijra*), Year 1 in the Muslim calendar.

In 630 Muhammad returned, defeated Mecca, converted most of its people to the new faith – Islam – and established religious rites at the *Ka'aba*, an ancient black stone. By 632, the year of his death, Muhammad had conquered most of western Arabia for Islam. 100 years later, Islam had reached as far as the Atlantic Ocean in the west and the borders of China in the east.

The Caliphs (632–61)

A succession crisis arose after Muhammad's death. One group claimed that he had chosen Ali, his cousin and son-in-law, to succeed him; another that Abu Bakr, his friend and father-in-law, should become the new leader, or caliph. In the event, Abu Bakr (r. 632–34) became first caliph, securing the entire Arabian peninsula for Islam, taking the new faith to the frontiers of the Eastern Christian Empire in Syria, and declaring *jihad* (holy war) against the Byzantine state.

The second caliph, Umar (or Omar, r. 634-44), won the strategic battle of Yarmuk (636), and captured Christian Damascus (635) and the Christian holy city of Jerusalem (637) from the Byzantine Empire. In 642 he took the major Christian centre of Alexandria (Egypt).

Uthman (or Osman, 644–56), a member of the influential Umayyad family, succeeded Umar, and continued the expansion of Islam, capturing Cyprus in 649, and arriving at the eastern borders of Persia in 653. After his

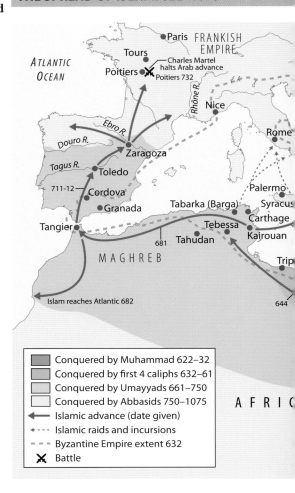

THE SPREAD OF ISLAM: 622–1075

	Conquered by Muhammad 622–32
	Conquered by first 4 caliphs 632–61
	Conquered by Umayyads 661–750
	Conquered by Abbasids 750–1075
←	Islamic advance (date given)
◄----	Islamic raids and incursions
---	Byzantine Empire extent 632
✘	Battle

assassination in 656, the Islamic community underwent the historic split between the majority orthodox Sunni and the minority Shi'ites, who followed descendants of Ali.

The Umayyad Dynasty

The first Sunni caliphate, the Umayyad dynasty, ruled from Damascus and lasted until 750. By the 8th century Muslim armies had crossed the Mediterranean from North Africa and in 711 began to conquer Spain, where the population remained largely Christian under Muslim rule. By 732 a Muslim army

map 12

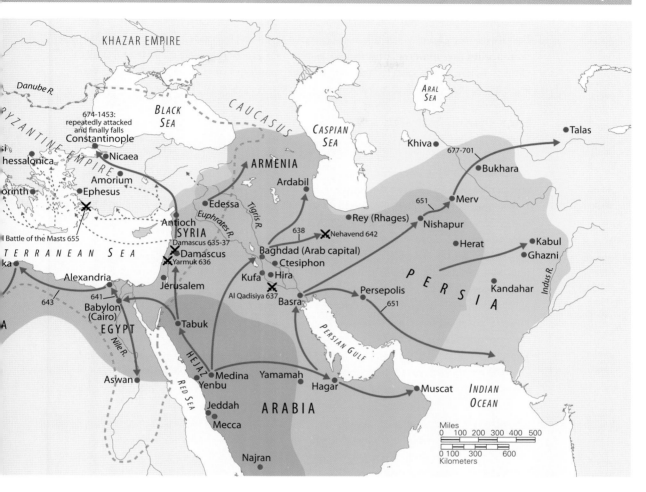

had crossed the Pyrenees and penetrated as far as Tours, south-central France, where it was checked at the Battle of Poitiers by the Frankish leader Charles Martel (r. 718–41) in a victory that saved Western Christendom.

Strife within Christendom – battles between Orthodox and Montanists, Donatists, and Arians in North Africa, and the secession of the Nestorians and Monophysites – made the victory of Islam much easier. Many Christians crossed over to Islam, with its clear statement of faith and strong call to brotherhood.

From its original base in Arabia, Islam spread by force extraordinarily quickly throughout the Middle East, central Asia, and North Africa, overrunning more than half of Christendom within a century. The majority of the population within the new Islamic empire remained non-Muslim. In the early years, Islam allowed indigenous cultures to continue, with little attempt at religious conversion. The Monophysite and Nestorian churches of Egypt, Ethiopia, and the Middle East all survived the coming of Islam, and even shared a common enemy: Byzantium, the Eastern Empire.

From the time of the Council of Chalcedon (451), two increasingly different Christian traditions were developing, one centred on Rome, the other on Constantinople. With diverging emphases, the Western and Eastern churches gradually grew apart, with the East developing its own traditions of spirituality, worship, and church life. The tradition now known variously as Orthodox Christianity, Eastern Orthodoxy, or the Orthodox Church began as the eastern half of early Christendom. The Orthodox tradition was fixed in the Apostolic Age and confirmed by Seven Ecumenical Councils.

Emperor and Patriarch

Unlike the Western, the Eastern Church never attempted to claim independence of the state; rather, it formed in effect the spiritual arm of the government. The Emperor Constantine, who chaired the Council of Nicaea, guaranteed unity for the church in return for its independence. Succeeding emperors continued to work for Christian tranquillity and unity by browbeating and overawing the church. The Bishop of Constantinople became in effect the imperial court-preacher and needed to retain the emperor's favour in order to succeed. Those who – like the great preacher John Chrysostom (c. 344–407) – criticized the emperor were likely to be punished.

As the Islamic forces swept across the east, the Eastern Church was drastically pushed back. With the capture of Jerusalem, Antioch, and Alexandria, the two surviving major centres of Christianity emerged as rivals: Rome under the guidance of the pope, and Constantinople under the leadership of the patriarch. At first the Orthodox Patriarch appeared to be the more powerful, especially since he presided over the wealthier – and still viable – Eastern Roman Empire (Byzantium). However, the patriarch continued to be subservient to the Eastern Emperor who, in practice, ran both church and state.

Iconoclasm

In the East, complex theological controversies continued to rage, especially over the nature and person of Jesus Christ. The East also contrasted with Rome in glorying in images and representations of God. Icons decorated with gold – symbolically representing Christ, Mary (*theotokos*, or the God-bearer), and the saints – were employed to help people worship and to illustrate the mystery of holiness.

However these icons provoked bitter controversy. The Seventh Ecumenical Council (Nicaea II, 787) took place amid a dispute over their use. Emperor Leo III of Syria (c. 675–741) – who saved the Eastern Empire by defeating Muslim armies in 718 and 740 – set out to prohibit the worship of icons, which he possibly believed to be an obstacle to converting Jews and Muslims. This council eventually approved the making and veneration – but not worship – of religious images. The Fourth Council of Constantinople (879), summoned by the learned Patriarch Photius (r. 858–67, 877–86), condemned both Monophysites and Iconoclasts, thus creating further divisions within the empire.

Yet finally icons triumphed, continuing as an essential feature of Eastern Christianity. Among the chief defenders of their use was John of Damascus (c. 675–c. 749), a monk and theologian who grew up under the Muslims. His writings marked a high point of Eastern Orthodox thought into the modern period.

Cyril and Methodius

In this period the most important expansion of Christianity in the East was effected by the brothers Cyril (826–69) and Methodius (c. 815–85) from Thessalonica. In 862 Prince

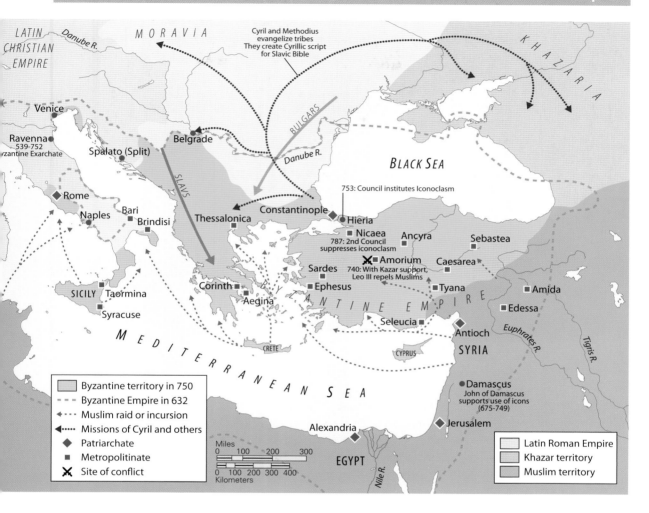

Legend:
- Byzantine territory in 750
- Byzantine Empire in 632
- Muslim raid or incursion
- Missions of Cyril and others
- ◆ Patriarchate
- ■ Metropolitinate
- ✗ Site of conflict
- Latin Roman Empire
- Khazar territory
- Muslim territory

Rastislav of Great Moravia (r. 846–70) asked the emperor to send him missionaries to translate the Bible into Slavic. Cyril (who knew both Arabic and Latin) and Methodius were selected and proceeded to devise the 'Glagolitic' alphabet for the Slavic language – not previously reduced to written form. They then translated into 'Old Church Slavonic' the New Testament, the Psalms, and other parts of the Old Testament, as well as sections of the liturgy.

After the death of Methodius, his followers were exiled from Moravia and found refuge in Bulgaria, which accepted Christianity in 865. The Slavic translation of Cyril and Methodius was enthusiastically accepted, and under Tsar Simeon I ('the Great', r. 893–927) Slavic literacy and liturgy flourished. Unlike the Western church, which was unified by its use of the Latin liturgy, the Byzantines permitted each nation and people to foster its own independent, autocephalous church with a liturgy conducted in the vernacular.

Celtic Monks and Missionaries

For much of earlier Christian history, the pattern of Christian conversion was familial and tribal. Following military defeat or political subjugation, chiefs and leaders accepted baptism and their people followed. Missionary work could be perilous, especially if tribal religion involved ritual human sacrifice, or if Christian missionaries were regarded as part of an expansionist imperial strategy.

Monasticism played a vital role in the Christianization of Europe. In the fifth-century the Briton Ninian founded a monastery at Whithorn (*Candida Casa*) and preached among the Picts of southern Scotland. Columba (c. 521–97) founded several monasteries in his native Ireland before sailing to the island of Iona, off the west coast of Scotland, in 563. He and his followers then evangelized in Scotland, and one disciple, Aidan (d. 651), journeyed to Northumbria, north-east England, in 633 to found the monastery of Lindisfarne, on Holy Island.

Part of the missionary impulse of these Irish monks was the concept that exile in Christ's name (*peregrinatio*) was per se a useful spiritual discipline. The monks often travelled in groups of twelve, in imitation of the Twelve Apostles, establishing churches, holy days, and cults of saints to supplant the shrines and beliefs of the northern pagan cults.

Another disciple of Columba, Columban (or Columbanus, c. 543–615) travelled to France, founding monasteries at Annegray, Luxeuil, and at Bobbio, northern Italy. Amandus (d. 675), born near Nantes, Brittany, became a monk, then a hermit, and evangelized in Flanders, founding a number of monasteries. Willibrord (658–739), 'Apostle to the Frisians', founded the monastery of Echternach, which grew into a major missionary centre.

Possibly the most remarkable missionary of this period was Winfrith, better known as Boniface (c. 675–754), the 'Apostle of Germany'. Likely born at Crediton, Devon, Boniface founded several monasteries, including Fulda (c. 743), where he was buried after his martyrdom. Boniface's courage in felling Thor's Oak at Geismar much impressed the pagan tribespeople.

Ansgar (or Anskar, 801–65), the 'Apostle of the North', came originally from Amiens, but was educated at Corbie, where he became a monk. Appointed Archbishop of Hamburg in 832, he entered Denmark under royal protection before moving on to Sweden. Though travelled widely in Scandinavia, Anskar found its people resistant to conversion. Sigfrid (d. 1045) – probably English, and certainly from the monastery at Glastonbury – evangelized remote areas of Sweden before moving to Denmark, where he was consecrated Bishop of Växjo.

Reversing the Celtic missionary trend, in 596 Pope Gregory the Great sent Augustine (d. c. 604), prior of the Abbey of St Andrew, Rome, to Canterbury with a group of around 40 monks to preach to the Anglo-Saxons. Arriving in 597, he converted Aethelbert and became the first Bishop of Canterbury. Paulinus (d. 644) followed Augustine's group with a second mission that arrived in England in 604, later converting King Edwin of Northumbria.

Miles
0   100   200   300
0 100 200   400
Kilometers

to Iceland
and Greenland

Trondheim
1029

NORWAY

Bergen c.1070

SWEDEN

Uppsala 1164

Birka

Legend:
— Mission c. 400–750 with missionary name
— Mission c. 750–1000 with missionary name
■ Archbishopric – date of foundation
● Bishopric – date of foundation
● Monastery – date of foundation
▨ Area of Celtic monasticism

NORTH
SEA

Sigfrid

Sigfrid 852-54

Växjö

BALTIC
SEA

Boniface (Winfrid) 716

Wilfrid/Willibrord
678, 690

DENMARK

Ãrhus 948

Roskilde

umba 563

SCOTLAND

Aidan

Iona 563

Lindisfarne 635

Ribe 948

Sigfrid

Ninian

Hexham
678

Monkwearmouth/
Jarrow

Hedeby

PRUSSIA

andida Casa, Whithorn 397

Aidan, Cuthbert 634-64

Hamburg 834

Anskar 826

Bangor
559

Ripon

Whitby 664

Gniezno
1000

Armagh

Kentigern
(Mungo)

York 625

Paulinus of York
627-33

Bremen 788

h

Clonard

Fursey 648

Utrecht
696 Ewalde

Magdeburg 958

IRELAND

ENGLAND

Dunwich
669

Corvey
815

POLAND

WALES

London
604

Suidbert

Adalbert c. 995

Glastonbury

Rochester

Canterbury
597

Amandus

HESSE

Fulda
744

Prague
973

MORAVIA

Krakow
1004

Winchester 676

Ghent

Mainz
743

Bamberg
1007

BOHEMIA

Corbie

Echternach
698

Eichstätt 742

Regensburg 739

Rouen

Rheims

Kilian 686

Freising
780

Passau 739

Gran
1001

TLANTIC
OCEAN

Columbanus 590

Sens

Reichenau 724

Gallus

BAVARIA

Salzburg 798

Tours

Luxeuil
c.590

Gallus

St Gall
c.673

CARINTHIA

Bourges

Gallus

Boniface (Winfrid) 716

Aquileia

FRANCE

Vienne

Amandus

Ravenna

Bobbio c.614

CROATIA

Toulouse

ITALY

Narbonne

Augustine 596-7

Danube R.

NAVARRE

CORSICA

Rome

SPAIN

MEDITERRANEAN SEA

SARDINIA

Tagus R.

Toledo 1085

Charlemagne

The Pope and Western Emperor struggled for power time and again. When the leaders of the Christian community in the West were not trying to stem the Muslim tide or absorb barbarian invasions from the East, they were battling with great temporal leaders such as Charlemagne ('Charles the Great', r. 800–14) for control of the church.

A pious man, the Frankish King Charles attempted to reform the church by encouraging Benedictine monasticism, appointing effective bishops, attacking paganism, spreading the Roman liturgy, and sponsoring an intellectual and artistic revival that became known as the 'Carolingian Renaissance', strongly guided by Alcuin of York (c. 735–804).

Charles made it clear that he, and not the pope, would govern the church in his expanding kingdom. The popes tried to curb him, but when some Roman aristocrats accused Pope Leo III (795–816) of misconduct, drove him out of office, and attempted to kill him, Charles rescued the hapless pontiff. Leo was restored to office – in return for dependence upon the emperor.

In an attempt to establish his independence from the Eastern Church, on Christmas Day 800, Pope Leo crowned Charlemagne emperor, so reviving the Empire in the West. Charlemagne abhorred the idea of owing his crown to the pope, and for the following fourteen years strove to dominate the papacy. Charlemagne was King of the Franks, but the pope had created him emperor; did this mean the pope alone could create an emperor? The popes believed this to be the case – but Charlemagne's successors disputed it. As the ninth century continued, the imperial title went to the most powerful contender – and the popes were constantly embroiled in politics.

THE EMPIRE OF CHARLEMAGNE

map 15

Byzantine Empire 732
Umayyad Caliphate 732
Frankish Kingdom 732
Empire of Charlemagne 814
Borders
Site of conflict
Patriarchate
Monastery

Miles
0   100   200
0   100 200 300
Kilometers

NORSE
SVEAR
GÖTAR
DANES
BALTIC SEA
BALTS
MAZOVIANS
POMERANIANS
conquered and tianized after ears' conflict
Hamburg
ABODRITES
Bremen
WILTZITES
Hildesheim
SAXONS
Magdeburg
recht
Paderborn
SORBS
POLES
Vistula R.
DEREVLIANS
gne's capital
Fulda
Elbe R.
Oder R.
Prüm
Frankfurt
794 Synod affirms use of icons
BOHEMIANS
Metz
St Emmeram
Regensburg
VOLHYNIANS
asbourg
Rhine R.
Passau
Danube R.
ISH OM
Augsburg
St Gallen
Salzburg
AVAR CALIPHATE
GOTHS
Milan
Aquileia
nne
Pavia
Venice
CROATS
BULGAR KHANATE
KINGDOM OF THE LOMBARDS
Bobbio
Ravenna
SERBS
Danube R.
BLACK SEA
Split
DUCHY OF SPOLETO
VLACHS
Charlemagne uers Lombardy Takes title of the Lombards"
CORSICA
Farfa
Ragusa
Rome
Monte Cassino
Christmas 800: Leo III crowns Charlemagne
Benevento
Thessalonica
Constantinople
SARDINIA
Naples
DUCHY OF BENVENTO
D I T E R R A
Cagliari
BYZANTINE EMPIRE
(EASTERN ROMAN EMPIRE UNTIL 610)
SICILY
Athens
N E A N
Tunis
Corinth
Ephesus
Syracuse
S E A
CRETE
CYPRUS
ATE

For generations England was first plundered, then settled by raiding tribes from Scandinavia and Germany. During the late 5th century Saxon invaders destroyed many of the old centres of Christianity, and descendants of the original inhabitants were pushed into outlying areas. Celtic Christianity survived largely in mountain strongholds and island fastnesses.

For a time the Celtic and Roman varieties of Christianity co-existed uncomfortably. However in 664 King Oswiu (or Oswig, 612–79) of Northumbria, whose own family was divided and hence celebrated Easter on different dates, called a church council. At the Synod of Whitby (664) this dispute was settled in favour of the Roman rite and calendar, though Celtic practices of private confession and disciplinary penitence were adopted. Some monks were unhappy with this and withdrew to Ireland and Scotland; Celtic Christianity eventually disappeared in England.

By 600 a group of larger English kingdoms – Wessex, East Anglia, Kent, Mercia, and Northumbria – had emerged, having gradually absorbed smaller neighbours such as Sussex, Essex, the Hwicce, and the Western Marches. By 700 every kingdom had become Christian with the consolidation of the conversion in the south initiated by Augustine in 597, and in the north by Irish missionaries early in the seventh century.

Alfred the Great

During the 9th century Wessex emerged as the strongest kingdom in England. Alfred the Great (849–99) reinforced this position, successfully beating off Viking attacks, reaching an agreement with the Vikings in the Danelaw, and reoccupying London (886). The king fostered a religious and educational renaissance that turned the tide against tribal gods and priests. Alfred's sons and grandsons, Edward the Elder (r. 899–924), Aethelstan (r. 924–39), Edmund (r. 939–46), and Eadred (r. 946–55), extended their power to Mercia, the Danelaw and, ultimately, Northumbria, paving the way for the unification of England. The writings of the Venerable Bede (c. 673–735) witness to the energy of the British church in adversity. Yet England remained vulnerable to Danish attacks, which culminated in the reign of the Danish king Cnut (or Canute, r. 1016–35), who ruled Norway and Denmark as well as England.

English kings had always been closely allied with the church; from about 900 this connexion was strengthened with the introduction of a Christian ceremony of royal coronation. The leading English churchman of the time, Archbishop of Canterbury Dunstan (c. 909–88), a strict ascetic, enforced the Benedictine Rule as abbot and reformed both secular and religious administrations as advisor to King Edgar (r. 959–75).

SHETLAND

St Ninian's Isle

to same scale as main map

Gaelic
Pictish
Anglo-Saxon
British
+ Major church
■ Celtic bishopric
■ Anglo-Saxon bishopric

Birsay
ORKNEY

CAITHNESS

Udal

+Applecross

MORAY
Deer+

PICTLAND

Brechin

+Dunkeld

Iona+

DAL RIATA

Dunblane
Govan
Glasgow
STRATHCLYDE

Abercorn
Edinburgh

Coldingham
■Lindisfarne
Melrose

ATLANTIC
OCEAN

NORTH
SEA

Whithorn

Corbridge
Hexham

Jarrow
+Monkwearmouth
Whitby

+Derry
NORTHERN
UÍ NÉILL

ULAID

Ripon

NORTHUMBRIA

York

Inishmurray+

AIRGIALLA
Clogher
Armagh

+Nendrum
Downpatrick

LINDSEY
+Lincoln

SOUTHERN
UÍ NÉILL
Monasterboice

CONNACHT
Kells+
Ardagh ■Trim
+Clonmacnoise

IRISH
SEA

Bangor
GWYNEDD
St Asaph

Shannon R.

Kildare
Glendalough
Inishcaltra ■Sletty
LAIGIN

Kilfenora+

POWYS

Lichfield
Leicester
Crowland
Elmham

Emly +Cashel
Ferns

Llanbadarn Fawr+
CEREDIGION
BUILTH

Peterborough
Ely

EAST
ANGLIA
Dunwich

+Ardfert MUNSTER Lismore

Severn R.
Worcester

Ipswich

Inisfallen
Cork

St David's
DYFED
BRYCHEINIOG
Hereford

St Albans
ESSEX

+
Skellig
Michael

GLYWYSING
Llanilltud Fawr+
Dinas Powys

Dorchester
London
Barking

Thames R.
Rochester

CELTIC
SEA

WESSEX
Winchester

KENT Canterbury

Sherborne
SUSSEX

Wimborne+
Selsey

DUMNONIA
Bodmin

ENGLISH CHANNEL

Miles
0 10   30   50

0 10 30 50
Kilometers

From the late 630s the Eastern Empire struggled for survival against Arab Islamic forces that dwarfed it both militarily and economically. The Arab conquests of the seventh century rapidly reduced the East Roman Empire to a core in Anatolia. The imperial authorities faced almost annual Arab raids into their remaining territories, yet the Byzantine army fought a lengthy guerrilla war against the invaders, believing theirs was the empire of Christ and they could win with his aid.

The Abbasid revolution in the mid-eighth century fragmented the Islamic world, which started to alter the military balance. The Byzantine army was now better able to resist the invaders. By the early tenth century, Byzantine forces, aided by local knowledge of the terrain and lengthy experience of Byzantine-Arab warfare, began to advance into Arab-held territory. In the 930s the Byzantine general John Kourkouas (Curcuas) led victorious Byzantine forces into the cities of Melitene and Samosata, and even began to advance beyond the River Euphrates. Armenia and Georgia, which had been under Muslim rule, were now annexed by Byzantium.

Slav incursions

Meanwhile Slav incursions into the Balkans left the Eastern Empire with only minimal control beyond its coasts. From the 6th century various peoples migrated across the south Russian steppe to lands north and south of the River Danube. The Slavic-speaking people who settled throughout the Balkan peninsula were followed by the Turkic Bulgars, who dominated north of the Balkan mountains on both sides of the Danube. Two centuries later, the Magyars conquered the Carpathian Basin and ended Bulgar rule north of the river. All these peoples interacted with the Byzantine Empire, which had till now dominated the region.

Conversion

In 687/88 Emperor Justinian II (r. 685–95, 705–11) confronted the Bulgars, and in 758 Emperor Constantine V (r. 741–75)

launched a full-scale attack on the Balkan Slavs. However the Turkic Bulgars established a powerful empire that was able to withstand Byzantine attempts to recover the northern Balkans. In 811 Emperor Nikephoros I and his army were slaughtered by forces led by the Bulgar Khan Krum. Yet, following defeat by a Byzantine army in 864, Khan Boris (852–89) was baptized into the Eastern Church.

Byzantine missionaries such as Clement of Ohrid (c. 840–916) and Naum of Preslav (c. 830–910) were sent to Bulgaria to help convert its people, utilizing the Glagolitic script previously created by Cyril and Methodius. Patriarch Photius of Constantinople provided Boris with guidelines for a Christian ruler. Gradually the Byzantines brought the Slav population of the southern Balkans to Orthodox Christianity, and during the reign of Emperor Basil II (976–1025) overcame the rival Bulgar Empire.

In 895–6 the Magyars arrived in the Carpathian Basin and proceeded to raid lands to the west, until the German Otto I ('the Great', r. 934–70) defeated them at the decisive Battle of Lechfeld (955). The Magyar Stephen I (c. 975–1038) was converted to Christianity around 1000; Pope Sylvester II sent him a crown for use at his coronation.

In southern Italy too, Byzantium once more became a force to be reckoned with, leading the Christians of the region against the Muslim invaders. By the 11th century, Constantinople was again capital of the greatest power in Christendom.

Orthodox Church: Greek rite
Orthodox Church: Slavonic rite
Orthodox Church: Georgian rite
Latin Church
Islam

LETTS

NOVGOROD

Ladoga

Beloozero (Belozersk)

VIATKA

Novgorod the Great

Yaroslavl

Rostov

SUZDAL

Volga R.

Riga

TEUTONIC ORDER

LITHUANIANS

Dvina R.

POLOTSK

SMOLENSK

Moscow

Vladimir

Nishni Novgorod

Murom

Smolensk

Ryazan

RYAZAN

BULGARS

PRUSSIANS

Vistula R.

CHERNIGOV

Elbe R.

Oder R.

Pinsk

Turov

VOLHYNIA

KIEV

Chernigov

Kursk

POLAND

Krakov

Vladimir-in-Volhynia

PEREJASLAV

Kiev

Prague

Olmutz

Belgorod

Dnieper R.

Volga R.

BOHEMIA

Galich

GALICIA

Dniester R.

CUMANS

Don R.

Salzburg

Danube R.

HUNGARY

PATZINAKS

KHAZARS

Venice

Zagreb

Bosporos

CROATIA

Cherson

Alania

Silistra

BLACK SEA

Rome

Turnovo

Sardica

SERBIA

BULGARIA

Veles

Philippopolis

Constantinople

GEORGIA

Tiflis

Dyrrachium

Thessalonica

Nicaea

Ankara

Neocaesarea

ARMENIA

Smyrna

Antioch

Melitene

SICILY

Ephesus

Laodicea

Iconium

Syracuse

Rhodes

Antioch

Tigris R.

Euphrates R.

Candia

CRETE

CYPRUS

ABBASID CALIPHATE

MEDITERRANEAN SEA

Jerusalem

Miles
0　100　200　300

0　100 200　400
Kilometers

- - - Byzantine Empire extent until late 12th century
◆ Patriarchal see
■ Metropolitan see or archbishopric

According to tradition, the Russian church was founded by the Apostle Andrew, said to have visited Scythia and Greek colonies on the Black Sea during the first century AD. As we know, between 863 and 869 Eastern Orthodox missionaries – Cyril and Methodius – travelled to eastern Europe and translated parts of the Bible into the Old Slavonic language for the first time – having first apparently invented the Glagolitic alphabet, paving the way for the Christianization of the Slavs.

Kievan Rus'

The Rus' were probably a multi-ethnic group of merchants, mercenaries, and peasants, which included Slavs, Balts, and Finns, whose trading activity extended across the Caspian Sea into central Asia. They established their capital at Kiev, which became an archbishopric after they converted to Christianity.

Around 866 it seems the first Christian bishop was sent to Kiev from Constantinople by Patriarch Photius I. Princess Olga of Kiev was the first ruler to convert to Christianity, in 955 or 957. Soon a Christian community arose among the Kievan nobility, led by Greek and Byzantine priests, although paganism still dominated the region.

Olga's grandson, the regent Vladimir Syatoslavich (Prince Vladimir I of Kiev, 980–1015), established the Kievan state of Rus'. Much impressed by the splendour of Byzantine worship, architecture, and culture during a trip to Constantinople in 988, when he returned to Kiev, Vladimir instigated the mass baptism of his people (988). This marked the official founding of the Russian Orthodox Church.

Russia imported many features of Byzantine culture, including a literary language, styles of masonry and mosaics, music and liturgy, monasticism, and an elaborate theological system.

Initially the Russian Church belonged to the Patriarchate of Constantinople, but in 1051 a Russian primate was established,

Statue of Saints Cyril and Methodius, inventors of the Glagolitic (Cyrillic) alphabet, Kiev, Ukraine.

and a separate, distinctive Russian Orthodox Church began to develop, eventually claiming to be the true successor of Rome and Constantinople. By the 12th century, the Russian church had become an important force, unifying the Russian people at a time of acute division.

The Russian Metropolitan's residence was initially in Kiev. However the Kievan state became unstable, partly as a result of uncertainties over the succession, leaving it vulnerable to external attacks, especially by the Pechenegs. From 1237 the invading Mongol armies of Batu Khan (c. 1207–55), grandson of Chinggis (Genghis) Khan, finally destroyed Kiev's supremacy. As a result, Metropolitan Maximus moved to Vladimir in 1299; by 1326 his successors, Metropolitans Peter and Theognostus, moved on to Moscow.

Division between East and West can arguably be traced to the early 3rd century, when Latin became the language of theological discourse in the West. The two wings of the church continued to drift apart after the Council of Nicaea in 325, for many different reasons of theology, church government, and liturgy.

The Eastern Church never accepted the so-called *filioque* clause, added to the Nicene Creed in the sixth century, which stated that the Holy Spirit proceeded from both the Father 'and the son' (*filioque*). This addition was intended to reaffirm the divinity of the Son; but Eastern theologians objected both to the unilateral editing of a creed produced by an ecumenical council and to the word changes themselves. For Eastern Christians, both the Spirit and the Son have their origin in the Father.

Other differences between the two churches included the question of whether the clergy could be married (East) or must remain celibate (West). The two churches also disputed the Christian calendar, and the date when Easter should be celebrated. The fact that East and West worshipped in different languages also played a part in the divorce.

The Roman West

After Charlemagne, the Western Empire gradually disintegrated into warring principalities, and political division was accompanied by economic disintegration. Between 970 and 1048 a total of 48 years' famine reduced many in the West to subsistence level. Trade declined, communications collapsed, and travel became perilous. Robber barons dominated small regions, preying on travellers and terrorizing the peasantry. As government fell apart, and the administrative structures created by Roman emperors and their successors broke down, patterns of political power reverted to tribal practices. Only the church – and particularly monastic communities – tried to sustain a more civilized way of life.

During this period, conflict also increased between rulers and popes, particularly when a reforming pope such as Leo IX (r. 1049–54) attempted to re-establish the dignity of his office and protect the church's conduct of its own affairs. At the Easter Synod (1049), Leo led a campaign against the sale of church offices (simony) and for clerical celibacy. However he was decisively defeated by Norman military forces at the Battle of Civitate (1053), and lived to see the Latin church of the West and Eastern Orthodoxy permanently divided.

Schism

Byzantium no longer enjoyed intellectual pre-eminence. Patriarch Michael Cerularius (r. 1043–58) was spiritual head of an Eastern kingdom torn apart by internal intrigue and crushed between the powerful empire of the Bulgars and the expanding Islamic empire of the Turks. After 1025 Orthodox Christianity suffered severe military setbacks in Asia Minor, and in 1080 the Turks captured Nicaea, less than 100 miles from Constantinople.

In 1054 a serious dispute over authority finally brought matters to a head between East and West. The papacy claimed direct succession from the Apostle Peter – and thus supreme church authority – claiming support from a document known as the 'Donation of Constantine' (later discovered to be a fake). Finally an immovable Pope (Leo IX) excommunicated an equally uncompromising Patriarch (Michael Cerularius). In response, the patriarch excommunicated the legates of Leo IX, who personally delivered the sentence of excommunication and anathematized the pope.

Following this apparently irrevocable 'Great Schism', a glimmer of hope for

Legend:
- Roman Catholic West
- Orthodox East
- Muslim northern limits by 1050
- ◆ Patriarchate

reconciliation appeared at the beginning of the Crusades, when the West came to the aid of the East against the Turks. But especially after the Fourth Crusade (1200–04), when Western Crusaders brutally sacked and occupied Constantinople, the ultimate outcome was heightened hostility between the two churches. The assault on Constantinople led eventually to the loss of the Byzantine capital to the Muslim

Ottomans in 1453, and has never been forgotten by the Eastern Orthodox Church.

It was now clear that the East/West break was final and that the unity of the church was completely severed. Although the Schism was the last straw, this separation was neither sudden nor unexpected. For centuries there had been a multitude of significant religious, cultural, and political differences between the Eastern and Western churches.

Part 3

The Middle Ages

There is one Universal Church of the faithful, outside of which there is absolutely no salvation.

CANONS OF THE 4TH LATERAN COUNCIL, 1215, CANON 1

During the centuries of barbarian invasion and political disorder, the monasteries became centres of learning much valued for their libraries. Their prestige began to be derived from cultural achievement rather than the original ideals of piety and self-denial. Spiritual discipline frequently became lax, and large and valuable buildings were often acquired through the donations of the faithful.

From the 10th century, spiritual renewal started to sweep through the monasteries of Western Europe, beginning around 910 with the founding of Cluny in Burgundy by William the Pious (875–918). A series of gifted leaders, notably Abbot Odo (r. 927–42) and Abbot Odilo (r. 994–1048), steered this reform movement, stressing personal spiritual life, common worship, and manual labour. Cluny became a model for monastic reform, and eventually more than 1,000 daughter houses followed.

Cluny aimed to reinvigorate Christian monasticism by stricter observance of the Benedictine rule, reverting to the purity of the monasteries initiated by Benedict of Nursia, and his stress on the daily cycle of worship as monks' core activity. But whereas Benedict had striven to segregate monks from society, Cluny tried to integrate monasticism with society. The reformers wanted to present lay people with an alternative way of life from that of the ordinary clergy, some of whom had become affluent and even dissolute.

Cluniac monks usually joined as young boys and received their training solely within the cloister. By contrast with earlier monasteries, which had essentially been independent, linked only by shared practices, beliefs, and sometimes shared founders, the powerful abbots of Cluny insisted that every monk in their daughter houses owed ultimate obedience to them rather than to the prior of his respective monastery.

Cluniac leaders wished to stamp out the practice of buying and selling church offices and positions (simony), recall the clergy to celibacy, eliminate corruption in the church, and encourage greater piety among ordinary Christians. Their aim was top-down reform through a spiritually revitalized pope who shared their reforming goals – something they accomplished with the election of Hildebrand as Pope Gregory VII (r. 1077–88) in the following century.

The Cluniac reforms were repeated in monasteries in the Low Countries, Lorraine, and Anglo-Saxon England, and became the catalyst of a wider reform movement in the church in the West. In England Archbishop Dunstan (909–88) worked to reform the church and promote Benedictine monasticism, while his contemporary Bishop of York, Oswald (d. 992), also eliminated abuses in the church and established new monasteries.

La Grande Chartreuse Monastery, France.

Legend:
- ◆ Major Cluniac monastery
- ■ Daughter house of Cluny
- ● Cluniac monastery

- Main area of first 100 years' Cluniac reform
- Other areas of 1st C Cluniac reform

NORTH SEA

IRELAND

ENGLAND

FRIESLAND

SAXONY

Elbe R.

Hildesheim

THURINGIA

München-Gladbach

Bermondsey ●

Lewes ■

Ghent ●

St Trond ●

Cologne ●

Siegburg ●

Hersfeld ●

Merseburg ●

St Vaast ●

Liège ●

Malmédy ●

Fulda ●

Brogne ◆

Stablo ●

GERMANY

ATLANTIC OCEAN

Fécamp ●

LORRAINE

Lorsch ●

FRANCONIA

Feuchtwangen ●

BOHEMIA

Rouen ●

Verdun ●

Metz ●

Regensburg ●

Seine R.

Paris ■

Gorze ◆

Rhine R.

Danube R.

NORMANDY

Hirsau ◆

SWABIA

BAVARIA

Ebersburg ●

BRITTANY

Fleury ◆

Auxerre ●

Vézelay ●

St Blaise

Tegernsee ●

Loire R.

La Charité ■

Dijon ◆

Einsiedeln

Souvigny ■

Cluny ◆

KINGDOM OF BURGUNDY

VENICE

FRANCE

AQUITAINE

Sauxillanges ■

Fruttuaria ●

Po R.

Classe ●

Rhône R.

SAVOY

KINGDOM OF ITALY

Moissac ●

COUNTY OF TOULOUSE

Marseille

ADRIATIC SEA

GASCONY

Miles
0   100   200

0   100   200
Kilometers

MEDITERRANEAN SEA

CORSICA

Farfa ●

Subiaco ●

LEÓN

Sahagún ●

NAVARRE

Rome ● ●

Pope Leo IX 1048-54

PAPAL STATES

Monte Cassino ●

ARAGON

Ebro R.

Pope Gregory VII 1073-85

KINGDOM OF SICILY

CASTILE

SARDINIA

Charterhouse

The Cluniacs were not the only reforming movement in medieval monasticism. Indeed, they began to attract the criticism of others for their excessive attention to ceremony and splendour. In 1084 Bruno of Cologne (c. 1030–1101), former master of a cathedral school in Rheims, founded the monastery of La Grande Chartreuse in southern France 'on a high and dreadful cliff under which there is a deep gorge in a precipitous valley'. Against common practice, this house reverted to a hermit-type organization, with the monks living solitary lives in a cluster of individual cells. The Carthusian order (English, 'Charterhouse'), which started here, remained the most austere form of monasticism throughout the Middle Ages, its leaders claiming it was never reformed because it was never corrupted.

The Cistercians

Some monastic leaders believed the Cluniac reforms did not go far enough. A much more austere form of monastery was founded by Robert of Molesme (c. 1029–1111) at Cîteaux, near Dijon, Burgundy, in 1098. This rapidly gave rise to the new order of Cistercian monks, who reverted to a strict observance of the Benedictine Rule.

Cistercian monasteries were deliberately built in remote locations to avoid contact with town-dwellers. The Cistercians – often known as 'White Monks' from the colour of their habit – emphasized silence and rigour, and renewed emphasis on hard, manual work. They rejected 'the use of coats, capes, worsted cloth, hoods, pants, combs, counterpanes and bed-clothes, together with a variety of dishes in the refectory'.

Like the Cluniacs, the network of Cistercian monasteries had a centralized form of organization, headed by the Abbot of Cîteaux, with an annual assembly of all abbots at the mother house. Leading Cistercians included Bernard of Clairvaux (1090–1153), celebrated for his spirituality and for his impact on both church and state – and on the first Crusade. Just two years after he entered Cîteaux, Bernard was despatched to establish Clairvaux, which became one of the most influential houses of the Cistercian order. With his rigorous asceticism, spirituality, and popularity as an effective preacher, Bernard played a major role in political and religious life.

Rapid growth

By the year of Bernard's death in 1153, there were already some 360 Cistercian monasteries in Europe, including 122 in Britain, 88 in Italy, 56 in Spain, and 100 in German-speaking lands; and by the end of the thirteenth century there was a total of 694 Cistercian houses in Western Europe.

With their strictness of life and lofty spiritual expectations, the Cistercians soon became a significant force for reform within the church and eventually in the papacy. By their example of selfless living, by their high esteem among lay people, and by skilful political strategy they supported the continuing fight against simony, nepotism, and lay manipulation of church offices and finances.

Cistercian monks often cultivated the wasteland around their monasteries, rapidly acquiring expertise in sheep farming. Ironically, this was to be the seed of their downfall. To help clear the land and meet the growing demand for their wool, the monasteries employed illiterate 'lay brothers' who were only part-members of the order, so diluting the purity of the monastic ideal. The Cistercians' financial success – resulting from the sale of wool – soon made the order extremely rich, so an order that started by seeking extreme austerity ended by being fiercely criticized for its greed and avarice.

Augustinians

Other new orders of the mid-eleventh century included the less austere Augustinians (known in England as 'Austin Canons'), who claimed their rule of life was based on principles first set out by Augustine of Hippo (354–430). Among other activities, they helped set up schools, hospitals for the care of the sick and for pregnant women, and hospices for people suffering from leprosy.

Monasteries were generally not slow in succumbing to worldly temptations. Wealthy benefactors made lavish donations to monastic houses in return for prayers for prosperity in this world and the next, which led to successful monasteries acquiring vast estates. The monastic life began as a calling but often became corrupted into a profession; monastic scholarship frequently stultified into dry traditionalism.

Major Cistercian house
Daughter house of Cîteaux
Other Cistercian house 1130–1300
Political boundary

Lyse
NORWAY
Hovedø
SWEDEN
Alvastra
DENMARK
Esrom
BALTIC SEA
Holme
Løgum
SCOTLAND
NORTH SEA
Melrose
Furness
Rievaulx 1132
Fountains
Roche
Mellifont
IRELAND
WALES
Tintern
ENGLAND
Waverley 1128
Doberan
Chorin
Amelungsborn
Magdeburg
Pforta
Bukowo
Oliwa
Vistula R.
Lad
POLAND
Lubiaz
Sulejów
HOLY ROMAN EMPIRE
Rhine R.
Elbe R.
Oder R.
SILESIA
Szepes
HUNGARY
Clairmarais
Seine R.
Longpont
Royaumont
Savigny
Orleans
Loire R.
Pontigny
Fontenay
1112: Bernard makes monastery head of Cistercian order
Clairvaux
Morimand
Molesme
1098: Monks from Benedictine abbey leave to found Cîteaux
Cîteaux
La Ferté
Bebenhausen
Borsmonoster
Zirc
Belakut
Chiaravalle
VENICE
Tupuszco
FRANCE
Obazine
Rhône R.
Sénanque
Fontfroide
ATLANTIC OCEAN
BYZANTINE EMPIRE
LEÓN
NAVARRE
Moruela
Las Huelgas
ARAGON
Poblet
CASTILE
Santa Creus
CORSICA
PORTUGAL
baça
Tagus R.
SARDINIA
Fossanova
KINGDOM OF SICILY
ALMOHAD CALIPHATE
MEDITERRANEAN SEA

Miles
0   100   200
0   100 200 300
Kilometers

The Crusades

In the 11th century the Seljuk Turks conquered Asia Minor (modern Turkey), parts of which had been Christian since the missions of the Apostle Paul. The Byzantine Empire was now reduced to little more than the area of modern Greece. In 1095 the Eastern Emperor, Alexius I Comnenus (1081–1118), pleaded for aid from the Christian West, as the Turks were now threatening Constantinople, the home of Eastern Christianity. The Crusades were a response to more than four centuries of Islamic conquest, during which Muslims had captured two-thirds of the Christian world.

At the Council of Clermont (1095) Pope Urban II (r. 1088–99) called on Christendom to resist and push back Islam. He presented the Crusaders with a number of goals: rescue of the Eastern Christians, recovery of the Holy Land – particularly the holy city of Jerusalem – from Muslim occupation, and free access to the Holy Land for Christian pilgrims. This triggered not just the First Crusade, but also the entire crusading movement that was to last for centuries.

Thousands of knights took a vow of the cross and prepared for war, partly as an act of penitence. Medieval Crusaders felt that they were both on a military expedition blessed by the pope and on a pilgrimage to the Holy Land, for which they expected to receive a special indulgence guaranteeing entrance to heaven.

The First Crusade (1096–99)

The First Crusade seemed always to be on the verge of disaster. It had no single leader, no effective supply lines, and no detailed strategy and huge numbers of its participants died in battle or from disease and starvation. Yet by 1098 the Crusaders

THE FIRST THREE CRUSADES

map 22

Legend:
- Muslim 1095
- Latin Christian 1095
- Orthodox Christian 1095
- Armenian Christian 1095
- First Crusade 1096–99
- Second Crusade 1146–48
- Third Crusade 1188–92
- Crusader States by 1144
- Area of anti-Jewish riots
- Battle

DENMARK

HOLY ROMAN EMPIRE

Prague

Regensburg (Ratisbon)

Elbe R.

Oder R.

Vistula R.

POLAND

RUSSIAN PRINCIPALITIES

Danube R.

Vienna

Salzburg

AUSTRIA

CARINTHIA

Venice

Genoa

Pisa

ITALY

Rome

CORSICA

SARDINIA

Tunis

Messina

SICILY

Bari

Brindisi

Taranto

NORMAN KINGDOM OF SICILY

BOHEMIA

HUNGARY

SERBIA

BYZANTINE EMPIRE

Nish

Sofia

BULGARIA

Ochrid

Philippopolis

Adrianople

Thessalonica

Dnieper R.

Dniester R.

Don R.

BLACK SEA

GEORGIA

Trebizond

1095: Emperor appeals to West for aid against Turks

Constantinople

Nicomedia 1096
Nicaea 1097
Dorylaeum
Dorylaeum 1097, 1147

EMPIRE OF NICAEA

Ephesus

Iconium

Halys R.

SELJUK SULTANATE OF RUM

ARMENIA

Attalia

Edessa 1144
Edessa

Tigris R.

Antioch 1098
Antioch

Aleppo

Euphrates R.

MEDITERRANEAN SEA

Candia

CRETE

CYPRUS

Limasol

Tripoli

SYRIA

Sidon

Damascus
Damascus 1148

Acre
Haifa

Hattin 1187

Arsuf 1191

Jerusalem

Ascalon 1099

Alexandria

FATIMID CALIPHATE

EGYPT

Nile R.

1078: Turks take Jerusalem and obstruct Christian pilgrims
1099: Crusaders besiege and massacre inhabitants

had restored Christian rule to Nicaea and to the major centre of Antioch, and in July 1099 captured Jerusalem itself. Over the next twenty years they established four Crusader States in the Levant.

Although it seemed the tide might finally be turning against the Muslims, the Crusaders had in fact attacked at a particularly opportune moment, when Islam was temporarily split by internal feuds. During the ensuing five centuries of struggle, only the First Crusade significantly resisted the military progress of Islam.

Anti-semitism

In 1095 a mob of Crusaders made its way down the River Rhine, Germany, robbing and murdering Jews. These warriors saw Jews – like Muslims – as enemies of Christ, and believed plundering and killing them to be no crime. The church condemned such anti-Jewish attacks. Fifty years later, a Cistercian monk named Radulf again stirred up Rhinelanders against the Jews, rousing Bernard of Clairvaux to travel to Germany, in an attempt to end the massacres.

Crac des Chevaliers Crusaders' castle, Syria.

The Second Crusade (1145–49)

When the Crusader State of Edessa fell to the Turks and Kurds in 1144, widespread support was voiced in Europe for a second crusade. Preached by Bernard of Clairvaux, this crusade was led by Louis VII of France and Conrad III of Germany, but failed miserably. Most of its warriors were killed en route, while those who actually reached Palestine made matters worse by attacking Muslim Damascus, which had been a strong ally of the Christians.

By the late 12th century, crusading had become a society-wide effort. Knights were asked to sacrifice wealth and life to defend the Christian East, and Christians at home supported the Crusaders through prayer, fasting, and almsgiving. Yet the Muslims continued to grow in strength. Their legendary leader Saladin (Salah ad-Din, 1137/8–93) united the Islamic Near East, preaching *jihad* against the Christians. At the Battle of Hattin (1187) he wiped out the Christian armies and captured a relic of the

True Cross. Christian cities surrendered to him, culminating in the disastrous capitulation of Jerusalem.

Third Crusade

The Third Crusade (1189–92), led by Emperor Frederick I 'Barbarossa' of Germany (r. 1155–90), Philip II Augustus of France (r. 1180–1223), and Richard I 'Lionheart' of England (r. 1189–99), appeared very grand. But the aged Frederick drowned crossing a river and his army returned home having never reached the Holy Land. After retaking Acre, Philip of France returned home too. Richard I led Christian forces on to victory, eventually retaking the entire coast of the Levant. But after two abortive attempts, Richard abandoned the struggle to reconquer Jerusalem, agreeing terms with Saladin that ensured peace in the region and free access to Jerusalem for unarmed pilgrims.

The Fourth Crusade (1201–04)

Feuding now broke out between the East and West that led to the diversion to Constantinople of the Fourth Crusade (1202), to support an imperial claimant who promised generous rewards. Once on the throne, he refused to fulfil his promises. Feeling cheated, the Western crusaders captured and sacked Constantinople (1204), the greatest Christian city of the contemporary world. Pope Innocent III (1198–1216), who had authorized this crusade, excommunicated the entire expedition and denounced the crusaders. But the events of 1204 closed the door for centuries on any rapprochement between the Roman Catholic and Greek Orthodox churches.

Numerous squalid military expeditions followed, and warriors, pilgrims, and traders travelled continually between Europe and the Holy Land. A few crusaders sustained a toehold in the Holy Land, but far from converting locals to Christianity, they often took up Eastern customs themselves.

The Crusades finally ended in 1270, leaving a poisonous heritage of ill-feeling between Christians and Muslims.

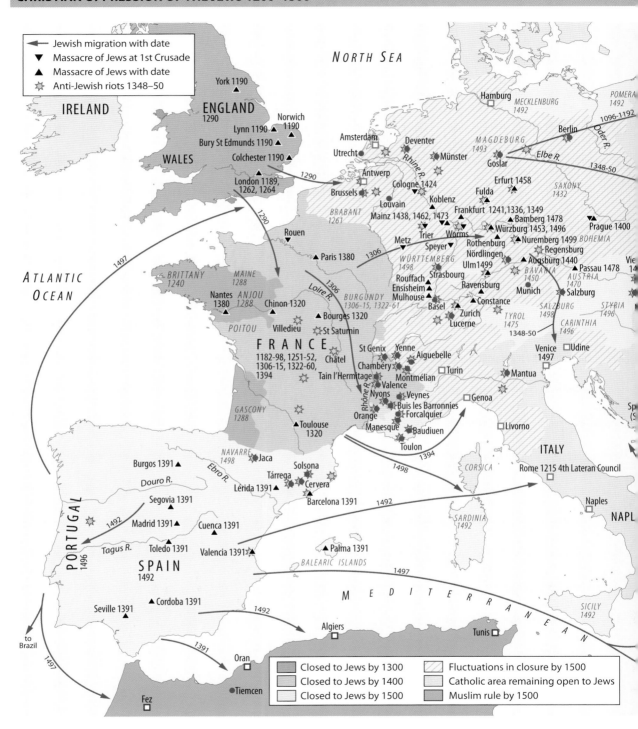

Legend:
- ← Jewish migration with date
- ▼ Massacre of Jews at 1st Crusade
- ▲ Massacre of Jews with date
- ✶ Anti-Jewish riots 1348–50

NORTH SEA

ATLANTIC OCEAN

IRELAND

ENGLAND 1290
York 1190
Norwich 1190
Lynn 1190
Bury St Edmunds 1190
Colchester 1190
London 1189, 1262, 1264

WALES

Amsterdam
Utrecht
Deventer
Münster
Hamburg
MECKLENBURG 1492
POMERA
MAGDEBURG 1493
Berlin
1096–1192
Oder R.
Goslar
Elbe R.
1348–50

Antwerp
Brussels
Cologne 1424
Louvain
Mainz 1438, 1462, 1473
BRABANT 1261
Rhine R.
Koblenz
Frankfurt 1241, 1336, 1349
Erfurt 1458
Fulda
SAXONY 1432
Bamberg 1478
Würzburg 1453, 1496
Prague 1400

Rouen
1290
1290

Metz
Trier
Worms
Speyer
Rothenburg
Nuremberg 1499
BOHEMIA
Nördlingen
Regensburg

BRITTANY 1240
MAINE 1288
Paris 1380
1306
WÜRTTEMBERG 1498
Ulm 1499
Augsburg 1440
BAVARIA 1450
Passau 1478
Vie
14

Nantes 1380
ANJOU 1288
Chinon 1320
Loire R.
1306
Rouffach
Ensisheim
Mulhouse
Strasbourg
Ravensburg
Munich
AUSTRIA 1470
Salzburg

POITOU
Villedieu
St Saturnin
Bourges 1320
BURGUNDY 1306–15, 1322–61
Basel
Zurich
Constance
Lucerne
SALZBURG 1498
STYRIA 1496
TYROL 1475
CARINTHIA 1496
1348–50

FRANCE
1182–98, 1251–52, 1306–15, 1322–60, 1394
Châtel
Tain l'Hermitage
St Genix
Chambéry
Yenne
Aiguebelle
Montmélian
Valence
Nyons
Veynes
Buis les Barronnies
Forcalquier
Baudiuen
Orange
Manesque
Toulon
1394
Venice 1497
Udine
Mantua
Genoa
Livorno
CORSICA
ITALY
Rome 1215 4th Lateran Council
Naples
NAPL

GASCONY 1288
Toulouse 1320
1498

NAVARRE 1498
Jaca
Solsona
Tárrega
Cervera
Lérida 1391
Barcelona 1391
Ebro R.
1492
SARDINIA 1492

Burgos 1391
Douro R.
Segovia 1391
Madrid 1391
Cuenca 1391
Toledo 1391
Tagus R.
Valencia 1391
Palma 1391
BALEARIC ISLANDS
1497

PORTUGAL 1496
1492
SPAIN 1492
MEDITERRANEAN

Seville 1391
Cordoba 1391
1492
Algiers
Tunis
SICILY 1492

to Brazil
1497
1391
Oran
Fez
Tiemcen

Legend (bottom):
- Closed to Jews by 1300
- Closed to Jews by 1400
- Closed to Jews by 1500
- Fluctuations in closure by 1500
- Catholic area remaining open to Jews
- Muslim rule by 1500

map 23

Under Muslim rule, Jews were generally free to practise their own religion. As a result, the Jews of Spain tended to welcome the Islamic conquest of the Arian Christian Visigothic Kingdom. By 950 Cordoba had become a major centre of Jewish scholarship.

The ancient Jewish communities of Italy had by 1095 spread north into the Rhineland, where the First Crusade resulted in attacks on the Jews. In acrimonious public debates, for example in Barcelona in 1263, Jews were pressed to convert. In northern Europe, Jews were excluded from craft guilds, so concentrated instead on money-lending – for which Christians criticized them as 'usurers'. In Spain the Almohad Muslims began to persecute the hitherto unmolested Jews, who as a consequence migrated towards Christian Toledo, which by 1100 supplanted Cordoba as the leading centre of Jewish scholarship.

Hostility to the Jews spread, with conversion campaigns by itinerant friars increasing tension. Jews were vulnerable to arbitrary decrees, religious fanaticism, economic exploitation, and mob violence – sometimes accompanied by baseless accusations of ritual murder of Christian children (the 'blood libel') and desecration of the Host (sacramental wafer).

Some rulers confined the Jews to crowded ghettoes, others expelled them. Around 1300 England, France, and Naples exiled the Jews. In the 1490s came a new wave of Jewish expulsions from Italy, Germany, and the Iberian peninsula. Spanish pogroms created many forced converts, who often continued to practise Judaism secretly, attracting the attentions of the Spanish Inquisition. After nearly 1500 years' settlement in Spain, the Sephardic Jews left for Italy and the Ottoman Empire.

The Jews Oppressed

Christian Pilgrimage

Pilgrimages to Christian holy sites had been undertaken ever since the 4th century, but became more common in the medieval period, when they offered the possibility of gaining God's grace – and even eternal life. Pilgrimage could replace public penance as an act to absolve sin, and from the 11th century journeys to holy sites were organized as a major enterprise.

Three main places were visited by pilgrims: Rome, with the traditional tombs of Saints Peter and Paul; Jerusalem, together with other sites in the Holy Land associated with Jesus; and Santiago de Compostela, where St James' alleged tomb was discovered around 830.

After the recapture of Jerusalem in 1099, during the First Crusade, the Holy Land became particularly popular with pilgrims – whilst the establishment of the Christian Orders of knights made travel there more secure. However, when the Muslim reconquest of Jerusalem in 1187 made the city inaccessible, the number of pilgrimages to Rome and Santiago de Compostela greatly increased.

The routes to Santiago through France, via Tours and Vézelay (which claimed to possess the relics of Mary Magdalene), were the most popular, largely as a result of Cluniac influence. As the idea of the sanctity of saints' relics and of their supernatural power developed, such relics proliferated along these routes. Local shrines, hospices, and owners of relics allegedly recovered from the Holy Land grew affluent at the expense of people undertaking pilgrimages.

Following the murder and canonization of Archbishop Thomas Becket (c. 1118–70), Canterbury became a favourite destination for English pilgrims, as famously described by Geoffrey Chaucer.

MEDIEVAL PILGRIMAGE ROUTES

○ Major pilgrimage destination
○ Pilgrim centre
— Major pilgrimage route c. 350–1500

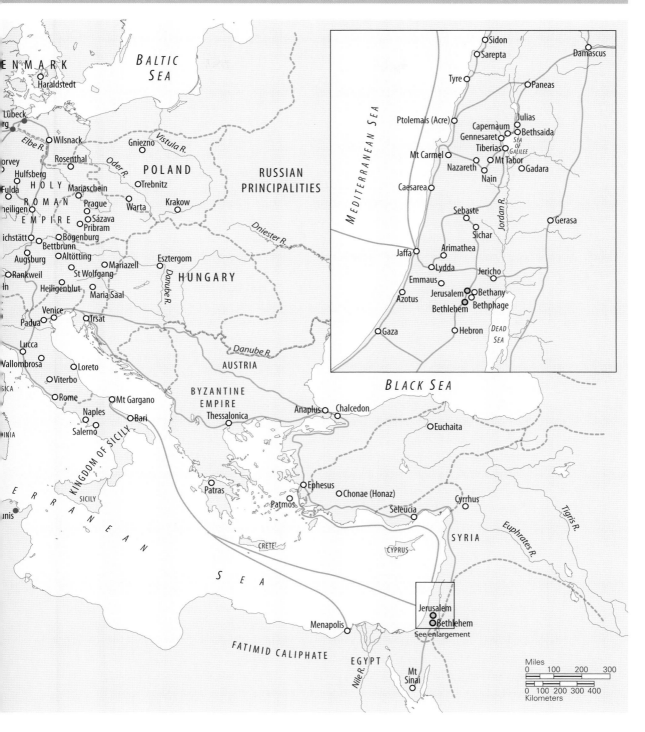

map 24

BALTIC SEA

DENMARK
Haraldstedt

Lübeck
rg

Wilsnack
Gniezno

Vistula R.

Elbe R.

orvey
Rosenthal

POLAND

Oder R.

Hulfsberg
Fulda

HOLY
heiligen
Mariaschein
Trebnitz

Warta
Krakow

ROMAN
Prague

EMPIRE
Sázava
Pribram

ichstätt
Bogenburg
Bettbrunn

Dniester R.

Augsburg
Altötting
Mariazell

Esztergom

Rankweil
St Wolfgang

HUNGARY

lh
Heiligenblut

Maria Saal

Danube R.

Venice
Trsat

Padua

Lucca

Danube R.

AUSTRIA

Vallombrosa
Viterbo

Loreto

BYZANTINE
EMPIRE

Rome

Mt Gargano

Thessalonica

Anaplus
Chalcedon

Naples
Bari

Salerno

KINGDOM OF SICILY

Euchaita

INIA

SICILY

Patras

Ephesus

Chonae (Honaz)

Patmos

Cyrrhus

Seleucia

CRETE

CYPRUS

SYRIA

Euphrates R.

Tigris R.

E
R
R
A
N
E
A
N

unis

SEA

BLACK SEA

Jerusalem
Bethlehem
See enlargement

Menapolis

FATIMID CALIPHATE

EGYPT

Nile R.

Mt Sinai

Enlargement:

MEDITERRANEAN SEA

Sidon
Sarepta

Damascus

Tyre

Paneas

Ptolemais (Acre)

Julias

Capernaum
Bethsaida

Gennesaret
SEA OF GALILEE

Tiberias

Mt Carmel
Mt Tabor

Nazareth
Gadara

Nain

Jordan R.

Caesarea

Sebaste

Gerasa

Sichar

Jaffa
Arimathea

Lydda

Jericho

Emmaus

Jerusalem
Bethany

Azotus
Bethlehem
Bethphage

Gaza

Hebron

DEAD SEA

Miles
0   100   200   300

0   100 200 300 400
Kilometers

The Rise of Learning

During the age of Charlemagne and the 10th and 11th centuries, education in Christian Europe was based mainly in monasteries and cathedral schools – largely the former until the 11th century. A learned monk would teach novices (new monks), and if he were well known adult monks from other houses would also come to study under him. Other young men from wealthy families would be sent to study under a monastic tutor.

By the 12th century, cathedral schools had overtaken the monastic establishments. The chancellor taught the seven liberal arts and theology to advanced students, while other teachers instructed younger scholars in Latin grammar. Most students were destined to become clerics. A licence to teach, given by the chancellor, was the predecessor of a university degree. During the 11th century, the leading cathedral schools in northern Europe were at Laon, Paris, Chartres, and Cologne. Debates in these schools reinvigorated intellectual life in Europe, drawing on the philosophy of ancient Greece, the Bible, and the teachings of the early Christian writers.

First universities

The cathedral schools culminated in the founding of the first universities. The term *universitas* was used to describe a guild, or corporation, of teachers or scholars who banded together. A city with a well-known cathedral might become the centre for a number of schools. Guilds of professors organized the universities of northern Europe, while in Italy the students themselves formed the guilds. The first universities obtained a charter from the pope; those established later applied to the secular ruler.

The gradual development of universities makes it difficult to date them precisely, but among the first were Bologna, Paris, Salerno, Oxford, Cambridge, Montpellier, Padua, Salamanca, and Toulouse. The universities typically taught the seven liberal arts, which included grammar, logic, rhetoric, arithmetic, geometry, astronomy, and music; however logic (philosophy) tended to dominate undergraduate education. Graduate faculties taught medicine, law, and theology. A few universities, such as Bologna, Padua, and Montpellier, devoted themselves to a single discipline – law or medicine. Paris, Cambridge, and Oxford became particularly noted for theology.

Medieval universities were relatively small by modern standards, the largest boasting between 3,000 and 4,000 students.

Scholasticism

Paris was the most important place of learning for theology, adopted by both Franciscans and Dominicans as their main training centre. Major scholars of this period who studied or taught at Paris include William of Ockham (c. 1288–c. 1348), Anselm of Bec (1033–1109), Peter Abelard (1079–1142), Peter Lombard (1100–60), Albertus Magnus ('the Great', c. 1200–80), Duns Scotus (c. 1265–1308), Thomas Aquinas (1225–74), and Lothar of Segni (later Pope Innocent III, r. 1198–1216). Their legacy – a systematic account known as 'scholasticism' – attempted to harmonize the theology of Augustine with the philosophy of classical Greek thinkers, especially Aristotle. The synthesis of Catholic dogma and reasoning by logic was the achievement of Aquinas in his *Summa Theologica*, a cornerstone of future Catholic theology, although some of his teaching was condemned by the Church in 1277.

By 1500 there were more than 60 universities in Europe.

map 25

Legend:
- ● Major monastic school
- ▲ Important cathedral school
- ■ University founded before 1300
- ■ University founded 1301–1400
- ■ University founded 1401–1500

NORWAY

NORTH SEA

SWEDEN

BALTIC SEA

SCOTLAND
■ Aberdeen 1494

■ Glasgow 1451
■ St Andrews 1410/13
● Jarrow
● Wearmouth
▲ York ● Rievaulx

IRELAND

ENGLAND
● Peterborough
■ Oxford 1167 ■ Cambridge 1209
■ London
WALES
▲ Canterbury

DENMARK
● Lübeck ■ Rostock 1419 ■ Greifswald 1456
■ Copenhagen 1478

POLAND

Elbe R.
Oder R.
Vistula R.

▲ Utrecht ▲ Hildesheim ▲ Magdeburg
● Corvey ■ Leipzig 1409
■ Cologne 1388 ■ Erfurt 1379
▲ Tournai Rhine R. ● Fulda
▲ Trier 1473 ▲ Mainz 1477 ■ Würzburg 1402 ▲ Bamberg
● Worms ■ Heidelberg 1386 ■ Prague 1348
■ Krakow 1364

● Caen 1432 ▲ Rouen
● Bec ▲ Laon
▲ Rheims
■ Paris c.1150
▲ Chartres ■ Tübingen 1477 ▲ Regensburg
Seine R. ▲ Clairvaux ■ Ingolstadt 1472
● Mont St Michel
● Savigny ● Fleury ■ Freiburg 1457 HOLY
■ Angers 1337 ▲ Basel 1460 ROMAN Danube R.
Loire R. ■ Orleans 1235 ■ Besançon 1485 ● St Gall EMPIRE
■ Nantès 1460 ▲ Tours ▲ Cîteaux SWISS
■ Bourges 1463 ● Cluny CONFEDERATION
■ Poitiers 1431 ■ Dôle 1422

■ Vienna 1365 HUNGARY
■ Pressburg 1467
■ Buda 1389
■ Pécs 1367

FRANCE
● La Chaise Dieu
■ Cahors 1331 ■ Valence 1452
■ Bordeaux 1441 ■ Grenoble 1339
■ Toulouse 1229 ■ Orange 1365
■ Avignon 1303 ■ Aix 1409

■ Vercelli 1228 ▲ Milan ■ Vicenza 1204 ■ Treviso 1318
▲ Pavia 1361 ● Venice
■ Padua 1222
■ Turin 1404 ■ Piacenza 1248 ■ Bologna 1088 ■ Ferrara 1391 ▲ Ravenna
■ Pisa 1343 ■ Florence 1321 ■ Arezzo 1215
■ Siena 1240
■ Perugia 1308

BYZANTINE EMPIRE

ATLANTIC OCEAN

NAVARRE
LÉON ■ Palencia 1208 ■ Huesca 1354
■ Valladolid 1241 ARAGON
CASTILE ■ Sigüenza 1489 ■ Lérida 1300
■ Salamanca 1134 ■ Barcelona 1450
PORTUGAL ▲ Alcalá 1499
Tagus R. ▲ Toledo
bon 1290 ■ Valencia 1499
■ Montpellier 1289
■ Perpignan 1349

CORSICA
SARDINIA
■ Rome 1303 ▲

● Monte Cassino
■ Naples 1224
■ Salerno 1231

KINGDOM OF SICILY
▲ Monreale ▲ Messina
■ Catania 1434

■ Seville 1254

MEDITERRANEAN SEA

Miles
0 100 200 300
0 100 200 400
Kilometers

The Rise of the Friars

The Italian Francis of Assisi (1181/2–1226) rejected his family fortune in obedience to Christ's words in the Gospels, and took up a wandering life, followed by a few friends. They begged from the rich, gave to the poor, tended the sick, and preached to anyone they met.

In time Francis' followers became recognized as a new Christian order, the Franciscans – often nicknamed 'Grey Friars' from their grey habits. Though they took similar vows to other monks, the Franciscans were known as 'friars' (brothers), and as 'mendicants' were constantly on the road, not based in a single location or building. They broke away from the monastic ideal of living apart from the world, desiring to bring the faith to ordinary people by living among them.

Although Francis is often associated with the birds and wild creatures, his efforts were largely devoted to the cities of medieval Italy. His friend Clare (c.1193–1253) established an order for women similar to the Franciscans, known as the Poor Clares.

Mission was a key concern for the Franciscans. Francis travelled to Egypt in 1219; and Franciscans later journeyed to Hungary, Spain, and the East, establishing a presence in Eastern Europe, North Africa, and the Middle East in the 13th century. Franciscan missionaries later travelled as far as Central Asia and India.

Dominic

The Dominicans, 'Black Friars', or the Order of Friars Preacher, were founded by the Spaniard Dominic de Guzmán (1170–1221) in 1214. Like the Franciscans, these preaching-monks spent much of their time in the towns and cities, gaining respect by their simple living and caring. The Dominicans pursued learning keenly and were closely involved in the rise of the new universities.

Miles
0   100   200

0   100   200   300
Kilometers

Edinburgh

York

Dublin

No
ENGLAN

Oxford   Lon
Canter

ATLANTIC
OCEAN

Angers

Li

To

Léé

Salamanca   SPAIN

PORTUGAL   Tagus R.   Toledo

Franciscan houses established by 1300
Dominican houses established by 1500

SWEDEN

Skanninge

Visby

BALTIC SEA

RTH SEA

Ribe

Lund

Roskilde

Lübeck   Stralsund

Bremen

Vilnius

RUSSIA

Magdeburg

Oder R.

Vistula R.

POLAND

Cologne

GERMANY

Elbe R.

Lublin

Trier   Mainz   Prague

Krakow

vais

Strasbourg   Rhine R.

HUNGARY

Dniester R.

s

Basel

Danube R.

SWITZERLAND

Vienna

Bern

AUSTRIA

Cluj

Pécs

Padua

BULGARIA

Genoa   Bologna

Danube R.

ellier   Florence

Rhône R.

Perugia

Dubrovnik

Rome   ITALY

CORSICA

Naples

SARDINIA

ORCA

Palermo

ITERRANEAN

Syracuse

SEA

Missions to the Mongols

An extraordinary achievement of the Franciscans and Dominicans was their missions outside Christendom. The Mongol invasions had opened up the road to the East, and by 1239 Dominicans had penetrated east of the middle Volga. Ten years later Andrew of Longjumeau reached Tabriz, in modern north-west Iran. For some 100 years Dominicans worked in central Asia, India, and Samarkand, while Franciscans reached as far as Peking (Beijing), capital of the Mongol empire, where they established a bishopric. These pioneering missionaries discovered Nestorian Christians in China and thousands of Christians who had been carried off to Asia by the Mongols after their raids on Europe.

The Mongols first entered Christendom in 1237, attacking Kievan Rus' and destroying its great trading cities. Pope Innocent IV (r. 1243–54) was so impressed by the Mongols' military might – they were not yet committed to Islam – that between 1245 and 1247 he dispatched Giovanni Carpini (c. 1185–1252) far into Asia to propose an alliance with them. A few years later Louis IX of France ('St Louis', r. 1226–70) sent another ambassador, the Franciscan William of Rubruck (c. 1220–c. 1293), which encouraged others to make similar journeys. In 1294 an Italian Franciscan, John of Montecorvino (1247–1328), arrived at the court of the Khan in Peking bearing a letter from the pope. He remained for 30 years, building churches, translating the New Testament, and winning converts. However in 1368 the Mongols were overthrown and the Ming dynasty once again closed China to foreigners.

After Montecorvino's death, the khan asked Pope Benedict XII to send another spiritual adviser to his court. In response, Giovanni de' Marignolli (John of Marignola,

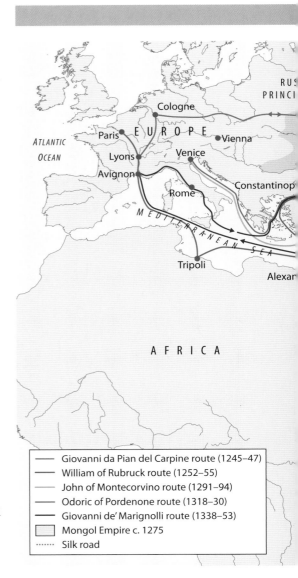

| Giovanni da Pian del Carpine route (1245–47) |
| William of Rubruck route (1252–55) |
| John of Montecorvino route (1291–94) |
| Odoric of Pordenone route (1318–30) |
| Giovanni de' Marignolli route (1338–53) |
| Mongol Empire c. 1275 |
| Silk road |

fl. 1338–53), originally from Florence, set out from Avignon in 1338. Travelling via Constantinople and the Black Sea to Caffa, his company arrived at the court of Mohammed Uzbeg, Khan of the Golden Horde, at Sarai, before crossing the steppes to Armalec (Kulja), where he built a church. He reached Cambalec (Beijing) in 1342, where he was welcomed by the last of the Mongol dynasty

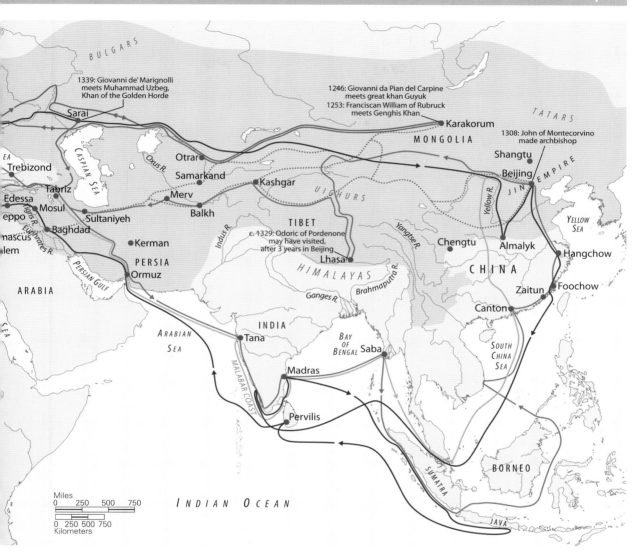

BULGARS

1339: Giovanni de' Marignolli
meets Muhammad Uzbeg,
Khan of the Golden Horde

1246: Giovanni da Pian del Carpine
meets great khan Guyuk
1253: Franciscan William of Rubruck
meets Genghis Khan

TATARS

Karakorum

MONGOLIA

1308: John of Montecorvino
made archbishop

Shangtu

Sarai

CASPIAN SEA

Oxus R.

Otrar

Samarkand

Kashgar

Beijing

JIN EMPIRE

EA

Trebizond

Tabriz

Merv

UIGHURS

Yellow R.

Edessa

Mosul

Balkh

YELLOW SEA

eppo

Baghdad

Sultaniyeh

TIBET
c. 1329: Odoric of Pordenone
may have visited,
after 3 years in Beijing

Chengtu

Almalyk

nascus

Kerman

Indus R.

Yangtse R.

CHINA

Hangchow

lem

PERSIA

Lhasa

HIMALAYAS

Brahmaputra R.

Zaitun

Foochow

Euphrates R.

Tigris R.

PERSIAN GULF

Ormuz

Ganges R.

Canton

SEA

ARABIA

INDIA

ARABIAN
SEA

Tana

BAY
OF
BENGAL

Saba

SOUTH
CHINA
SEA

MALABAR COAST

Madras

Pervilis

Miles
0   250   500   750

0   250 500 750
Kilometers

INDIAN   OCEAN

SUMATRA

BORNEO

JAVA

in China. Marignolli left China in 1347,
travelling back to Europe via Malabar, Java,
Pervilis, Sri Lanka, Ormuz, Baghdad, Mosul,

Aleppo, Damascus, and Jerusalem. He finally
arrived in Avignon in 1353, delivering a letter
from the great khan to Pope Innocent VI.

The reforming monastic orders' new emphasis on poverty encouraged some to challenge affluent clergy and corrupt monasteries. Peter Valdes (or Waldo, d. c. 1210), a rich merchant from Lyons, sold all he possessed, translated the New Testament into the vernacular, and preached without authorization. His followers – known as Waldensians – criticized ecclesiastical authority, which soon led to their condemnation as heretics. Nevertheless the movement grew, and by the close of the 13th century had spread through much of Europe. Followers in northern Italy became more radical.

A more extreme sect, the Cathars, or Albigensians – from Albi, France – had appeared early in the 11th century, and by the 1160s was established in Languedoc and Lombardy. Its adherents appear to have believed that all created matter was evil, and the incarnation and crucifixion false. In 1209 Pope Innocent III launched a savage 20-year crusade against both the Albigensians and Waldensians.

At the Council of Constance (1414–18) Jan Hus (John Huss, c. 1372–1415), a reformer from Bohemia whose denunciation of the morals of the clergy angered the church authorities, was convicted of heresy and burnt to death. His views had much in common with Lollardy in England, which drew on the writings of John Wyclif (1330–84). Hus became a national hero and the Czechs established the Hussite church, or Bohemian Brethren, which formed a national focus for rebellion against the papacy.

In the Low Countries from the late 14th century the Brethren of the Common Life propagated the *devotio moderna* reform movement among both lay people and members of religious orders.

Legend:
- Hussites
- ○ Hussite centre
- Lollards
- ● Lollard centre
- Albigensians (Cathars)
- ● Albigensian centre
- Bogomils (Paulicians)
- ● Bogomil centre
- Waldensians
- ● Waldensian centre
- Fraticelli
- ○ Fraticelli centre
- Brethren of the Free Spirit
- ● Brethren of the Free Spirit centre

DENMARK

Hamburg

HOLY ROMAN EMPIRE

POLAND

Warsaw

Vistula R.

Deventer

roonendaal

Cologne

Liège

Elbe R.

Oder R.

Melnik

Cesky Brod

Prague

Kutná Hora

Tábor

Trier

Metz

Toul

Rhine R.

Regensburg

Sankt Oswald

Pupping

Neustadt

Sankt Christophen

Danube R.

Jonvelle

Besançon

HUNGARY

Vienne

Bergamo

Legnano

Vicenza

Milan

Turin

Pavia

Verona

Parma

Ferrara

Valence

Genoa

Modena

Bologna

Montélimar

Faenza

Florence

Rimini

Avignon

Arles

Pisa

Siena

ADRIATIC SEA

Nish

Aix

Antibes

Arezzo

Sofia

ellier

Asciano

Belyatovo

Orvieto

Philippopolis

Viterbo

CORSICA

Rome

BYZANTINE

Naples

EAN   SEA

SARDINIA

KINGDOM OF SICILY

EMPIRE

Christian Muscovy: 1221–1510

In the mid-13th century the Mongols invaded the Rus' and had by 1240 captured Kiev. Although Aleksandr Nevskii (1221–63) attempted to stem the tide, by 1262 the Mongols controlled all the lands of the Rus'. Yet this was not a unqualified disaster for Christianity; the Mongol Kipchak Khanate, for example, based at Sarai on the lower Volga, tolerated the Christian church.

Metropolitan Kirill (r. 1242–82) strove to sustain religious cohesion, but in 1299/1300 Maximus of Kiev (r. 1283–1305) transferred the Metropolitan seat of the Russian Orthodox Church from Kiev to Vladimir, 100 miles east of Moscow, and his own residence to Moscow itself – moves that subverted the importance of Kiev.

Following the Mongol invasions, a collection of principalities formed in the Ukraine, Belarus', and Greater Russia, including Tver and the urban republics of Novgorod and Pskov, with Moscow becoming increasingly dominant. In 1331 the ruler of Moscow was given the title 'grand prince', and his attacks on other princes, such as those of Tver, gained the support of the Mongols.

The church was pivotal in the survival and life of the Russian state. Sergius of Radonezh (1314–92), Metropolitan of Kiev and all Russia, who established the Monastery of the Holy Trinity, encouraged resistance to the Mongols, while Metropolitan Alexius (1296–1378) helped his people both to withstand years of Tatar oppression and to expand economically.

During the 14th century Novgorod – founded in 1221 by Iurii Vsevolodovich – reached the height of its success, based on the profits of the Baltic trade. But in the following century the princes of Moscow challenged its independence. Prince Ivan III of Muscovy ('Ivan the Great', r. 1462–1505) defeated Novgorod in 1471.

Third Rome

By 1448, the Russian Church had become independent of Constantinople. Metropolitan Jonah (or Jonas, r. 1448–61), installed by the Council of Russian bishops in 1448, was given the title Metropolitan of Moscow and All Rus. In 1472 Ivan III married Zoe, niece of the last Greek Emperor of Constantinople; from this time dates the claim of Russian rulers to succeed the Greeks as protectors of Orthodox Christianity and successors to Byzantium, dubbing Moscow 'the Third Rome' and its ruler 'Tsar' (Caesar).

Monastic life flourished in Russia, focusing on prayer and spiritual growth. Disciples of Sergius founded hundreds of monasteries across Russia, some of the most notable in the north, to show that the faith could flourish even in inhospitable lands. Artists such as the icon painter Andrei Rublev (c. 1360–1427/8 or 1430) adorned many Moscow churches – for example the Kremlin, the monastery of St Sergii, the Dormition cathedral in Vladimir, and the Church of the Trinity, Zvengorod.

Possessors and Non-Possessors

In 1503 Nilus of Sora (1443–1508) clashed with Joseph, Abbot of Volokolamsk (1439/40–1515) in a dispute concerning the role and duty of monastics. Joseph stressed the social obligations of monks, while Nilus insisted that a monk's primary role is prayer and separation from the world. A split occurred: Joseph's 'Possessors' believed church and state should be closely allied, and that monks should care for the sick and the poor; Nilus' 'Non-Possessors' opted for a life of holy detachment.

Muscovy in 1300

Grand Principality of Moscow in 1462

☐ Important monastery

Territory acquired by Ivan III, Grand Prince of Moscow, between 1462 and 1505

Territory acquired by Vasily III, Grand Prince of Moscow, between 1505 and 1533

Part 4

The Reformation and After

...A reformation of the Church is near at hand..., and while God opens new ways for the preaching of the Gospel by the discoveries of the Portuguese and Spaniards, we must hope that he will also visit his Church and raise her from the abasement into which she has fallen...

JACQUES LEFÈVRE D'ÉTAPLES
(c. 1455–1536)

The West in 1500

Throughout the Middle Ages pope and emperor had been engaged in a contest for supremacy, a conflict that generally resulted in victory for the papacy, but created bitter antagonism between Rome and the Holy Roman Empire. Such antagonism increased in the 14th and 15th centuries as national feelings grew – particularly in German-speaking countries. Resentment of papal taxes and against submission to officials of a distant, foreign papacy became common in Europe.

During the 15th century the papacy began to reap the results of centuries of compromise. The Avignon papacy (1303–78) and Great Schism (1378) saw two – even three – men claiming to be pope; whilst the Council of Constance (1414–18) became a power struggle between bishops and pope, all damaging papal government and harming the church's reputation in the eyes of the laity.

The church continued to sell offices and indulgences, and remained the political tool of princes and a useful source of income for second sons and the corrupt. Criticism of clerical abuses had been widespread in Europe for centuries. But as society became more urbanized, better educated, and richer, the literate laity turned up the volume of criticism of the church and clergy.

Yet in 1500 the Catholic Church seemed to stand undivided and virtually unchallenged. Its dioceses and archdioceses neatly divided up Western Europe, its bureaucracy was widely envied, and its wealth was almost unmatched.

THE WESTERN CHURCH IN 1500

map 30

Legend:
- Habsburg Lands
- Union of Calmar
- Venetian territory
- ■ Archbishopric
- National borders
- Regional borders
- Archdiocese boundaries
- Limit of Islamic influence c. 1500

Miles
0   100   200

0   100   200   300
Kilometers

DENMARK-NORWAY

SWEDEN

BALTIC SEA

Lund

Riga

RUSSIA

Bremen

Danzig

Vistula R.

LITHUANIA

Magdeburg

Gnesen (Gniezno)

Warsaw

SAXONY

Elbe R.

POLAND

logne

HOLY ROMAN EMPIRE

Prague

Oder R.

Krakow

Lvov

rier   Mainz

Rhine R.

Salzburg

Danube R.

AUSTRIA

Gran

Buda Pest

MOLDAVIA

Besançon

Kalocsa

HUNGARY

Tarantaise

SAVOY

Udine

Venice

WALLACHIA

Bucharest

Embrun

Milan

Ravenna

Zara

OTTOMAN

BLACK SEA

on   Genoa

Florence

PAPAL STATES

Spalato

Danube R.

Siena

Bagusa

CORSICA

Rome

Antivari

Constantinople

Sassari

Siponto

Benevento

Brindisi

EMPIRE

Oristano

Naples

NAPLES

Otranto

Cagliari

Rossano

Palermo   Messina

Ephesus

Monreale   SICILY

KHANATE OF CRIMEA

DITERRANEAN   SEA

Charles V

As a descendant of Ferdinand of Aragon (r. 1479–1516) and Isabella of Castile (r. 1474–1504), Charles inherited the Spanish crown in 1516, taking the title Charles I. He also ruled Sardinia, Sicily, the Kingdom of Naples, and the Balearic Islands, while the newly colonized Spanish territories in the New World poured wealth into his treasury. Charles inherited from his grandparents much of the Netherlands, Franche-Comté, Luxembourg, and the Habsburg lands of Germany; while Charles' Habsburg family also claimed Hungary, Bohemia, Moravia, and Silesia. In 1519 Charles was elected Holy Roman Emperor.

Reformation

However Charles' extensive holdings and ambitions did not afford him an easy rule. In 1517 Martin Luther made the first moves in what soon grew into a major dispute within the church. Charles might have crushed the Reformation in its early stages, in concerted action with the other major powers, had Pope Clement VII (r. 1523–34) not allied himself with the French king, Francis I (r. 1515–47).

At the Imperial Diet at Augsburg (1530), attended by Charles V, there was optimism about re-uniting the opposing religious parties. The Lutherans submitted their beliefs in the form of the Augsburg Confession (or *Augustana*) but the Roman Catholics rejected all the reformers' submissions and the Emperor ordered a recess. The Protestant princes realized that Charles V now intended to make war on Protestantism, and in response formed the Schmalkaldic League.

CHARLES V AND THE EUROPEAN REFORMATIO

map 31

NORWAY

SWEDEN

DENMARK

BALTIC SEA

●Bremen

●Magdeburg

Danzig●

Vistula R.

●Warsaw

POLAND

LITHUANIA

SAXONY

HOLY
ROMAN
EMPIRE

Elbe R.

●Prague

Oder R.

●Cologne

●Mainz

Trier●

●Worms

Hagenau●

Rhine R.

Krakow●

●Kiev

1530: Lutherans present Charles V
with Augsburg Confession
1548: Augsburg Interim: Charles
makes some concessions
to Protestants
1555: Peace of Augsburg:
Lutheranism recognized

1540–41: Charles V attempts
reconciliation with Protestants
●Regensburg (Ratisbon)

●Augsburg

●Salzburg

Danube R.

HUNGARY

Venice●

Milan●

Genoa●

ignon

Florence●

PAPAL
STATES

Danube R.

OTTOMAN

BLACK SEA

Rome●

1519: Charles V crowned
Holy Roman Emperor

Naples●   NAPLES

CORSICA

EMPIRE

Constantinople●

●Cagliari

Palermo●

SICILY

MEDITERRANEAN SEA

Ragusa●

▨	Roman Catholic
▨	Protestant c.1555
▨	Territory of Charles V
——	Holy Roman Empire boundary
- - -	Borders

Christian Europe: 1560

In 1517 Martin Luther (1483–1546) posted his 95 Theses at Wittenberg. Huldreich Zwingli of Zurich (1484–1531) also revolted against Rome, and the Frenchman John Calvin (1509–64) later became convinced he should restore the church to its original purity.

Luther's teachings were condemned by Charles V at the Diet of Worms (1521), whilst a Catholic majority at the Diet of Speyer (1529) attempted to prohibit the further spread of Lutheranism and to ensure toleration for Catholics in Lutheran territories. Lutheran princes 'protested' against this, thereby coining the term 'Protestant'.

But the Reformation was motivated as much by politics as by religion; rulers of Europe took advantage of the church's unpopularity to seize much of its wealth and power. In 1534 Henry VIII (1491–1547) declared himself Head of the Church of England, while many of the German princes supported Luther for both political and religious reasons.

Under the Peace of Augsburg (1555) it was agreed that the ruler of every German state – there were about 300 – should choose between Roman Catholicism and Lutheranism, enforcing his chosen faith upon his subjects (*cuius regio, eius religio*). Meanwhile Reformed Protestantism, or 'Calvinism', took root – at least for a time – in France, Poland, Hungary, and Scotland.

The longstanding concept of the religious unity of a single Christian community throughout Western Europe under the supreme authority of the pope had been destroyed once for all.

REFORMATION EUROPE: 1560

map 32

NORWAY

Oslo

Stockholm

SWEDEN

BALTIC SEA

DENMARK Copenhagen

COURLAND

LIVONIA

Catholic
Catholic minority
Lutheran
Anglican
Calvinist/Reformed/Zwinglian
Hussite/Moravian
Orthodox
Muslim

PRUSSIA

RUSSIAN PRINCIPALITIES

Elbe R.

BRANDENBURG

Hanover

Münster

Vistula R.

Warsaw

POLAND

Wittenberg

Oder R.

SAXONY

HESSE HOLY

NASSAU ROMAN

EMPIRE

Dresden

SILESIA

Krakow

LITHUANIA

Rhine R.

Prague

BOHEMIA

MORAVIA

PALATINATE

Nuremberg

HUNGARY

Strasbourg

WÜRTTEMBERG

Augsburg

Vienna

BAVARIA

AUSTRIA

Danube R.

Basel

FRANCHE-

COMTÉ

SWISS

CONFEDERATION

Bern

TYROL

TRANSYLVANIA

Geneva

SAVOY

VENETIAN

REPUBLIC

Venice

WALLACHIA

MODENA

GENOA

Florence

TUSCANY

PAPAL

STATES

BOSNIA

Danube R.

BLACK SEA

CORSICA

Rome

O T T O M A N

NAPLES

SERBIA

SARDINIA

E M P I R E

M E D I T E R R A N E A N   S E A

GREECE

Athens

SICILY

Calvinist influenced
Lutheran influenced
Anabaptist minority
Socinian minority
Waldensian minority
Holy Roman Empire boundary
Ottoman Empire boundary

The Counter Reformation

Revival in the Roman Catholic Church, the 'Catholic Reformation', was in part a response to the rise of Protestantism. But reform of the Catholic religious orders had already begun independently as early as the 1520s.

In 1534 the Society of Jesus was founded by Ignatius Loyola (1491–1556) to spearhead the Catholic revival. It soon became largely responsible for reinforcing the Catholic faith in southern Europe.

The Roman Catholic Church summoned the Council of Trent (1545–63) to re-establish doctrines of the Catholicism challenged by Protestantism. At the council, leaders of the Latin Church tightened discipline and doctrine, and re-invigorated the church. A leaner, more focussed, Roman Catholic Church emerged and the supremacy of the pope was re-affirmed.

In the late 16th and early 17th centuries, wars of religion shook every country in Europe. The Peace of Augsburg (1555) had not ended conflict in central Europe, but merely provided a breathing space. The territorial expansion of Protestantism reached its widest extent in central Europe around 1566, after which it began to recede confronted by the militant forces of the Catholic Counter-Reformation.

The reforms, divisions, and revolutions of the sixteenth century led to a redefining, tightening, and redrawing of geographical, ecclesiastical, and theological boundaries. But the major divide remained between Roman Catholic insistence upon the finality of papal authority and Protestant insistence upon the finality of Biblical rule.

CHRISTIAN EUROPE: 1600

SCOTLAND
Edinburgh
NORTH SEA
IRELAND
Dublin
ENGLAND
WALES
London
Plymouth
ATLANTIC OCEAN
Rouen
La Fièche
Loire R.
Bou
FRA
Bordeaux
Toulouse
Santiago de Compostela
NAVARRE
Valladolid
Barcelon
Salamanca
Madrid
PORTUGAL
Tagus R.
Toledo
Valencia
Lisbon
SPAIN
Seville

Miles
0   100   200

0   100   200   300
Kilometers

map 33

Christiania

Stockholm

ESTONIA

DENMARK - NORWAY

SWEDEN

LIVONIA

COURLAND

Riga

BALTIC
SEA

Copenhagen

PRUSSIA

Danzig

Elbe R.

Stettin

BRANDENBURG

dam

Hanover

HOLY

Münster

ROMAN

Wittenberg

EMPIRE

Vistula R.

Warsaw

P O L A N D

werp

Rhine R.

SAXONY

Oder R.

HESSE

Fulda

Dresden

SILESIA

Glatz

NASSAU

Mainz

Bamberg

Prague

Kuttenberg

Krakow

L I T H U A N I A

Trier

Würzburg

PALATINATE

Nuremberg

BOHEMIA

n

Strasbourg

Dillingen

Ingolstadt

MORAVIA

H U N G A R Y

Molsheim

WÜRTTEMBERG

Augsburg

Brünn
(Brno)

MOLDAVIA

Basel

BAVARIA

Vienna

Trnava

ANCHE
OMTE

SWISS
CONFEDERATION

TYROL

AUSTRIA

Danube R.

TRANSYLVANIA

Bern

Graz

Geneva

Milan

VENETIAN
REPUBLIC

Neuhaus

SAVOY

MODENA

Parma

Venice

WALLACHIA

ignon

Genoa

Danube R.

GENOA

Florence

O

BLACK SEA

CORSICA

TUSCANY

PAPAL
STATES

T

BOSNIA

T

Rome

O

M

SERBIA

A

NAPLES

N

Sassan

Naples

SARDINIA

E

M

Cagliari

GREECE

P

I

D

Palermo

Messina

R

Athens

E

SICILY

I
T
E
R
R
A
N
E
A
N   S
E A

Legend:

- Roman Catholic
- Recovered to Catholicism by 1600
- Lutheran
- Anglican
- Calvinist/Reformed/Huguenot
- Calvinist influenced
- Moravian
- Orthodox
- Muslim
- ○ Major Jesuit seminary or centre
- — Holy Roman Empire boundary
- ← Route of Spanish Armada

The Thirty Years' War

The Thirty Years' War (1618–48) was a disaster for central Europe. Rival armies marched across the region, sometimes fighting, constantly plundering. Great military leaders appeared, flourished, and fell again. After lengthy negotiations, compromise finally prevailed, and the Peace of Westphalia was signed in October 1648.

Although ostensibly a religious conflict, this war did not significantly change the confessional map of central Europe. The Peace of Westphalia reaffirmed the Peace of Augsburg, except that Reformed Churches were now awarded the same legal recognition as Roman Catholics and Lutherans, choice of permitted faith depending upon the government of the respective territory. With the exception of lands of the Austrian Habsburgs, where Counter Reformation gains were allowed to stand, areas that were Protestant or Catholic in January 1624 were to remain so.

The heaviest losers in the war were the German people. For thirty years armies had lived off their lands, looting, murdering, raping, and destroying. Plague and famine followed the mercenary armies – and even cannibalism was reported in several areas.

The Treaty of Westphalia marked the end of the final significant religious war in Europe. Whereas up to 1648 religion had been a major factor determining internal and external politics, it became much less so after the devastating Thirty Years' War.

	Catholic
	Catholic influenced
	Lutheran
	Anglican
	Calvinist/Reformed
	Calvinist influenced
	Hussite/Moravian
	Orthodox
	Muslim
——	Holy Roman Empire boundary
····	Extent of Ottoman Empire

Christiania (Oslo)

Stockholm

DENMARK–NORWAY

SWEDEN

LIVONIA

BALTIC SEA

COURLAND

Riga

Copenhagen

PRUSSIA

RUSSIA

Danzig

Stettin

Elbe R.

Hanover

BRANDENBURG

Vistula R.

LITHUANIA

Warsaw

POLAND

HOLY ROMAN EMPIRE

SAXONY

Dresden

SILESIA

Oder R.

Krakow

Prague

Dnieper R.

PALATINATE

Nuremberg

BOHEMIA

MORAVIA

...phine R.

WÜRTTEMBERG

BAVARIA

AUSTRIA

HUNGARY

Dniester R.

...sbourg

Augsburg

Vienna

Basel

Danube R.

TRANSYLVANIA

MOLDAVIA

SWISS CONFEDERATION

Bern

...a

VENETIAN REPUBLIC

Venice

WALLACHIA

Florence

TUSCANY

BOSNIA

BLACK SEA

CORSICA

PAPAL STATES

Rome

SERBIA

OTTOMAN EMPIRE

NAPLES

Naples

SARDINIA

GREECE

...ITERRANEAN SEA

SICILY

Athens

Portugal colonized Brazil, while the remainder of South America fell within the Spanish sphere of influence, as agreed in the Treaty of Tordesillas (1494). The Pope instructed both colonial powers to take missionaries to the New World and set up new bishoprics in a network of dioceses.

Missions to America

The Spanish conquered the Aztec kingdom in Mexico and the Incas of Peru, employing particularly brutal methods. Despite the appalling way in which they were treated, many Native Americans converted to Christianity: it was claimed that between 1524 and 1531 more than one million were baptized. In reality enthusiastic missionaries exaggerated their success, and conversions were often quite superficial, with 'converts' possessing minimal understanding of their new faith. Generally the Spanish treated the natives as inferiors. A few priests protested, the best known of them being Bartolomé de las Casas (1484–1566), who became convinced Spanish treatment of Native Americans was contrary to Christian teaching.

Ignatius Loyola

In 1534 the Spaniard Ignatius Loyola (c. 1491–1556) with six friends vowed to practise poverty, chastity, and celibacy, and to devote the rest of their lives to mission, thus initiating the 'Society of Jesus', better known as the Jesuits. In 1540 this new order received written authorization from Paul III, and set out to fulfil its mission to carry the gospel to the peoples of newly discovered continents. The Jesuits regarded themselves as a spiritual élite, at the pope's disposal to use however he felt appropriate for spreading the 'true church'. The order grew rapidly: when its founder Loyola died in 1556, there were already more than 1,500 Jesuits, mainly in Spain, Portugal, and Italy, but also in India, Brazil, Japan, Africa, and almost every other country in Europe.

The Jesuits focussed on three main tasks: education, counteracting Protestantism, and missionary expansion into new areas. In France, the Low Countries, southern Germany, and particularly eastern Europe, the Jesuits led the counter-attack against Protestants. Several Jesuits served as papal representatives, or legates, tying countries such as Ireland, Sweden, and Russia more firmly to Rome. Other Jesuits served as court preacher or confessor to the emperor, the kings of France and Poland, and the dukes of Bavaria.

Jesuit missions

When they sailed to America, Africa, and Asia in search of converts, Jesuit priests often travelled in Spanish and Portuguese ships searching for new colonies. They endowed their converts with their own enthusiastic brand of Catholicism. The Jesuits played a leading role in the conversion of Brazil and Paraguay, and, together with the Dominicans, Franciscans, and Augustinians, led the Church of Rome in a period of rapid overseas expansion between 1550 and 1650. As a result of their enterprise, almost all of Mexico, Central, and South America, along with much of the population of the Philippines, became adherents of the Roman Catholic Church.

In Brazil and Paraguay the Jesuits introduced a controversial method of protecting Native Americans from exploitation. Between 1583 and 1605 they created a system of around 30 native reservations, or *reductions*, offering settlement and refuge to Guarani Indians who had been enslaved by Spanish colonists. Residents led a rather regimented life,

isolated from the 'corruption' of wider society, in a system that has been criticized for its paternalism.

Francis Xavier

The pioneering Jesuit missionary Francis Xavier (1506–52) – 'apostle to the Indies and Japan' – was born in Navarre, Spain. When John III of Portugal asked the Jesuits for missionaries for his empire, Xavier responded, arriving in Goa, India, in 1542. Respected for his ability to live and work alongside the poor, Francis soon moved on to Sri Lanka, the Molucca Islands, the Banda Islands, and the Malay Peninsula, preaching and baptizing wherever he went. In 1549

Xavier landed at Kagoshima, Japan, adopting local mores to attract converts. Before he could gain entry to China, he died of fever, still aged only forty-six.

Other Jesuits carried on Xavier's work, achieving considerable success, and by 1600 the Japanese church numbered more than 300,000 members. However, after rivalry erupted between the Western powers and Christian orders, the Japanese shogun (governor) instigated brutal persecution of Christians. In 1640 the Japanese government set up an Office of Inquisition for Christian Affairs to detect and punish Christians. Before long the Japanese church was almost completely eradicated.

HUDSON
BAY

Quebec 1674
NEW FRANCE

1603

Azores 1534
PORTUGAL SPAIN

Colorado R.
Mississippi R.

*NEW
GALICIA*

Baltimore 1789

Ce
Tangi
Safi 1487

*NORTH
ATLANTIC
OCEAN*

Funchal 1514
Las Palmas 1404

Sonora 1779
Durango 1620

Linares
1777

New Orleans 1793

Havana
1787 Santiago

1494

Guadalajara 1548
Morelia 1536
Puebla 1527
Oaxaca 1535
Tegucigalpa (Tegus) 1531

Mexico
1546

Mérida
1561

1522 La Vega 1511
San Juan 1511

Chiapas 1538

Cartagena
1534

Santo Domingo 1511

Cacheo *GUIN*
*SIERRA
LEONE*

Guatemala 1743
Managua 1531

St Marta 1534

Caracas 1531

Sao Th

Panama
1513

Mérida
1778

St Thomas 1790

*PACIFIC

OCEAN*

Popoyan 1546 Bogotá 1564

Quito 1546
Cuenca 1769

Amazon R.

Belém 1720
Sao Luis 1677

Trujillo 1577
Lima 1546

BRAZIL

Recife 1676

Ayacucho 1609
Cuzco 1537

San Salvador 1676

Arequipa 1577 La Paz 1605
Charcas 1609 Santa Cruz 1605

Mariana 1745
Rio de Janeiro 1676

*NEW
CASTILE*

Asunción
1547

Sao Paulo 1745

*SOUTH
ATLANTIC

OCEAN*

Córdoba 1570

Paraná R.

Santiago 1561
Concepción 1546

Buenos Aires 1620

1541

St Franci

TRISTAN DA CUNHA

PATAGONIA

Line of demarcation:
Treaty of Tordesillas, 1494

Miles
0   500   1000   1500

0   1000   2000
Kilometers

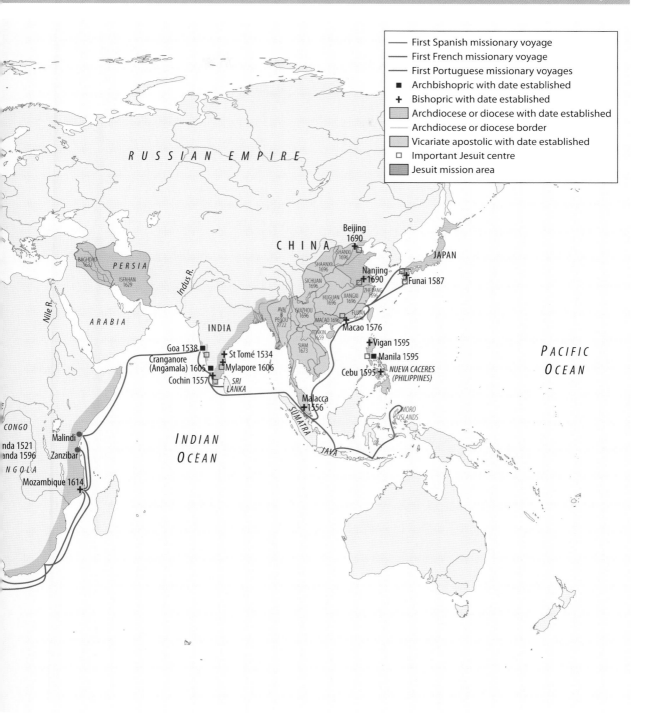

map 35

First Spanish missionary voyage
First French missionary voyage
First Portuguese missionary voyages
■ Archbishopric with date established
✝ Bishopric with date established
Archdiocese or diocese with date established
Archdiocese or diocese border
Vicariate apostolic with date established
□ Important Jesuit centre
Jesuit mission area

RUSSIAN EMPIRE

CHINA

Beijing 1690

SHANXI 1696

SHAANXI 1696

Nanjing 1690

SICHUAN 1696

ZHEJIANG 1696

HUGUAN 1696

JIANGXI 1696

JAPAN

Funai 1587

GUIZHOU 1696

FUJIAN 1696

AVA & PEGOU 1722

MACAO 1696

Macao 1576

PERSIA

BAGHDAD 1632

ISFAHAN 1629

ARABIA

Indus R.

INDIA

TONKIN 1659

SIAM 1673

Vigan 1595

Manila 1595

Cebu 1595

NUEVA CACERES
(PHILIPPINES)

Goa 1538

Cranganore
(Angamala) 1605

✝ St Tomé 1534

Mylapore 1606

Cochin 1557

SRI
LANKA

Malacca
1556

SUMATRA

JAVA

MORO
ISLANDS

PACIFIC
OCEAN

Nile R.

CONGO

...nda 1521

...anda 1596

Malindi

Zanzibar

NGOLA

INDIAN
OCEAN

Mozambique 1614

Christianity in the Philippines

A Spanish expedition from America, which included five Augustinian friars, seized the Philippines in 1561–62. Other religious orders soon followed, and at the Synod of Manila (1580) the Jesuits, Augustinians, Dominicans, and Franciscans divided up the islands between them for proselytization. Mass conversions followed, and more than half a million people were baptized within 30 years.

By the early 17th century, Spanish rule had been firmly established, though less oppressively than in the New World. Church institutions covered the islands and around half the population had converted. The Philippines became themselves a base from which missions were launched into other parts of Asia.

At the beginning of the 19th century, the Philippines had been a mainly Christian country for about 200 years. There were Muslim communities in the south, and some remote mountainous areas had still not yet been successfully evangelized. Pre-Christian beliefs and practices had not entirely disappeared, and a Filipino 'folk' Catholicism evolved.

Opposition to Spanish domination of the church, and the wealth of, and corruption within, the religious orders, helped fuel nationalist feeling. Few Filipinos were able to join the orders, and even in the secular priesthood they tended to have low status, which caused much bitterness, particularly among the growing numbers of educated Filipino clergy. From the 1850s onward some Filipino priests began to urge political reform.

After the United States annexation of the Philippines in 1898, the Roman Catholic hierarchy sided with the Americans. In the following decade, church and state were separated, Spanish religious orders gradually withdrew, and many non-Spanish Roman Catholic clergy arrived. Spanish bishops were gradually replaced by Americans, rather than Filipinos. The widely-resented Roman Catholic Church now faced competition from both the nationalist Iglesia Filipina Independiente and from American Protestant missionaries.

Aglipay

The Iglesia Filipina Independiente traces its foundation to 1899. A Filipino priest named Gregorio Aglipay (1860–1940) became its leader in 1902, and it had soon attracted around 25 per cent of Filipino Catholics. Influenced by Isabelo de los Reyes (or Don Belong, 1864–1938), the new 'Aglipayan' church betrayed Unitarian leanings. It attracted fierce opposition from the Roman Catholic Church, which gradually regained stability, with Filipino priests playing an increasingly significant role.

Apart from the Episcopal (Anglican) Church, which worked among remote non-Christian tribes and Muslim communities, Protestant denominations concentrated on evangelizing Roman Catholics. Splits occurred as independent churches were formed by Filipinos keen to control their own religious affairs. 'Quasi-Christian' churches also appeared, most important among them the *Iglesia ni Cristo*, formed in 1914 by Felix Manalo (Ka Félix, 1886–1963), who claimed it was the only true church. This organization grew rapidly after World War II.

In 1946 the Philippines gained independence, but Christianity continued to play an important role in the country. The Roman Catholic Church still depends heavily on foreign clergy, mostly from religious orders. The Philippines is the only country in Asia with a predominantly Christian population; church attendance is high and religious life vigorous. The church still exerts political influence, evidenced in its active role in the campaign to bring to an end the Marcos regime in 1986.

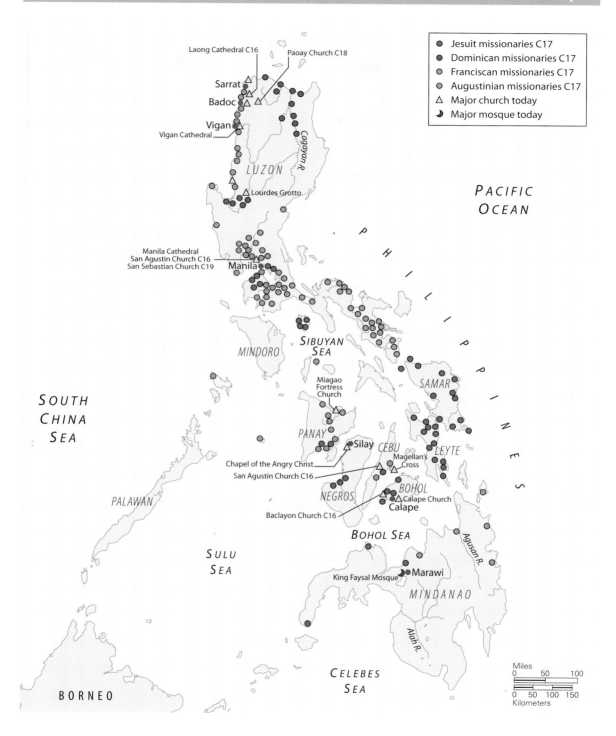

Laong Cathedral C16
Paoay Church C18
Sarrat
Badoc
Vigan
Vigan Cathedral

Jesuit missionaries C17
Dominican missionaries C17
Franciscan missionaries C17
Augustinian missionaries C17
Major church today
Major mosque today

LUZON

Cagayan R.

PACIFIC OCEAN

Lourdes Grotto

Manila Cathedral
San Agustin Church C16
San Sebastian Church C19
Manila

P
H
I
L
I
P
P
I
N
E
S

MINDORO

SIBUYAN SEA

SAMAR

SOUTH CHINA SEA

Miagao Fortress Church

PANAY

CEBU

Silay

LEYTE

Chapel of the Angry Christ
San Agustin Church C16

Magellan's Cross

PALAWAN

NEGROS

BOHOL

Calape Church
Calape

Baclayon Church C16

BOHOL SEA

SULU SEA

Agusan R.

King Faysal Mosque
Marawi

MINDANAO

Aldh R.

CELEBES SEA

BORNEO

Miles
0   50   100

0   50   100   150
Kilometers

Early in the seventeenth century Protestants began to colonize North America, starting with settlements on the Atlantic coast. The pioneer colonists sometimes combined commercial motives with missionary zeal and a desire for freedom of worship. In 1607 a community was set up at Jamestown, Virginia, with Robert Hunt (c. 1568–1608) acting as Anglican chaplain. However Anglicanism was never the most popular form of Christianity in the New World.

Pilgrim Fathers

The 'Pilgrim Fathers' who disembarked at Plymouth, New England, in 1620, were Independents who had already left the English national church to seek ecclesiastical asylum in Holland. They subsequently left Europe on board the *Mayflower* to find somewhere they could practise their faith freely and set up an ideal Christian commonwealth. They drew up the 'Mayflower Compact', translating into political terms their understanding of the voluntary basis of human associations that made them radical Puritans in church matters. Plymouth Colony remained relatively democratic, and its congregational covenant spread to the Massachusetts Bay Colony.

Great Migration

Religious conflict worsened in England under Charles I (r. 1625–49) and many Puritans decided to leave the country. The 'Great Migration' of 1629–40 saw some 80,000 people leave England, about 20,000 migrating to each of Ireland, New England, the West Indies, and the Netherlands. The 'Winthrop fleet' of eleven ships took around 800 passengers to the Massachusetts Bay Colony in 1630. By 1641, a total of around 200 ships had arrived, carrying about 21,000 immigrants, among them 129 clergymen and theologians.

Both the Pilgrims and the Massachusetts Bay Colony believed in the ideal of a Christian commonwealth governed by Christian principles, seeking to achieve the earthly prototype of the heavenly city. The first governor of Massachusetts Bay Colony, John Winthrop (1588–1649), stated: 'We shall be as a city upon a hill, the eyes of all people are upon us.' Massachusetts established a state church, a representative assembly – and by 1636, Harvard College.

Further settlements were set up in what became New Hampshire and Maine, committed to remaining in the Church of England and working for reform from within.

Dissent

Conflict arose early between establishment orthodoxy and dissenters such as Anne Hutchinson and Roger Williams, who moved to frontier settlements where they could better explore religious freedom and political democracy. In 1636 Williams (c. 1603–83) founded Providence Plantation on Rhode Island, a colony characterized by religious diversity. The Baptists who settled there committed to another characteristic of future American politics: separation of church and state. William Penn (1644–1718), a member of the Society of Friends, or 'Quakers', set up Pennsylvania as a refuge for his own group fleeing persecution in England.

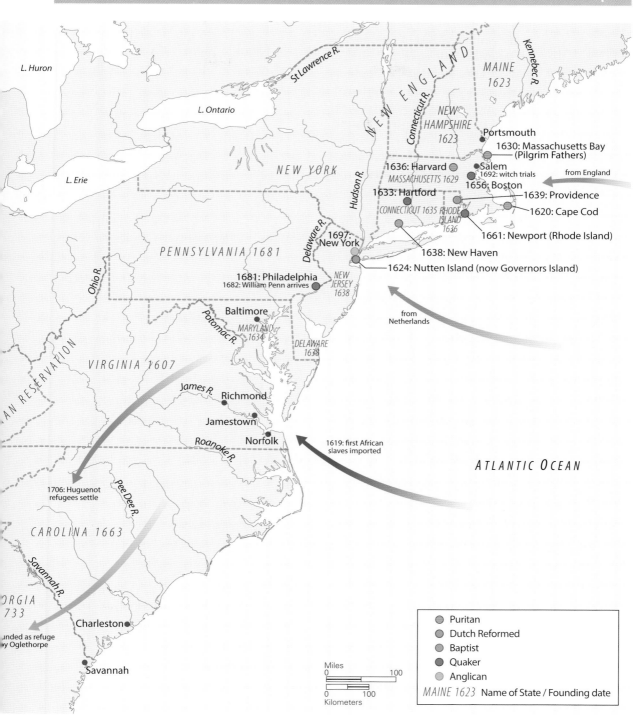

L. Huron

L. Ontario

St Lawrence R.

Kennebec R.

NEW ENGLAND

MAINE
1623

L. Erie

NEW
HAMPSHIRE
1623

Portsmouth

1630: Massachusetts Bay
(Pilgrim Fathers)

NEW YORK

1636: Harvard
MASSACHUSETTS 1629

Salem
1692: witch trials

1656: Boston

from England

Hudson R.

1633: Hartford

1639: Providence

1620: Cape Cod

CONNECTICUT 1635

RHODE
ISLAND
1636

1661: Newport (Rhode Island)

Delaware R.

1697:
New York

1638: New Haven

PENNSYLVANIA 1681

1624: Nutten Island (now Governors Island)

Ohio R.

1681: Philadelphia
1682: William Penn arrives

*NEW
JERSEY
1638*

from
Netherlands

Baltimore

*MARYLAND
1634*

*DELAWARE
1638*

AN RESERVATION

VIRGINIA 1607

James R. Richmond

Jamestown

Potomac R.

Roanoke R.

Norfolk

1619: first African
slaves imported

ATLANTIC OCEAN

1706: Huguenot
refugees settle

Pee Dee R.

CAROLINA 1663

Savannah R.

ORGIA
733

Charleston

unded as refuge
y Oglethorpe

Savannah

Miles
0 _____ 100

0 _____ 100
Kilometers

⬤	Puritan
⬤	Dutch Reformed
⬤	Baptist
⬤	Quaker
⬤	Anglican

MAINE 1623 Name of State / Founding date

Christian Europe: 1700

By 1700 Europe had settled into broad religious divisions. The north of Europe was predominantly Protestant, countries to the south and east of Europe were predominantly Roman Catholic, whilst Russia and the Baltic nations were largely Orthodox Christian. At this period, the Balkan countries formed part of the Muslim Ottoman Empire: Christianity there was heavily oppressed, and any Christian activity had to be carried out in secret.

While countries such as Spain, Italy, Portugal, and France were almost entirely populated by Roman Catholics, Britain – though officially Protestant – was more heterogeneous in its religious make-up.

Meanwhile secularization was spreading in West European society, culture, and thought. Christianity was becoming more a matter of intense personal decision – with secularization the inevitable counterpart.

Christianity was evolving in ethos and doctrine, finding new emphases, new inspirations, and appealing in novel ways to new classes of people, as the world changed around it. European life was being secularized; religion was becoming personalized and individualized: the two developed together and were interdependent.

THE CHURCH IN EUROPE IN 1700

map 38

Legend

- Catholic
- Catholic influenced
- Lutheran
- Anglican
- Calvinist/Reformed
- Calvinist influenced
- Pietism
- Orthodox
- Muslim
- ○ Pietist centre
- ── Holy Roman Empire boundary

Christiania (Oslo)

DENMARK–NORWAY

Stockholm

SWEDEN

ESTONIA

LIVONIA
Riga

BALTIC SEA

COURLAND

RUSSIA

Copenhagen

PRUSSIA

Danzig

Elbe R.

Stettin

BRANDENBURG

Hanover

Vistula R.

LITHUANIA

Halle

Herrnhut

Warsaw

SAXONY

SILESIA

HOLY ROMAN EMPIRE

Dresden

Prague

POLAND

Krakow

UKRAINE

BOHEMIA

Oder R.

Dnieper R.

PALATINATE

Nuremberg

MORAVIA

hine R.

WÜRTTEMBERG

BAVARIA

AUSTRIA

IMPERIAL HUNGARY

TRANSYLVANIA

Dniester R.

asbourg

Augsburg

Vienna

MOLDAVIA

Basel

SWISS CONFEDERATION

Bern

ra

MILAN

Venice

VENETIAN REPUBLIC

Danube R.

CROATIA

HUNGARY

WALLACHIA

AVOY

BOSNIA

BLACK SEA

Florence

TUSCANY

PAPAL STATES

SERBIA

MONTENEGRO

OTTOMAN EMPIRE

CORSICA

Rome

SARDINIA

Naples

NAPLES

GREECE

SICILY

Athens

MEDITERRANEAN SEA

After 1650 Spain – weakened militarily and financially – continued as a major colonial power, but lost her ability to compete with her northern neighbours. Portugal's population was too small, the grip on her colonies too weak, and the colonies too spread out to protect them successfully.

Spain suffered territorial losses in the Caribbean and along the Gulf coast. Britain occupied the islands of Barbados and Trinidad, and seized Jamaica in 1655. In 1697 France added Haiti to her colonies of Martinique, Guadeloupe, and Saint Christophe. The Dutch, French, and English each grabbed their respective Guiana on the north-east coast of South America, between Spanish and Portuguese colonies.

In 1622 Pope Gregory XV (r. 1621–23) founded the Sacred Congregation for the Propagation of the Faith (the '*Propaganda*') in an effort to secure direct control of Catholic missions. This new policy aimed to replace the patronage system employed in missions since the end of the 15th century. Patronage had been granted by the pope to the monarchs of Spain and Portugal, giving them responsibility for Christianizing natives, establishing dioceses, and appointing clergy in their colonies.

However in Latin America the patronage system continued, despite pressure from the pope. The cross and the crown were more closely linked here than elsewhere in the Catholic world. The Council of the Indies, in Madrid, continued to control important ecclesiastical positions in Latin America.

Every major religious order – mobilizing tens of thousands of priests – contributed to the almost total – but superficial – Christianization of Latin America. A minority opposed the political and economic oppression suffered by native populations. For example, António Vieira (1608–97), a Portuguese ambassador who subsequently became a Jesuit, won concessions from the Portuguese government for Brazilian Indians and blacks.

Jesuit reductions

The Jesuits continued to pioneer mission methodology in the vast, uncolonized areas of Paraguay. To protect, defend, and Christianize the Indians, priests gathered them into the self-contained and self-sustaining villages called reductions, in an experiment that flourished between 1650 and 1720. Natives were instructed in basic Christianity, their lives were organized into set times for prayer, for work in the fields or at trades, for religious festivals, and recreation. At their height there were approximately sixty *reductions*, involving overall more than 100,000 people. However what proved to be a controversial trial collapsed in the 18th century, in part through Spanish-Portuguese boundary disputes, and in part as a result of increasing opposition to the Jesuit order.

Cartagena
Panama
Orinoco R.
Bogotá
1565
NEW GRANADA
Quito
Japura R.
Amazon R.
Belém
Sao Luis
Trujillo
PERU
Madeira R.
Olinda
Lima 1546
Cuzco
Tapajos R.
Xingu R.
Tocantins R.
BRAZIL
San Salvador 1676
La Paz
Arequipa
Cuiabá
Sao Francisco R.
Charcas 1609
PACIFIC
OCEAN
Paraguay R.
Parana R.
Rio de Janeiro
Asunción
Córdoba
de Tucamán
Salado R.
Santiago
Buenos Aires
Rio de la Plata
SOUTH
ATLANTIC
OCEAN
Concepción
Imperial
Colorado R.
PATAGONIA

Miles
0   500   1000
0   500   1000   1500
Kilometers

Jesuit mission
Franciscan mission
Dominican mission
Capuchin mission
◦   Jesuit Reduction
■   Archbishopric with date of establishment
+   Bishopric (selected)

Miles
0   100   200   300

0   100 200 300 400
Kilometers

1721: Egade's
Pietist mission
to Greenland

1716: Pietist mission
to Lapps

Trondheim
Seminary founded

NORTH
SEA

Bergen

Christiania
(Oslo)

Bishop encourages Pietism

Stockholm

SWEDEN

Linköping

BALTIC
SEA

Riga

COURLAND

SCOTLAND

Edinburgh

Johann Arndt (1663-1727):
forerunner of Pietism

Copenhagen

DENMARK-NORWAY

1670-72: Labadie
gathers house church

1747-55: von Mosheim
church historian

1672: Labadie flees here
Altona

Stettin

Danzig

PRUSSIA

Dublin
IRELAND

ENGLAND

1738: John Wesley's
'warming experience'

WALES

1728: Moravian church

Oxford

London

John Wesley and
George Whitefield
return from America
influenced by Pietism

1732: Moravian mission
to St Thomas, Caribbean

ATLANTIC
OCEAN

UNITED
PROVINCES

Amsterdam

Antwerp

SPANISH NETHERLANDS

Moravian brethren
influence Christians
in London

1675, 1680:
Spener publishes
major Pietist works

Hanover

Herford

Göttingen

Frankfurt

Brunswick

Berlin

Frederick William I
influenced by Francke

1692-1727: Francke
sets up Pietist
institutions

Warsaw

LITHU

Elbe R.

BRANDENBURG

Halle

SAXONY

Dresden

Herrnhut

SILESIA

1722: Zinzendorf sets up refugee asylum

Oder R.

Vistula R.

POLAND

HOLY
ROMAN
EMPIRE

Prague

BOHEMIA

Krakow

PALATINATE

WÜRTTEMBERG

Seine R.

Paris

1819-: Centre of
Württemberg Pietism

Korntal

Denkendorf

Strasbourg

Nuremberg

MORAVIA

AUSTRIA

Danube R.

Vienna

IMPERIAL HUNGARY

TRANSYLVANI

Loire R.

FRANCE

Rhine R.

Basel

SWISS
CONFEDERATION

Bern

Geneva

SAVOY

BAVARIA

Augsburg

1713-41: Bengel
publishes Pietist works

HUNGARY

In the early 17th century German Lutherans continued Philipp Melanchthon's efforts to construct a distinctive systematic theology, with many scholars displaying a tendency to sterile dogmatic debate. Advocates of a more personal, devotional form of Christianity – such as the mystic Jakob Boehme (1575–1624) and author Johann Arndt (1555–1621), author of the widely-read *Wahres Christentum* (True Christianity) – were fore-runners of the influential Pietist movement.

Spener

The founder of 'Pietism' – initially a term of ridicule used by its opponents – was

Philipp Jakob Spener (1635–1705). Born in Alsace, Spener became convinced of the need for moral and religious reform within

map 40

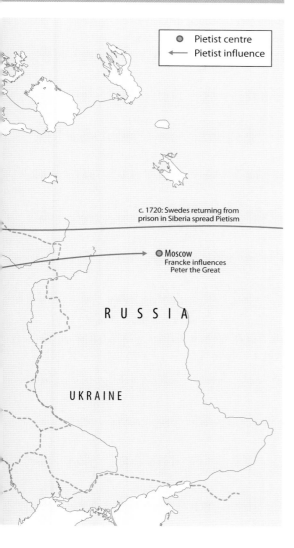

Pietist centre
← Pietist influence

c. 1720: Swedes returning from
prison in Siberia spread Pietism

◉ Moscow
Francke influences
Peter the Great

R U S S I A

U K R A I N E

Spener's lines, but soon met opposition and left to found the University of Halle, which became a Pietist centre. Guided by Francke, Pietism spread throughout central and northern Germany, its influence reaching Sweden and as far as Moscow. Francke also founded a celebrated orphanage at Halle in 1695.

Spener's emphasis on separation from the world led Pietists to avoid 'worldly' entertainments such as dancing and the theatre, while some insisted that 'new birth' must be preceded by agonized repentance.

Pietism reached its greatest strength in the mid-18th century, its individualism ironically helping prepare the way for secular Enlightenment thinking. Pietism aided the revival of biblical studies in Germany, helped make religion again a matter of the heart and daily life, and brought a new emphasis on the role of the laity in the church.

Moravians

No distinct Pietist church was formed until in 1722 Count Ludwig von Zinzendorf (1700–60) – Spener's godson – founded a colony at Herrnhut, on his estates in Saxony, which became known as the Moravian Brethren. This denomination later despatched dynamic missionaries throughout Europe and overseas. Among its pioneers were Bartholomäus Ziegenbalg (1682–1719) and C. F. Schwartz (1726–60) in India, and Georg Schmidt (1709–85) in South Africa. Moravian pietism also influenced the Norwegian Lutheran missionary Hans Egede (1686–1758) – known as 'the Apostle of Greenland' – and inspired Alexander Mack (1679–1735) to begin the New Baptists, or Brethren group in Germany – today known as the Church of the Brethren. Pietism and the Moravian Christians were a major influence on John Wesley and others who launched the Methodist movement in England, and upon the Great Awakening.

Lutheranism. In 1669 he started to hold religious meetings (*collegia pietatis*) in his home. In 1675 he published *Pia desideria*, which suggested methods of restoring life to the church, including Bible-study meetings and greater lay involvement. His book had considerable impact throughout Germany.

Some theologians at Leipzig, including August Hermann Francke (1663–1727), started to lecture on Christianity along

In its early years the 1607 Jamestown, Virginia, settlement looked unlikely to survive; yet it overcame unrest, starvation, Indian uprising, and economic collapse to become England's most populous North American colony. The Church of England was given official status there as early as 1619, and by the middle of the 18th century Virginia boasted some 100 Anglican churches. The Church of England had become stronger here than anywhere else in the New World.

Although Maryland was founded in 1634 under the auspices of English Catholics, by the end of the century the Church of England was officially established there too, as it was in South and North Carolina – though the latter colony had in addition a major Quaker settlement and a growing Baptist presence. Georgia was not founded till 1733 – the last of the 13 colonies that were to become the United States – but also established the Anglican Church.

At the time of the American Revolution, Anglicanism dominated the South, especially the areas of earliest settlement. However, the Revolution badly impaired both the prestige and appeal of the Church of England, and within a generation it had been reduced to a minority denomination throughout the region.

Congregationalism in New England

The situation in New England differed considerably from that of the South. Slavery was a much smaller institution, life expectancy was greater, and serious theological debate more common.

The Congregational Church enjoyed legal favour in the colonies of Massachusetts and Connecticut, and grew steadily, with educated ministers supplied by Harvard (founded in 1636), and Yale (1701). The Great Awakening of the 1740s intensified enthusiasm and led some to separate from the official church.

The American Revolution was strongly supported by Congregationalists.

By contrast the colony of Rhode Island and Providence Plantations continued to practise the religious variety and diversity encouraged by its founder, Roger Williams. The Baptists profited from this religious liberty, as did the Quakers, who established Newport, Rhode Island, as their main New England base.

The Middle Colonies

Located between the South and New England, the Middle Colonies included diverse ethnicities, nationalities, languages, and denominations. The Dutch, who came first to the area we now know as New York, brought with them their national church. Although the British took over the Dutch colony in 1664, the Dutch Reformed religion continued in New York and New Jersey, and the Dutch Reformed Rutger's College was founded in 1766. The Calvinist Dutch joined in the Great Awakening of the 1740s, as did the Scottish and Irish Presbyterians of the Middle Colonies, who had begun to settle in this region early in the 18th century.

Led by the Quaker William Penn, Pennsylvania became a haven not solely for persecuted Quakers, but for many other religious dissenters too. Though not founded until 1682, by 1750 Philadelphia had become the cultural capital of America.

Legend:
- Approximate extent of 13 colonies
- Anglican/Episcopalian
- Baptist
- Roman Catholic
- Congregationalist
- Lutheran
- Presbyterian/Reformed
- Quaker

Miles
0　　100

Kilometers
0　　100

ATLANTIC OCEAN

Part 5

The Modern Church

Congress shall make no law
respecting an establishment
of religion, or prohibiting the
free exercise thereof…

FIRST AMENDMENT,
UNITED STATES CONSTITUTION

The Great Awakening

The Great Awakening, America's first major revival, was possibly the most momentous religious occurrence of the colonial period. It arose out of Pietist beliefs that German, Scottish, and Scotch-Irish migrants brought with them across the Atlantic between the 1680s and 1730s.

The first evidence of the Awakening appeared in the 1720s among Pietists in the Middle Colonies. In the Delaware Valley, the Irish Presbyterian William Tennent Sr. (1673–1746) spread enthusiastic piety and offered training to ministers at his 'log college' at Neshaminy, Pennsylvania. (Johann) Conrad Beissel (1691–1768) arrived in Germantown, Pennsylvania, in 1712, and from 1722 led revivals among the newly arrived German Dunkers; whilst the Dutch Reformed minister Theodore Frelinghuysen (1691–1748) led several revivals in the Raritan Valley, New Jersey. In the early 18th century the Congregationalist Solomon Stoddard (1643–1729) saw revivals among his congregation in Northampton, Massachusetts; whilst from 1734 till the early 1740s his grandson, the theologian Jonathan Edwards (1703–58), inspired fervent conversions here and in frontier towns throughout the Connecticut Valley.

An extraordinary tour by the British Anglican evangelist George Whitefield (1714–70) transformed these local events into an inter-colonial phenomenon. Arriving from England in October 1739, his integrity, rhetorical skills, and unusual mix of Anglicanism, Pietism, and Calvinism contributed to his wide appeal. Whitefield preached in churches and in the open air – sometimes to crowds of more than 20,000 – often defying the opposition of local clergymen. Whitefield achieved his greatest success in New England, but engendered religious excitement and revival throughout the colonies.

The Awakening peaked in the late 1730s and early 1740s, as other evangelists followed Whitefield. In 1741 Gilbert Tennent (1703–64) retraced Whitefield's route through New England; Long Island preacher James Davenport (1716–57) aroused enthusiasm in Connecticut and Massachusetts; and the German Moravian leader Nikolaus Ludwig von Zinzendorf arrived in Pennsylvania and encouraged ecumenical evangelicalism among the German Pietists.

The South

The Awakening was initially most effective in the middle and northern colonies, but by the mid-1740s the revival began to wane there. It developed later and more slowly in the South, hampered by unsympathetic Anglican clergymen and scattered settlements. But in the late 1740s and 1750s itinerant preachers solidified the Awakening here too. Samuel Davies (1723–61) and other 'log college' graduates took 'New Side Presbyterianism' into Virginia, and Separate Baptists from New England began to arrive in 1754. The Anglican Devereux Jarratt (1733–1801), minister at Bath parish, Virginia, worked with the Methodist societies that began to appear in the area in the 1760s and 1770s. In 1784 some Anglicans defected to join the Methodist denomination, while others, including Jarratt, formed the basis of an Evangelical party within the Episcopal (US Anglican) Church.

Controversy over revivalism caused a schism within Presbyterianism, conflict among Congregationalists, and the growth of rival parties within Anglicanism. Yet the revivals appealed to men and women of all regions, classes, and Protestant denominations and churches. Their egalitarian and anti-authoritarian nature were especially popular in the rural interior. Critics of the Awakening denounced the revivalists' 'enthusiasm'.

Georgian Bay

L. Huron

St Lawrence R.

L. Champlain

L. Ontario

MAINE

Kennebec R.

NEW HAMPSHIRE

York

Hudson R.

Connecticut R.

L. Erie

NEW YORK

Solomon Stoddard revives church

MASSACHUSETTS

Harvard

Northampton

Boston

Hartford

Plymouth

RHODE ISLAND

Connecticut Valley 1734-1740s: Jonathan Edwards spreads revival

CONNECTICUT

PENNSYLVANIA
1741-42: Zinzendorf revives German Pietists

Delaware R.

NEW JERSEY

Yale

New Haven

Southold

1740: James Davenport spreads revival in Connecticut and Massachusetts
1750s: Shubal Stearns evangelizes and sets up Baptist churches

Raritan Valley 1726: Theodore Frelinghuysen revives church

New York

Elizabeth

Delaware Valley 1720s: William Tennent Snr. spreads pietist fervour

Neshaminy 1720s Gilbert Tennent

Ohio R.

Germantown 1722: Conrad Beissel revives German Dunkers

Philadelphia

1736: Evangelist George Whitefield arrives from England

MARYLAND

Potomac R.

Dover

DELAWARE

Early C18: Pietists from Germany via England

1740s-50s: Samuel Davies revives Virginia

Annapolis

VIRGINIA

1739: George Whitefield from England

James R.

HANOVER COUNTY

ATLANTIC OCEAN

Richmond

Williamsburg

Bath parish 1760s-70s: Devereux Jarratt revivalism among Methodists

Norfolk

Roanoke R.

Halifax

Hertford

NORTH CAROLINA

New Bern

Pee Dee R.

SOUTH CAROLINA

Georgetown

Jan 1741 Whitefield returns to England

Savannah R.

Charleston

GEORGIA

Beaufort

1735: Wesley brothers arrive as missionaries

Savannah

Miles
0   100

0   100
Kilometers

★ Centre of Awakening

Log college: sends out revivalists

← Whitefield's tour (overland)

Between the 1790s and the 1830s a further series of nationwide religious revivals, known as the 'Second Great Awakening', made revivalism an enduring feature of American Christianity. This phenomenon was closely linked to the westward expansion of the newly independent nation

The Second Awakening commenced in rural Connecticut and New Hampshire in the late 1790s. In New England it gained strength when in 1801 Yale College students attended revivals and then – as ministers – spread revivalism throughout the region's Congregational churches. New England revivalism led to the formation of a plethora of voluntary missionary, philanthropic, and reform societies. Yale and Andover seminary graduates, stimulated by the Awakening, became missionaries and educators and accompanied the westward 'Yankee migration' into the states of New York and Ohio. There under the 'Plan of Union' (1801)

Congregationalists and Presbyterians joined forces to found churches and schools.

Frontier revivals

A different – and more lively – Awakening occurred in the 1790s among the swelling number of Americans crossing the Cumberland Gap into Kentucky and Tennessee – mainly Methodists, Baptists, and Scots-Irish Presbyterians from western Virginia and the Carolinas. The Scots-Irish Presbyterian James McGready (1758–1817) and some Methodists from North Carolina conducted revivals in 1799 and 1800 at Muddy River, Red River, and Caspar River, south-western Kentucky. The Presbyterian Barton Stone (1772–1844), minister of Concord and Cane Ridge churches, western Kentucky, arranged a huge 'camp meeting' at Cane Ridge in 1801. It was attended by some 10,000 people and lasting a whole week. Presbyterian, Baptist, and Methodist preachers present at this 'Great Revival' went on to hold numerous camp meetings across Kentucky, Tennessee, and southern Ohio over the ensuing three years.

Particularly suited to the sparsely settled Western frontier, these gatherings spread Protestantism throughout the region, and gave denominations such as the Baptists and Methodists new national prominence. Presbyterians in the east denounced these emotional revivals, provoking revivalist Presbyterians in Tennessee to form the breakaway Cumberland Presbyterian Church in 1810.

Charles Grandison Finney at age of 80.

Revivalism

New York State was a rapidly developing region in this period, populated largely by 'Yankee migrants'. Charles Grandison Finney (1792–1875) and others conducted countless revivals here during the 1820s and early 1830s, creating an atmosphere of evangelism, reform, and religious experiment that was so intense that western New York State was often dubbed the 'burned-over district'.

Although the revivals eventually subsided, their impact did not. The Awakenings helped shape the religious and cultural life of the United States profoundly and lastingly.

African Christianity

Christianity had been strongly established in North Africa in Roman times, but during the 7th century it all but disappeared, following the Arab invasions and spread of Islam. However substantial Christian minorities of ancient churches that had resisted Byzantine and Roman control – Copts, Jacobites, and Nestorians – persisted despite the Muslim conquest.

Ethiopia

Christianity was present in Ethiopia from very early times, with an extensive network of monastic communities. In the mid-13th century a new flowering of Christian work began under an able *Abuna* (patriarch).

Several popes sent legates to Ethiopia who tried in vain to bring the Coptic church there into communion with Rome. Ethiopian delegates also participated in the Council of Florence (1441–42), and further embassies reached Lisbon in 1452 and Rome in 1481. Although nothing came of their specific purpose – to set up an alliance against the Muslim powers based in Cairo and Baghdad – these visits aroused Western interest in Africa.

Sub-Saharan Africa

Christianity was introduced to sub-Saharan Africa much later. From the late-15th to the mid-17th centuries efforts were made by Portuguese priests and traders. In 1487 Portuguese explorers reached Timbuktu overland from the coast.

Portuguese rulers hoped to prevent the further spread of Islam by converting to Christianity the peoples south of the Sahara. The introduction of Christianity to Africa also provided a means for successive Portuguese kings to gain control over parts of the continent.

Portuguese Catholic missionaries directed their attention to the rulers of African kingdoms, sending delegations to the courts of Benin, Warri, Kongo, and Mutapa. These missionary endeavours were combined with commercial and political interests. In Kongo, for instance, the king converted to Catholicism in the late 15th century, and attempted to spread his new faith amongst his subjects. However he was offered teaching aids and priests by Portugal only in return for handing over huge numbers of slaves. In Mutapa, too, the kings converted, recognizing the dominance of Portugal; but Christianity failed to spread beyond the royal family.

Decline

With the collapse of her empire in the 17th century, Portugal's monopoly on missionary activity in Africa ended. This – together with the disruption caused by the slave trade – led to a steady decline of Christianity in Africa. By 1700 there were very few African Christians, despite several centuries of missionary activity. Some converts lived in trading posts established along the coast, whilst a small number in the Kongo maintained the Catholic faith.

New moves by other European powers laid the pattern of events for the following centuries. In 1686 Louis XIV of France annexed Madagascar, where the French had first settled in 1626. In 1652 the Dutch founded what was to become the strategic settlement at Cape Town. And in 1713, under the Asiento Treaty, Britain acquired the right to import slaves from Africa into Spanish America, commencing this extensive, lucrative, and shameful trade.

Lisbon

MEDITERRANEAN SEA

Tangier

ATLAS MOUNTAINS

Algiers

Tunis

Tripoli

Cairo

Nile R.

Ghat

S A H A R A

RED SEA

Suakin

Massawa (1541)

Arguin (1443)

GULF OF ADEN

Socotra (1507)

Cape Verde Is (1444)

Awdaghost

Timbuktu

Bilma

Walata

Senegal R.

Jenne

Niger R.

Kano

Zeila

ETHIOPIAN HIGHLANDS

ADAMAWA

Freetown

1792: Freed slaves

Lagos

Elmina (1471)

Accra

Warri

Fernando Po (1472)

GULF OF GUINEA

São Tomé (1480)

Mogadishu

INDIAN OCEAN

Lamu

Malindi

Mombasa

to India

Congo R.

Mpindi (1504)

Luanda

Kilwa Kisiwani (1505)

ATLANTIC OCEAN

Benguela

Zambezi R.

Quelimane

Sofala (1505)

Limpopo R.

KALAHARI DESERT

Orange R.

Cape Town

Dutch, German and French colonists after 1652

Roman Catholic mission activity C16–C17
Coptic Church
Reformed/Calvinist in late C18
Islam
⊙ Portuguese settlement (date)
← Portuguese route

Miles
0   500   1000

0   500   1000   1500
Kilometers

The First U.S. Missions

The American Board of Commissioners for Foreign Missions (A.B.C.F.M.), formed in 1810 as a result of the Great Awakening, was the earliest American missionary society. In 1806 a group of students at Williams College, Massachusetts, committed to foreign missions and organized a 'Society of Brethren'. Some went on to Andover Seminary, Newton, Massachusetts, where they made more recruits, notably the pioneer missionary to Burma, Adoniram Judson (1788–1850). By 1810 Congregationalist ministers in Connecticut and Massachusetts had organized the American Board of Commissioners.

When Judson and his colleague Luther Rice (1783–1836) sailed – initially to India – in 1812, Samuel J. Mills, Jr. (1783–1818) remained at home to gather support. During their voyage, both Judson and Mills became convinced of Baptist views, which led to the founding of the Baptist General Convention for Foreign Missions (1814).

However the A.B.C.F.M. persisted, becoming active in home missions too. Between 1801 and 1826 Congregationalists and Presbyterians cooperated in the Ohio and Mississippi River Valley 'Plan of Union', supported by the American Bible Society, the American Tract Society, and other interdenominational associations founded

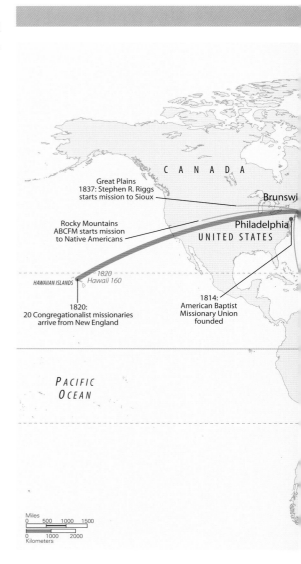

Great Plains
1837: Stephen R. Riggs
starts mission to Sioux

C A N A D A

Brunswi

Rocky Mountains
ABCFM starts mission
to Native Americans

Philadelphia
UNITED STATES

1820
Hawaii 160
HAWAIIAN ISLANDS

1820:
20 Congregationalist missionaries
arrive from New England

1814:
American Baptist
Missionary Union
founded

PACIFIC
OCEAN

Miles
0   500   1000 1500
0   1000   2000
Kilometers

Hopkins Hall and First Congregational Church, Williams College, Williamstown, Massachusetts.

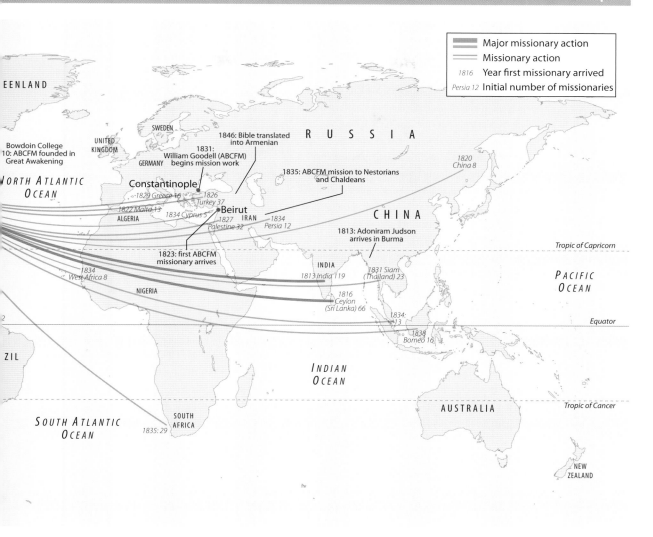

Major missionary action
Missionary action
1816 Year first missionary arrived
Persia 12 Initial number of missionaries

EENLAND

SWEDEN

RUSSIA

UNITED KINGDOM

Bowdoin College
10: ABCFM founded in
Great Awakening

1846: Bible translated
into Armenian

1831:
William Goodell (ABCFM)
begins mission work

GERMANY

1835: ABCFM mission to Nestorians
and Chaldeans

1820
China 8

NORTH ATLANTIC
OCEAN

Constantinople

1829 Greece 16   *1826*
Turkey 37

1822 Malta 13

ALGERIA   *1834 Cyprus 5*   Beirut

CHINA

1827   IRAN   *1834*
Palestine 32   *Persia 12*

1834
West Africa 8

1823: first ABCFM
missionary arrives

NIGERIA

1813: Adoniram Judson
arrives in Burma

Tropic of Capricorn

INDIA

1813 India 119

1831 Siam
(Thailand) 23

PACIFIC
OCEAN

1816
Ceylon
(Sri Lanka) 66

1834:
13

Equator

1838
Borneo 16

ZIL

INDIAN
OCEAN

SOUTH
AFRICA

1835: 29

AUSTRALIA

Tropic of Cancer

SOUTH ATLANTIC
OCEAN

NEW
ZEALAND

during an upsurge of voluntary religion linked to the Awakening. 'Societies of Inquiry' [into the claims of missions] spread rapidly among the eastern colleges, with Yale and Princeton becoming major recruitment centres for volunteers. 'Yale Bands' travelled West, having studied Native American languages – founding colleges and persuading legislatures to establish school systems. Congregationalists were also prominent in missions to Native Americans and freed slaves, operating chiefly through the A.B.C.F.M.'s sister organization, the American Missionary Association (1846). After the American Civil War (1861–65) they took the lead in founding institutions for African-Americans, such as the Hampton Institute (1868), Atlanta University (1865), and Fisk University (1866).

By 1790, missionary activity in Africa had reached a low point. The earliest new attempts to spread Christianity among Africans began at the Cape of Good Hope, where there had been white settlers since the mid-17th century. In 1792 the Moravians revived their mission at Baviaanskloof (Genadendal), Western Cape, followed by the Nederlandsche Zendinggenootschap at Bethelsdorp, under the controversial Dutchman Johannes van der Kemp (1747–1811), and the London Missionary Society at Kuruman under Robert Moffat (1795–1883).

The first sustained efforts in West Africa were in and around Freetown, Sierra Leone, by German members of the Church Missionary Society from 1804, and Wesleyans from 1811. The missionaries mainly worked among former slaves returning to Africa and others liberated from slave-trading ships. The Baptist Missionary Society (B.M.S., founded in 1792) and the Berlin Society (1824) were among the great Protestant societies formed at this period.

However until the 1840s missionary work was held back by poor geographical knowledge and by the depredations of climate and disease, particularly in West Africa. Foreign missionaries depended on African assistance, needing permission from African rulers to settle and teach, and requiring Africans to act as interpreters, translators, catechizers, and workers.

Mid-19th century

The Swiss Basel and British Wesleyan missions evangelized the Gold Coast, and from the 1840s to the 1870s missionaries began to evangelize the African interior. Protestant missions such as the Church Missionary Society in Britain were now stronger and better funded. From the 1830s African converts from Sierra Leone began to return to their homelands – many to western Nigeria – and requests for missionaries followed. Missionaries now started to work in East Africa and Zanzibar too.

Evangelicals regarded commerce such as the palm-oil trade as a means of opening the way for the gospel, whilst the increasing numbers of educated African Christians seemed to offer the possibility of indigenous churches. In 1864 Samuel Ajayi Crowther (c. 1809–91) was consecrated as the first African Anglican bishop.

Perhaps the greatest propagandist for 'commerce and Christianity' was Dr David Livingstone (1813–73). Many followed his example, from the Universities' Mission to Central Africa (U.M.C.A.) to Scots missions to Nyasaland (Malawi). Roman Catholic missions in Africa now revived too: the Holy Ghost Fathers were founded in 1848; the Society of African Missions in 1856; and the White Fathers were established by Cardinal Lavigerie (1825–92) in 1868.

However progress was slow. Influenced partly by American revivalism and millennialist theology, many Protestants began to call instead for a more individualistic approach: the rapid 'evangelization of the world in this generation'.

Scramble for Africa

After 1880, missionaries started to become caught up in the friction and conflict caused by the partition of Africa among the European powers. As missionary numbers grew, they began to compete – like traders and governments – for 'spheres of influence': Protestants against Roman Catholics, and evangelical faith missions against those working by older, more settled methods. The Congo Free State, for example, restricted British and American Baptists and Presbyterians, but favoured Catholic missionaries, after reaching agreement with the Vatican.

Legend:

- ▣ British Protestant mission
- ◉ French Protestant mission
- ★ US Protestant mission
- ▲ German Protestant mission
- ▣ British Catholic mission
- ◉ French Catholic mission
- ◆ Other mission

1868:
Charles Lavigerie
founds White Fathers
Algiers

Tangier
SPANISH MOROCCO
Casablanca
IFNI
1912 Spanish
Protectorate
MOROCCO
ATLAS MOUNTAINS
ALGERIA
Tripoli
Benghazi

MEDITERRANEAN SEA

LIBYA
1912 to Italy

Alexandria
Cairo
Asyut
EGYPT

SPANISH
SAHARA

RIO
DE ORO

S A H A R A

Tamanrasset

Nile R.

RED SEA

Bathurst
St Louis
GAMBIA
to Britain
PORTUGUESE
GUINEA
Freetown
SIERRA LEONE
to Britain
Monrovia

Senegal R.

FRENCH WEST AFRICA

UPPER
VOLTA
Niger R.
TOGO
to Germany
NIGERIA to Britain

NIGER

Khartoum
ANGLO-EGYPTIAN
SUDAN

ERITREA
1889 to Italy
Massawa

Djibouti
GULF OF ADEN

BRITISH
SOMALILAND

LIBERIA
IVORY
COAST
Kumasi
GOLD
COAST
Abidjan
Accra
Lagos
Ibadan
Calabar

KAMERUN
to Germany

FRENCH EQUATORIAL AFRICA

ETHIOPIA
Addis
Ababa

ETHIOPIAN
HIGHLANDS

ITALIAN SOMALILAND
1889 to Italy

1823: J.Ashmun founds
Liberia as home for freed slaves

GULF OF GUINEA
RIO MUNI to Spain

Yaounde

São Tomé
Lambarené
FRENCH
EQUATORIAL
AFRICA
CONGO
Brazzaville

Stanleyville

BELGIAN CONGO

Kampala
UGANDA

BRITISH EAST
AFRICA

Nairobi

David Livingstone
(1813–73) explores and
opens southern
Africa for missions

1913: Dr Albert Schweitzer
starts mission hospital

Congo R.

Léopoldville

Luanda

GERMAN
EAST AFRICA

Mombasa
Zanzibar
Dar es Salaam

INDIAN
OCEAN

ATLANTIC OCEAN

ANGOLA
to Portugal

NORTHERN RHODESIA

Zambezi R.

Blantyre

SOUTHERN
RHODESIA

Mozambique

MOZAMBIQUE

MADAGASCAR
1896 to France

Tananarive

GERMAN
SOUTHWEST
AFRICA
Windhoek

Walvis Bay

BECHUANALAND

Limpopo R.

Pretoria
SWAZILAND

Johannesburg
Kuruman
Orange R.
Kimberley
BASUTOLAND
Durban

UNION OF
SOUTH AFRICA

Cape Town

Miles
0   500   1000
0   500   1000   1500
Kilometers

Legend:

- - - - Political borders 1914
- ← Advance of Christian missions
- Ethiopian Coptic Church
- Islam
- Animist religions
- Christian mission activity

In the 18th century, European nations with trading and colonial interests targeted the Indian sub-continent, the British eventually emerging dominant. A century of religious unrest and war between Moguls, Hindus, and Sikhs helped open up the way for colonial control.

The first Protestant missions arrived in 1706, undertaken by Francke's Pietist missionary centre in Halle, but sponsored by the Lutheran King of Denmark. The German Bartolomäus Ziegenbalg (1683–1719) translated the New Testament and part of the Old into Tamil, supported by missionary societies in Germany and by the British Society for Promoting Christian Knowledge (S.P.C.K.), founded in 1698. Another German Lutheran, Christian Friedrich Schwarz (1726–98), starting in Tranquebar, made a substantial contribution to the growth of Christianity in India.

However at the outset of the 19th century many Europeans in Asia regarded the propagation of Christianity there as unimportant, seeing little purpose in provoking Hindus and Muslims by encouraging Christian proselytization. Dutch Calvinist missions in Ceylon, Java, and other parts of Indonesia had declined. Although the British administered large areas via the East India Company, before 1813 missionaries were not permitted to work inside its territories. Only in the Danish settlements of Tranquebar and Serampore was evangelization officially encouraged.

at Calcutta – and by their example exerted an influence far beyond in a huge expansion of Christian activity in Asia.

The East India Company's charter was revised in 1813 to permit missionaries to operate within its territories. Missions now spread rapidly in south and west India, moving later into central and northern regions. After 1833, missionaries were allowed to travel quite freely. The Anglican Church Missionary Society (C.M.S.) reached Amritsar in 1852, and Peshawar in 1855, and Anglican bishoprics were established at Calcutta (Kolkata) in 1814 and Madras (Chennai) in 1835. By 1851 19 Protestant missions were at work in India, and it was estimated there were more than 90,000 Protestant converts, mostly in the south.

Strong Catholic communities continued to exist in Ceylon and parts of Vietnam, and from the 1840s the revival of Roman Catholic missions began to impact the whole of Asia. In 1886 the Catholic Church organized a new hierarchy for India and Ceylon (Sri Lanka).

Fort Dansborg in the former Danish colony at Tranquebar, Tamil Nadu, India.

New era of missions

In 1799 three British Baptist missionaries, William Carey (1761–1834), Joshua Marshman (1768–1837), and William Ward (1769–1823), established themselves at Serampore – not far from the English centre

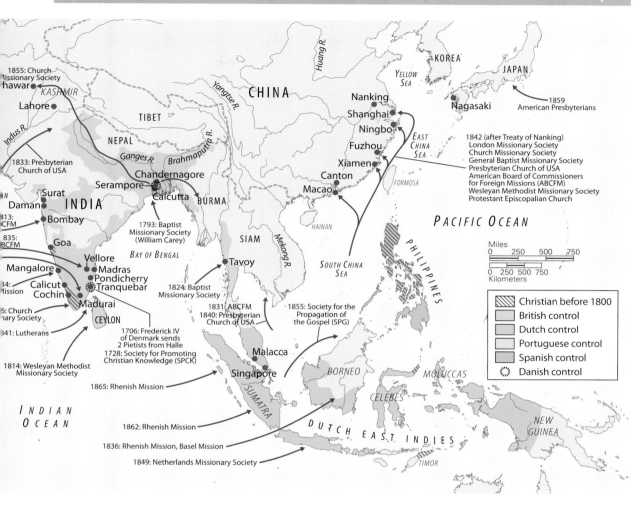

By 1910, only Afghanistan, Nepal, and Tibet remained closed to missionaries. Yet overall, Asian reactions to Christianity were typically indifferent or hostile.

China and Japan

Except for a tiny Dutch presence permitted at Deshima, near Nagasaki, Japan was totally closed to Westerners, whilst in China Europeans were restricted to commercial exchanges at Canton and the Portuguese colony of Macao. In Canton the Briton Robert Morrison (1782–1834) – the first Protestant missionary to China – began to evangelize and translate the Chinese Bible.

Inland, in both China and Japan Christianity was outlawed. Harsh persecution had almost eradicated earlier Roman Catholic activity. In the remainder of South and East Asia, Christianity was virtually non-existent.

Missions to China and Japan

Within China, the expansion of Christianity became possible only after Britain's acquisition of Hong Kong, the Treaties of Nanking (1842) and Tientsin (1858), and after the Peking Convention (1860) allowed missionaries into the interior. Within 30 years the number of Protestant missionaries shot up from 81 to 1,269, and doubled again to 2,818 by 1900. Roman Catholic priests, 639 in 1890, numbered 883 by 1900.

However the traditional hostility of most Chinese towards foreigners was now concentrated on the missionaries. After 1860, anti-foreign protests grew, culminating in the Boxer Rebellion of 1900. The suppression of the Boxers, the collapse of imperial authority, and the revolution of 1911 marked a further period of missionary expansion and relative success. Many Chinese began to see Christianity as a means of personal advancement and of establishing a modernized China

Japan

Western missionaries were finally admitted to Tokyo, Hakodate, and Nagasaki in 1859, but Christianity remained proscribed. Although some religious freedom was granted in 1873, not until the Meiji constitution of 1889 was this liberty permanently guaranteed. By that date around 450 Protestant missionaries were at work, but travel inland was still restricted, and Japanese Christianity remained an urban religion.

Some Japanese converts attempted to create a distinctively Japanese theology, resulting in the 'Nonchurch' Christianity (*Mukyokai*) of Uchimura Kanzo (1861–1930), whose adherents combined a personal experience of God with a puritan ethic, developed in small, independent Bible-study groups.

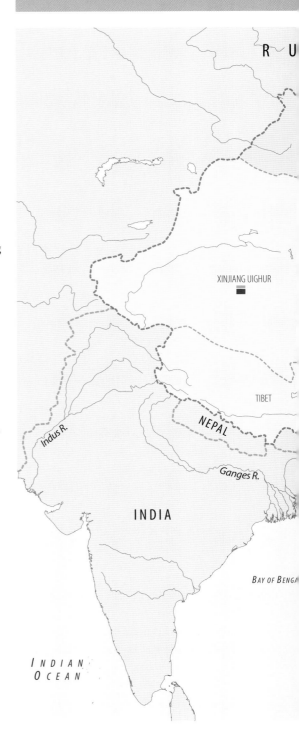

Approximate proportion of
Protestant/Catholic missions

■ Catholic ■ Protestant

○ Major mission centre

--- 1912 China border

Density of missions
per province c. 1920

More than 251
201–250
151–200
101–150
51–100
0–50

Catholicism in the U.S.A.

Roman Catholics had long been feared and disfranchised in many of the British North American colonies. The first mass immigration of Roman Catholics occurred as families fled the Irish Potato Famine of 1847, many settling as day labourers in Eastern cities.

Since the early years of the French Empire in North America, French priests had held the majority of senior posts in the Roman Catholic hierarchy. Now Irish priests gradually replaced them.

As Protestant Prussia increased its strength relative to other German states during the 19th century, many German Roman Catholics emigrated to North America. The German Chancellor Bismarck's anti-Catholic *Kulturkampf* (1871–76) strengthened the pull of America for German Catholics, especially those from Bavaria and the Rhineland. Many newly-arrived German immigrants soon moved on to the Mid-West.

American Catholics faced a bitter campaign of anti-foreignism displayed as vestryism (church ownership and control at local level), 'Know Nothingism' (aimed at restricting office to native-born citizens), and economic disadvantage. However they were ably led by such men as John Hughes (1797–1864) of New York, John England

Baltimore Cathedral, built in 1821, was the first Roman Catholic cathedral in the U.S.A.

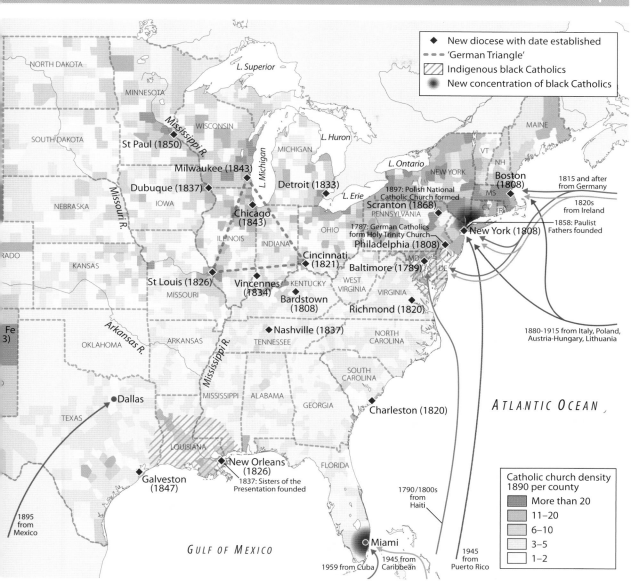

New diocese with date established
‑ ‑ ‑ 'German Triangle'
Indigenous black Catholics
New concentration of black Catholics

NORTH DAKOTA

MINNESOTA

L. Superior

WISCONSIN

SOUTH DAKOTA

St Paul (1850)

Mississippi R.

MICHIGAN

L. Huron

MAINE

Milwaukee (1843)

L. Michigan

Detroit (1833)

L. Ontario

NEW YORK

VT

NH

Boston (1808)

1815 and after from Germany

Dubuque (1837)

IOWA

NEBRASKA

L. Erie

1820s from Ireland

1897: Polish National Catholic Church formed

MS

CT RI

Missouri R.

Chicago (1843)

ILLINOIS

INDIANA

OHIO

Scranton (1868)

PENNSYLVANIA

1787: German Catholics form Holy Trinity Church

1858: Paulist Fathers founded

KANSAS

RADO

Cincinnati (1821)

New York (1808)

Philadelphia (1808)

NJ

St Louis (1826)

Vincennes (1834)

KENTUCKY

WEST VIRGINIA

Baltimore (1789)

MD

DE

Bardstown (1808)

VIRGINIA

Richmond (1820)

Fe 3)

Arkansas R.

OKLAHOMA

ARKANSAS

Mississippi R.

TENNESSEE

Nashville (1837)

NORTH CAROLINA

1880-1915 from Italy, Poland, Austria-Hungary, Lithuania

Dallas

TEXAS

MISSISSIPPI

ALABAMA

GEORGIA

SOUTH CAROLINA

Charleston (1820)

ATLANTIC OCEAN

LOUISIANA

New Orleans (1826)

1837: Sisters of the Presentation founded

FLORIDA

Galveston (1847)

1790/1800s from Haiti

Catholic church density 1890 per county

More than 20
11–20
6–10
3–5
1–2

1895 from Mexico

GULF OF MEXICO

Miami

1959 from Cuba

1945 from Caribbean

1945 from Puerto Rico

(1786–1842) of Charleston, and Cardinal James Gibbons (1834–1921), Archbishop of Baltimore from 1877. In the papal encyclical *Rerum novarum* (1891) Catholics won from the Vatican the important right to participate fully in labour unions.

A major achievement of American Catholicism was the construction of a full Christian school system: elementary, secondary, and university.

New Religious Movements

During the first half of the 19th century, many American frontier regions were settled by a variety of religious communities and communes seeking the freedom and space to practise their beliefs. People roused to commitment to a new life by the revivalists often moved on to one or other of these new movements: Oneida, the Shakers, or the Mormons – or to new denominations such as the Seventh-day Adventists and Church of God (Anderson), whose first settlement practised Christian communism.

These new movements included Puritan communities such as Brook Farm (1841–47), which burgeoned from religious discussions in Cambridge, Massachusetts. Oneida, New York State, was founded by the Congregational minister John Humphrey Noyes (1811–86), and initially thrived. But when Oneida experimented with 'complex marriage' (an organized form of promiscuity) and scientific birth control, it was assaulted by clergy and broke up. The Shakers, who formed 19 successful celibate communes, were also by-products of New England culture.

The Seventh Day Baptist (German) Johann Conrad Beissel (1691–1768) founded Ephrata, for a time the cultural centre of the Pennsylvania Dutch; whilst Count Zinzendorf set up Pietist colonies in Pennsylvania similar to the mother community at Herrnhut, Saxony. Followers of the German immigrant George Rapp (1757–1847) set up thriving 'Rappite' or 'Harmonist' communities at Economy, Pennsylvania, and Harmony, Indiana.

The Mormons – 'The Church of Jesus Christ of Latter-day Saints' – were the most successful of the religious communes with a New England background, established at Salt Lake, Utah, by Brigham Young (1801–77) in 1847, after a long trek westwards. There was

also a 'Reorganized LDS Church', founded by Joseph Smith, Jr. (1832–1914), with headquarters in Independence, Missouri, which didn't practise polygamy, and several splinter groups.

Like many other groups, the Jehovah's Witnesses, founded around 1870 by Charles

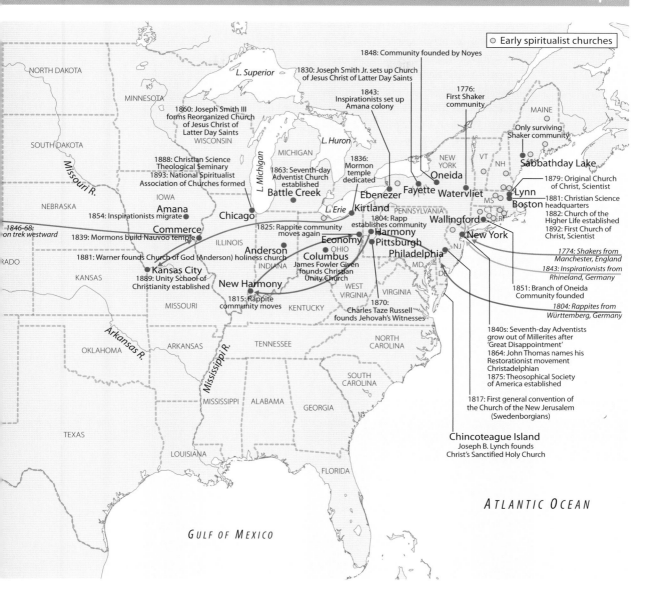

○ Early spiritualist churches

1848: Community founded by Noyes

1830: Joseph Smith Jr. sets up Church of Jesus Christ of Latter Day Saints

1843: Inspirationists set up Amana colony

1776: First Shaker community

1860: Joseph Smith III forms Reorganized Church of Jesus Christ of Latter Day Saints

Only surviving Shaker community

Sabbathday Lake

1888: Christian Science Theological Seminary
1893: National Spiritualist Association of Churches formed

1863: Seventh-day Adventist Church established

1836: Mormon temple dedicated

1879: Original Church of Christ, Scientist

1881: Christian Science headquarters

Battle Creek

Oneida

Fayette

Watervliet

Lynn
Boston

1882: Church of the Higher Life established
1892: First Church of Christ, Scientist

1854: Inspirationists migrate

Amana

Chicago

Ebenezer

Kirtland

1804: Rapp establishes community

Wallingford

New York

Missouri R.

1846-68: on trek westward

1825: Rappite community moves again

Harmony

Commerce

1839: Mormons build Nauvoo temple

Economy

Pittsburgh

Philadelphia

1774: Shakers from Manchester, England

1843: Inspirationists from Rhineland, Germany

Anderson

Columbus

1881: Warner founds Church of God (Anderson) holiness church

James Fowler Given founds Christian Unity Church

1851: Branch of Oneida Community founded

Kansas City

1889: Unity School of Christianity established

New Harmony

1815: Rappite community moves

1804: Rappites from Württemberg, Germany

1870: Charles Taze Russell founds Jehovah's Witnesses

1840s: Seventh-day Adventists grow out of Millerites after 'Great Disappointment'
1864: John Thomas names his Restorationist movement Christadelphian
1875: Theosophical Society of America established

1817: First general convention of the Church of the New Jerusalem (Swedenborgians)

Chincoteague Island
Joseph B. Lynch founds Christ's Sanctified Holy Church

ATLANTIC OCEAN

GULF OF MEXICO

Taze Russell (1852–1916), believed they were restoring New Testament Christianity. At their headquarters in Brooklyn, New Jersey, they practised a form of Christian communism modelled on Acts 4:32.

Mary Baker Eddy (1821–1910), founder of the 'Mother Church' of Christian Science

in Boston, claimed to have been healed by Phineas P. Quimby (1802–66) greatly admiring his New Thought system. In 1875 she brought out the first edition of *Science and Health*, and in 1908 founded *The Christian Science Monitor*, which became one of the leading daily newspapers in America.

The Rise of Pentecostalism

Pentecostalism in America arose out of the holiness movement, and appeared in holiness churches and camp meetings from the mid-1860s onwards. As the 20th century approached, there were increasing numbers of incidences of people speaking in tongues and other physical signs of the Holy Spirit's powers. The first Pentecostal churches started before 1901, including the mainly African-American Church of God in Christ (1897), the Pentecostal Holiness Church (1898), and the Church of God, headquartered in Cleveland, Tennessee (1906).

According to Pentecostalist tradition, on 1 January 1901 the first 'Pentecostals' are said to have appeared at Charles Parham's (1873–1929) Bethel Bible College, Topeka, Kansas, when Agnes Ozman received the baptism of the Holy Spirit and spoke in tongues. Parham now began to teach that tongues was 'Bible evidence' of baptism in the Holy Spirit, and a supernatural gift of human languages to aid in world evangelization.

Pentecostalism achieved worldwide attention in 1906 through the Azusa Street revival, Los Angeles, led by the African-American preacher William Joseph Seymour (1870–1922). His Apostolic Faith Mission conducted almost continuous services, where thousands of people claimed to have received the gift of tongues and baptism in the Holy Spirit.

Several holiness denominations soon joined the new movement, including the Pentecostal Holiness Church, the Fire-Baptized Holiness Church, and the Pentecostal Free-Will Baptist Church. The African-American Charles Harrison Mason (1866–1961) carried the tongues experience back to his Church of God in Christ at Memphis, Tennessee and the denomination

THE ORIGINS OF PENTECOSTALISM IN THE U.S

soon mushroomed. Having received tongues at Azusa Street in 1907, William H. Durham (1873–1912) returned to Chicago, where he led thousands into the Pentecostal movement, evolving into the largely white Assemblies of God denomination in 1914.

map 51

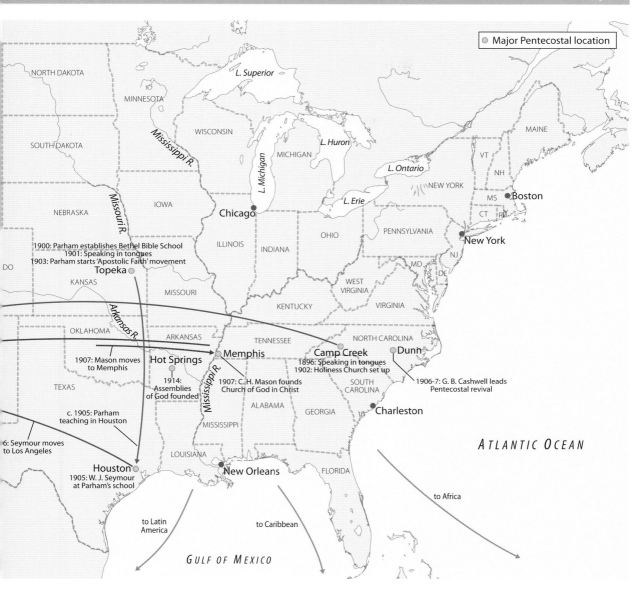

Major Pentecostal location

NORTH DAKOTA

MINNESOTA

SOUTH DAKOTA

L. Superior

WISCONSIN

L. Huron

MICHIGAN

L. Michigan

L. Ontario

MAINE

VT

NH

NEW YORK

MS ● Boston

Mississippi R.

Missouri R.

NEBRASKA

IOWA

Chicago ●

OHIO

PENNSYLVANIA

CT RI

New York ●

1900: Parham establishes Bethel Bible School
1901: Speaking in tongues
1903: Parham starts 'Apostolic Faith' movement

ILLINOIS

INDIANA

NJ

MD

DE

DO

Topeka ○

KANSAS

MISSOURI

WEST
VIRGINIA

VIRGINIA

KENTUCKY

Arkansas R.

OKLAHOMA

ARKANSAS

TENNESSEE

NORTH CAROLINA

Dunn ○

1907: Mason moves
to Memphis

Hot Springs ○

Memphis ○

Camp Creek ○
1896: Speaking in tongues
1902: Holiness Church set up

1906-7: G. B. Cashwell leads
Pentecostal revival

TEXAS

1914:
Assemblies
of God founded

1907: C. H. Mason founds
Church of God in Christ

SOUTH
CAROLINA

Mississippi R.

ALABAMA

GEORGIA

Charleston ●

c. 1905: Parham
teaching in Houston

MISSISSIPPI

6: Seymour moves
to Los Angeles

LOUISIANA

FLORIDA

ATLANTIC OCEAN

Houston ○
1905: W. J. Seymour
at Parham's school

New Orleans ●

to Africa

to Latin
America

to Caribbean

GULF OF MEXICO

THE RISE OF PENTECOSTALISM   135

African-American Churches

The first independent black churches arose in response to the indignities suffered by black Christians in white congregations. These new churches often borrowed the denominational name of the church they left. Richard Allen (1760–1831) led his people out of a white Methodist church to found the Bethel African Methodist Episcopal (A.M.E.) church in Philadelphia in 1794. The new denomination held its first General Conference in 1816. James Varick (1750–1827) founded the African Methodist Episcopal Zion (A.M.E. Zion) Church in New York in 1821. Black Baptist churches soon formed too, though Baptist conventions (denominational organizations) were not started until later. The first black foreign missionary, Lott Cary (or Carey, 1780–1828), of Richmond, Virginia, sailed to Liberia in 1821 for the African Baptist Missionary Society, founded in 1815.

After emancipation, the black churches were the sole major institution controlled by African-Americans, and became significant centres of black identity. A new militancy emerged with the National Association for the Advancement of Colored People (N.A.A.C.P.), founded in 1910, and the National Urban League, founded in 1911. National political initiatives combined with black congregations to empower the civil rights movement during and after World War II.

James L. Farmer, Jr. (1920–99) and George Houser (1916–) – a black and a white – both sons of Methodist ministers, founded the Congress of Racial Equality (CORE) in 1942. In 1957 the Baptist preacher Martin Luther King, Jr. (1929–68) organized the Southern Christian Leadership Conference (S.C.L.C.). King possessed the ability to

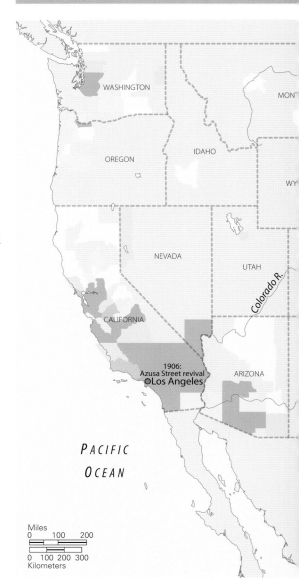

employ the language and traditions of the African American congregations and was supported by thousands of black Christians in his celebrated freedom marches seeking civil rights for black Americans.

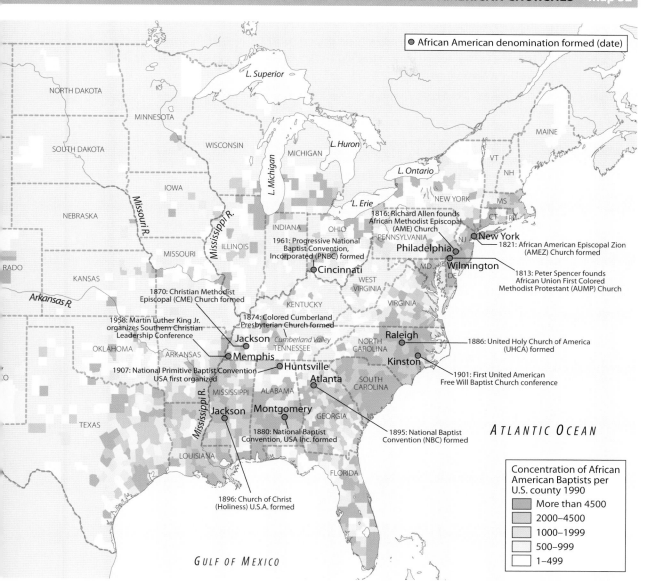

● African American denomination formed (date)

1816: Richard Allen founds African Methodist Episcopal (AME) Church

1821: African American Episcopal Zion (AMEZ) Church formed

1813: Peter Spencer founds African Union First Colored Methodist Protestant (AUMP) Church

1961: Progressive National Baptist Convention, Incorporated (PNBC) formed

1870: Christian Methodist Episcopal (CME) Church formed

1958: Martin Luther King Jr. organizes Southern Christian Leadership Conference

1874: Colored Cumberland Presbyterian Church formed

1886: United Holy Church of America (UHCA) formed

1907: National Primitive Baptist Convention USA first organized

1901: First United American Free Will Baptist Church conference

1880: National Baptist Convention, USA Inc. formed

1895: National Baptist Convention (NBC) formed

1896: Church of Christ (Holiness) U.S.A. formed

Cincinnati, Philadelphia, New York, Wilmington, Raleigh, Kinston, Jackson, Memphis, Huntsville, Atlanta, Jackson, Montgomery

NORTH DAKOTA, SOUTH DAKOTA, MINNESOTA, WISCONSIN, MICHIGAN, IOWA, NEBRASKA, MISSOURI, KANSAS, ILLINOIS, INDIANA, OHIO, KENTUCKY, TENNESSEE, OKLAHOMA, ARKANSAS, MISSISSIPPI, ALABAMA, GEORGIA, TEXAS, LOUISIANA, FLORIDA, WEST VIRGINIA, VIRGINIA, NORTH CAROLINA, SOUTH CAROLINA, PENNSYLVANIA, NEW YORK, MAINE, VT, NH, MS, CT, RI, NJ, MD, DE, RADO

L. Superior, L. Michigan, L. Huron, L. Ontario, L. Erie

Missouri R., Mississippi R., Arkansas R., Cumberland Valley

ATLANTIC OCEAN

GULF OF MEXICO

Concentration of African American Baptists per U.S. county 1990

	More than 4500
	2000–4500
	1000–1999
	500–999
	1–499

In the South Seas, missionary activity progressed generally from east to west. Hearing favourable reports about Tahiti, Western Protestant missionaries journeyed there first, moving on later to the more hostile Melanesian Islands in the west. Missionaries with the London Missionary Society were the first to reach the Society Islands; from there they progressed to the western islands of Polynesia: Tonga, Western Samoa, and Fiji.

Christianity was carried to Paumotu by native Protestants from Tahiti, just twenty years after missionaries arrived at the larger island. Similarly, the Christianization of Samoa and the Navigator Islands was begun in 1830 by native Methodists from Tonga. Rotuma, Fiji, New Hebrides, and the Loyalty Islands too were all first evangelized by native Christians.

After missionaries from the American Board (A.B.C.F.M.) brought Christianity to Hawaii, the major enterprise of crossing the Pacific was undertaken in 1852 by missions to the Marshall Islands and to the Caroline and Gilbert Islands.

Catholic missions

In the 17th century, Spanish Roman Catholics crossed from the Christianized Philippines to western Micronesia and converted the population of the Marianas Islands. But no further Catholic evangelization occurred in this region until the late 19th century.

The main Catholic missions in the area were French: in Melanesia, the Congregation of the Sacred Hearts of Jesus and Mary – the 'Pipcus Fathers'; and in Polynesia, the Marist Fathers. The arrival of Catholic missionaries frequently precipitated tension – even conflict – with Protestant converts. It was to avoid such problems that New Guinea was by agreement divided into separate mission fields, Protestant and Catholic. French Catholics also established themselves in New Caledonia and southern New Guinea, as well as on the far eastern islands of Tahiti, the Marquesas Islands, Mangereva, and Easter Island.

Australia and New Zealand

The English naval explorer James Cook (1728–79) first charted the coasts of Australia and New Zealand in 1770. When Britain set up a penal colony in Australia, an Anglican chaplain, Richard Johnson (c. 1753–1827), sailed out with the first convict ship in 1788. Wesleyans followed in 1815, and Presbyterians in 1823. Christianity was established not so much by missionary enterprise – though missionaries attempted to evangelize the Aboriginal and Maori peoples – or state imposition, as by the voluntary efforts of individual British settlers, soldiers, and officials.

By the time an Anglican establishment had been set up in the 1820s, Scottish Presbyterians and Irish Catholics had already become numerous, with Roman Catholic priests serving the mainly Irish Catholic population. Between 1860 and 1940 clergy recruited in Ireland continued to dominate the Australian Catholic church.

In New South Wales, the favoured Church of England initially received government grants of land on which to build churches and schools; but after 1836 these grants were made non-denominational. By 1871 a policy of religious voluntarism had been adopted, with state support for solely secular education.

The first European settlers arrived in New Zealand in 1805, and the first missionaries nine years later. It became a British colony in 1841, with a religious voluntarism similar to that in Australia adopted in 1877, despite early attempts at founding denominational

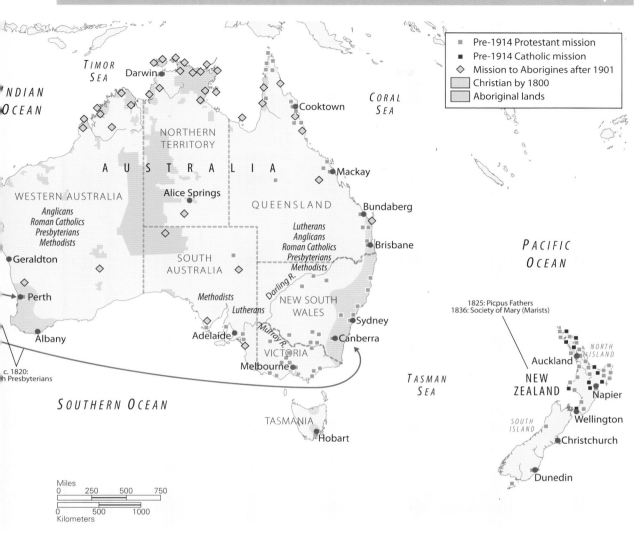

■	Pre-1914 Protestant mission
■	Pre-1914 Catholic mission
◇	Mission to Aborigines after 1901
	Christian by 1800
	Aboriginal lands

TIMOR SEA

Darwin

INDIAN OCEAN

CORAL SEA

Cooktown

NORTHERN TERRITORY

A U S T R A L I A

Mackay

Alice Springs

WESTERN AUSTRALIA

Anglicans
Roman Catholics
Presbyterians
Methodists

QUEENSLAND

Bundaberg

Lutherans
Anglicans
Roman Catholics
Presbyterians
Methodists

Brisbane

Geraldton

SOUTH AUSTRALIA

PACIFIC OCEAN

Perth

Methodists

Darling R.

NEW SOUTH WALES

Lutherans

1825: Picpus Fathers
1836: Society of Mary (Marists)

Albany

Adelaide

Murray R.

Sydney

Canberra

VICTORIA

Melbourne

Auckland

NORTH ISLAND

c. 1820:
h Presbyterians

TASMAN SEA

NEW ZEALAND

Napier

SOUTHERN OCEAN

TASMANIA

Hobart

SOUTH ISLAND

Wellington

Christchurch

Dunedin

Miles
0   250   500   750
0   500   1000
Kilometers

settlements in Christchurch (Anglican) and Otago (Presbyterian). Anglicans eventually came to form the majority of the population, with large minorities of Scottish Presbyterians, Roman Catholics, and Methodists.

During the 19th century Protestant missionaries began to come to Latin America from the USA. North American Protestantism proved attractive to the middle-class liberals who had led the Latin American republics' fight for political independence. Roman Catholic missions had been ejected, and a shortage of priests in South America brought about a decline in the faith. In the Caribbean, Methodist and Baptist missionaries arrived, often as part of the anti-slavery movement.

At the start of the 20th century, the Assemblies of God and Seventh-day Adventists were among the most evangelistic missions working in Latin America. By the outbreak of World War I, every Latin American republic had established Protestant missions. However, with only half a million converts in the entire region, they still represented only a fraction in comparison with the Catholic population.

By 1970 about 50 per cent of the Roman Catholic clergy of Latin America were foreigners. Many of them supported indigenous political movements striving for justice against repressive governments. Less dependent on their bishops than local priests, and often paid by missionary societies, foreign clergy felt freer to challenge the authorities. Yet some indigenous clergy – notably Archbishop Óscar Romero of El Salvador (1917–80), who was assassinated for his stance – also began openly to denounce their governments. Persecutions of the church followed; between 1964 and 1978 260 foreign missionaries were expelled from Latin American states, and more than 450 priests were arrested.

During the 1960s Protestant growth escalated, especially in poor urban districts. In much of Latin America the population was only nominally Catholic. The most spectacular Protestant growth in Latin America has been among the Pentecostal groups, especially in Brazil, Chile, Mexico, and Guatemala. The most widespread of the Pentecostal churches is the Assemblies of God, whilst the non-Pentecostal Seventh-day Adventists have also become very popular.

The interior of the National Cathedral, El Salvador, where Archbishop Óscar Romero was assassinated. His portrait is on the wall.

- ● Roman Catholic archbishopric
- ○ Distribution of Pentecostalism

MEXICO

CUBA

DOMINICAN
REPUBLIC
HAITI
JAMAICA

BELIZE
GUATEMALA
HONDURAS
EL SALVADOR
NICARAGUA
COSTA
RICA
PANAMA

PUERTO
RICO
San Juan

NORTH
ATLANTIC
OCEAN

Maracaibo
Caracas
Port of Spain
TRINIDAD

Pamplona
VENEZUELA
Orinoco R.
Georgetown
Paramaribo
Cayenne
GUYANA
SURINAME
FRENCH
GUIANA

Medellín
Manizales
Bogotá
Cali COLOMBIA

Quito
ECUADOR
Guayaquil
Cuenca

Belém
S. Luiz de Maranhao
Amazon R.
Manaus
Fortaleza
Teresina
Natal
Olinda-Recife
Maceió

PERÚ

BRAZIL

Tocantins R.

Trujillo

Lima
Cuzco

San Salvador

PACIFIC
OCEAN

Arequipa
La Paz
BOLIVIA
Sucre

Cuiaba
Goiânia
Brasilia
Diamantina
Paraguay R.
Belo Horizonte
Riberao Prêto
Mariana
Vitoria

PARAGUAY
Parana R.

Salta
Salado R.
Asunción
Sao Paulo

La Serena
Santa
Fe
Porto Alegre

CHILE

Santiago
Córdoba
Rosario
Parana
URUGUAY
Montevideo

Penco
Buenos
Aires

ARGENTINA

SOUTH
ATLANTIC
OCEAN

Miles
0   500   1000

0   500   1000   1500
Kilometers

Punta Arenas

FALKLAND ISLANDS

Distribution and strength of
Roman Catholicism
- 50–69% of population
- 75–89% of population
- Over 90% of population
- Mainly Protestant

By 1938 two-thirds of missionaries worldwide were sent out by the Free Churches. Most of those from established churches had either a Pietist (German, Swiss, Dutch, or Scandinavian) or Wesleyan background. During the 'Great Century of Christian Missions' (1792–1914), the base of Christian outreach shifted from the patronage of Christian rulers – its foundation for centuries – to a new basis: the voluntary donations of millions of ordinary Christians, and the recruitment of thousands of lay people as missionaries.

Modern missions

The birth of modern missions is often traced to the English Baptist cobbler William Carey's conviction of the claim of the Great Commission in Mark 16:15 upon his life. Carey (1761–1834) taught himself Latin, Greek, Hebrew, Dutch, and French and sailed to India as a pioneering missionary. In the USA the beginning of modern missions dates from the founding of the American Board of Commissioners for Foreign Missions in 1810.

Throughout the 19th century, missions emanated from churches with a strong belief in the active participation of their members in the work of worldwide evangelization. Some churches were specifically founded to give primary emphasis to missions: for instance the Swedish Mission Covenant Church, founded in 1877, and Christian and Missionary Alliance (C.M.A.), founded in 1897. A. B. Simpson (1844–1919), who started the C.M.A., was also founder of Nyack Missionary College, the earliest 'Bible institute' (1882). Similar Bible institutes and colleges soon became vital centres for the training of ministers and missionaries.

In 1854 a series of Anglo-American Missionary Conferences commenced, providing much of the impetus leading to the seminal Edinburgh Conference of 1910. In 1866

Distribution of Protestant Mission Stations in 1925

Continental Missionary Conferences started meeting at Bremen, Germany. In 1888 delegates were sent to the London Conference from 55 societies in Britain and its colonies, 66 societies in North America, and 18 in continental Europe; whilst at the New York Conference of 1900 168 different missionary societies were represented.

Among new agencies exhibiting the broader, democratic basis of foreign missions, and making use of diverse talents, the China Inland Mission (C.I.M.) was particularly influential. It was a 'faith mission' – dependent on the voluntary support of

people responding according to their belief, inclination, and ability – and became the largest single Protestant mission in China.

During the 19th century the United States became the major source of new Protestant missions and of missionary personnel. Of seminal importance there was student conference at Northfield, Massachusetts, in 1886, when the 'Mount Hermon Hundred' volunteered for mission work. By 1920 more than 20,000 young people had volunteered as missionaries after being challenged by the Student Volunteer Movement (S.V.M.).

A revolution during the 'Great Century' was the mushrooming of the participation of women in missionary work. At the start of the century there were very few women missionaries, but by the end of this period women comprised just over 50 per cent of overseas personnel.

During the 19th century about 160 new orders were established in the Roman Catholic Church, mostly devoted to home or foreign missions. France was the greatest source and support for these new Roman Catholic orders.

The Ecumenical Movement

In 1895 the interdenominational Young Men's Christian Association (YMCA), founded in 1844 by the Englishman George Williams (1821–1905), gave birth to the World Student Christian Federation (W.S.C.F.), which, together with the Student Volunteer Movement – a major mission organization – produced some of the great prophets of Christian unity.

The 1910 World Missionary Conference, held in Edinburgh and presided over by Student Volunteer Movement leader John R. Mott (1865–1955), reviewed the state of world evangelism. The largest Protestant gathering until that date, this conference was called to promote work for world mission across denominational lines. Mott's slogan – 'The Evangelization of the World in this Generation' – proved a memorable catalyst. The Edinburgh conference succeeded in establishing greater co-operation in missions but also helped launch the modern ecumenical movement.

By 1937, the Eastern Orthodox Church was also taking part in ecumenical discussions, as were churches in Africa and Asia. In 1945, the end of World War II spurred the churches to reconvene in Amsterdam in 1948 to form the World Council of Churches. W.C.C. headquarters were later moved to Geneva, and a series of world assemblies followed.

Roman Catholics

But Roman Catholics and Russian Orthodox remained notable absentees from ecumenical organisations. Pope John XXIII (r. 1958–63) changed this situation, calling for 'that unity for which Jesus Christ prayed' and summoning Vatican II Council (1962–65) to renew the Roman Catholic Church. A new openness to ecumenical affairs entered the Catholic Church after it was announced that other Christian communions were to be seen as 'separated brothers' rather than outside the church. In 1999 representatives of the Lutheran World Federation and Roman Catholic Church signed a joint declaration, apparently resolving the conflict over the nature of justification at the root of the Protestant Reformation.

But for the Eastern Orthodox, Christianity is the Church, and the Church is Orthodoxy. The Eastern Orthodox goal has been to reconcile all non-Orthodox back

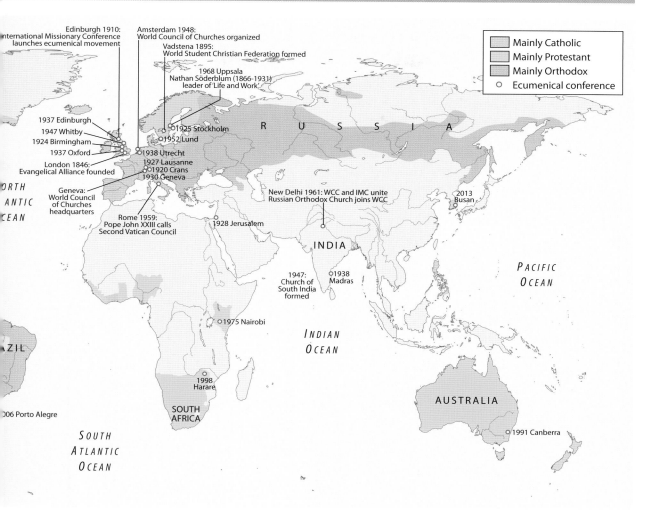

into Orthodoxy. Nevertheless in 1965 the anathemas (excommunications) that created the Great Schism of 1054 between Catholics and Orthodox were revoked by Pope John XXIII and the Ecumenical Patriarch of Constantinople. But reconciliation proceeded very slowly.

Unity locally

Worldwide ecumenism has been reflected in local and grass-roots moves towards unity.

In 1925 the United Church of Canada was formed in a merger of several denominations. Meanwhile many smaller denominations combined with one another in the U.S.A. In 1927 five denominations in China gathered in one Church of Christ. And in 1947 Anglicans, Methodists, Presbyterians, Congregationalists, and Reformed joined to form the Church of South India, serving as a model for others elsewhere.

The Church in the U.S.A.

Different geographical areas of the United States have historically been characterized by distinctive religious traditions. In the English colonies, Puritan Congregationalism was concentrated in New England; Anglicanism (later, Episcopalianism) in Virginia, Maryland, New York, and Connecticut; Presbyterianism in the backcountry; Quakerism in Philadelphia and the Delaware Valley; and German groups in western Pennsylvania. These patterns persist, though often overlain by newer ones.

During the 19th century, revivalism, religious innovation, immigration, and westward expansion produced new regional patterns that were clear by the turn of the century and form the basis for current American religious regions. New England is characterized by large numbers of Congregationalists, Unitarian-Universalists, Episcopalians, and Catholics. The Midland region to its south – from the mid-Atlantic states to the Rocky Mountains – contains many Methodists, Presbyterians, and German groups, as well as Baptists, Episcopalians, and Disciples of Christ. (The Pennsylvania German sub-region is populated largely by Amish, Mennonite, and similar groups.) The Upper Mid West – west from Lake Michigan through the Dakotas – is dominated by Scandinavian Lutherans, Catholics, and – a result of early 20th-century migration from New England – Congregationalists.

Baptists have predominated in the South since the rise of Evangelicalism in the 19th century, but Methodists also form a large minority. The Holiness and Pentecostal churches that grew from both denominations have been strong since 1900. The North Carolina Piedmont region has been occupied by Presbyterian, Quaker, and German groups

since the Colonial period. Peninsular Florida is peopled by a number of groups who have migrated there since the late 19th century; French Catholic Louisiana is a remnant of the French colonization of the Mississippi Valley; and Texas German the result of 19th-century immigration. Utah and the surrounding area became Mormon in the mid-19th century

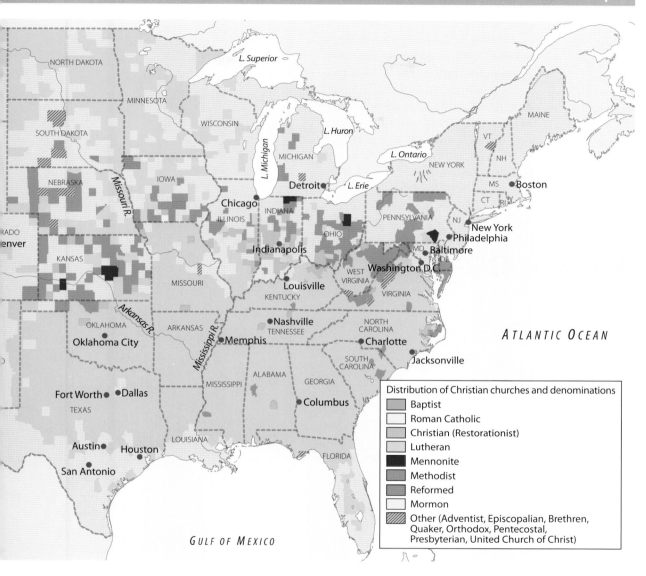

Distribution of Christian churches and denominations

- Baptist
- Roman Catholic
- Christian (Restorationist)
- Lutheran
- Mennonite
- Methodist
- Reformed
- Mormon
- Other (Adventist, Episcopalian, Brethren, Quaker, Orthodox, Pentecostal, Presbyterian, United Church of Christ)

and is still today religiously uniform. The Spanish Catholic region consists of Catholics of Hispanic descent and Native American Catholics, and is increasingly influenced too by Mexican Catholicism. The Western region has been settled largely by migrants from other areas of the country and has no single dominant group.

These regional divisions are far from exact and other patterns of religious settlement and persuasion co-exist and intersect. Some religious groups – such as Catholics, Episcopalians, and Unitarian-Universalists – are mainly urban; others – such as Churches of God, Disciples of Christ, Baptists, Amish, and Mennonites – principally rural.

From its outset the Russian Revolution of 1917 was hostile to Christianity. In a series of decrees Vladimir Lenin (1870–1924) enforced the separation of church and state, which entailed the church losing all its property and most of its rights. Lenin also launched a campaign to free Russian peasants and workers from the remains of 'superstition' (that is, religion). Between 1917 and 1923 more than 1,200 Orthodox priests and 28 bishops were killed.

In 1928 Lenin's successor, Joseph Stalin (1878–1953), introduced a law on religious associations that allowed a church to operate only if its members were registered, its appointments supervised, its activities were confined to the church building (leased from the state), and it published no 'propaganda'. Stalin's aim was to ensure that the church remained submissive and compliant.

'The Great Patriotic War' of 1941–45 radically changed matters for the Orthodox Church. Stalin needed support in strengthening the nation's morale to resist the Nazis, and the church was now utilized as thoroughly as it had previously been persecuted. In 1943, after meeting Stalin, Metropolitan Sergius (1867–1944) was elected Patriarch of Moscow, leader of the Russian Orthodox Church – though his predecessors had been eliminated.

In 1946, immediately after World War II, 4 million 'Uniates' in the Ukraine – Christians following the Eastern rite but in communion with the Pope – were forcibly converted to Orthodoxy. Attempts to undo this again after the collapse of the USSR in 1989 heightened tensions in the newly-independent Ukraine and damaged relations between the papacy and the Moscow patriarchate.

In the 1960s a new wave of religious persecution was unleashed by Nikita

THE RUSSIAN CHURCH TODAY

BARENTS SEA

Helsinki
St Petersburg
Shrine of Bishop Nikita
Talinn
Novgorod
Vologda
Pskov
Yaroslavl
Kostroma
Riga
Kalinin
Zagorsk
Ivanov
Hill of Crosses
Monastery with relics of St Sergius
Vladimir
Vilnius
Moscow
Meskuiciai (Siaullai)
Smolensk
Kaluga
Tula
Madonna of Ostra Brava
Minsk
Orel
POLAND
Chernikov
Kursk
Tambov
Voronezh
Lvov
Zhitomir
Kiev
Monastery of the Caves
Charkov
Ivano-Frankivsk
Vinnytsia
Poltava
Mukacheve
Czernowitz
UKRAINE
Rostov
Kischenev
ROMANIA
Simferopol
Krasnodar
Stavropo
BULGARIA
BLACK SEA
Sukhuumi
K'ut'aisi
P'ot'i
Bat'umi
Akhalts'ikhe
TURKEY
GULF OF BOTHNIA
GULF OF FINLAND
Arkhange
Elista

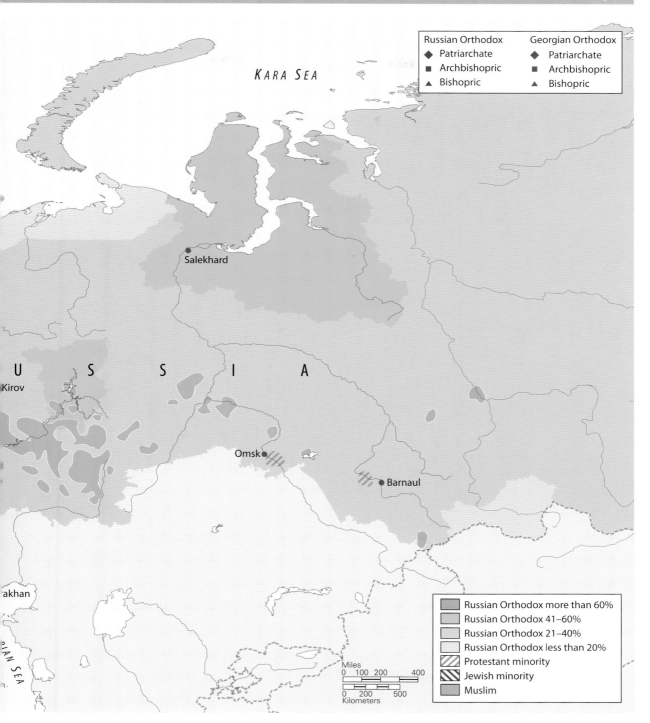

map 58

KARA SEA

Russian Orthodox
◆ Patriarchate
■ Archbishopric
▲ Bishopric

Georgian Orthodox
◆ Patriarchate
■ Archbishopric
▲ Bishopric

Salekhard

U S S I A

Kirov

Omsk

Barnaul

akhan

IAN SEA

Miles
0 100 200   400

0   200   500
Kilometers

Russian Orthodox more than 60%
Russian Orthodox 41–60%
Russian Orthodox 21–40%
Russian Orthodox less than 20%
Protestant minority
Jewish minority
Muslim

Khrushchev, Soviet leader between 1955 and 1964. Anti-religious propaganda was increased and half the remaining 63 monasteries closed (there had been more than 1,000 before 1917). President Yuri Andropov (r. 1982–84), one-time head of the KGB, further intensified the ideological campaign against Christians. Article 142 of the Soviet Penal Code banned offences against the separation of church and state, and was used to suppress private prayer and Bible-study meetings and to prevent anyone other than parents from teaching children religion. Such measures were an attempt to quash a religious revival that had been occurring in Russia. Underground, unregistered groups of Christians continued to meet privately – Orthodox, Baptist, Pentecostal, and Mennonite, as well as Roman Catholics in Ukraine and Lithuania.

Eastern Europe

Following World War II, treatment of Christianity varied in countries 'behind the Iron Curtain' (subject to Communist regimes). After initial attempts at suppression, the Communist government in Poland reached an accommodation with the Roman

Polish pilgrims celebrate the beatification of Pope John Paul II at the Vatican, Rome, Italy.

Catholic Church. Stalin used the subservient Moscow patriarchate to demonstrate to the Orthodox of Romania and Bulgaria that 'religious liberty' existed in the Soviet Union. In Albania religion was completely proscribed and all places of worship closed. In Hungary and Czechoslovakia so-called 'peace movements' were formed among the clergy, to promote compromise between them and the State.

In 1989 the collapse of the Soviet Union and break-up of the Soviet empire brought new freedoms to satellite states in Eastern Europe and led to a revival of Christianity. The Polish Pope John Paul II (r. 1978–2005) played a role in the demise of the Soviet Union with his visits to Poland backing the Solidarity Movement. Lutherans in East Germany and Catholics in Romania also had an important part in ending Communist domination in 1989. In the new Russian Federation President Boris Yeltsin (r. 1991–99) helped restore Orthodoxy to a prominent position.

Although Christianity has greatly declined in Western Europe, in some other regions of the world it has flourished. The demographic centre of gravity has moved south, particularly to Sub-Saharan Africa, Latin America, and the Pacific.

North America

In the USA the huge influence of Mexican, Cuban, and other Latinos has given Catholicism (and increasingly Protestantism) an Hispanic aspect, especially in the South-West and Florida. Eastern Orthodoxy is weaker, except possibly in New York, with its expanding Russian community. Korean and Chinese evangelicals are prominent in California.

Though the US constitution stipulates separation between Church and State, politics is strongly influenced by Christian forces.

Canada is generally more conservative than America, with Quebec overwhelmingly Catholic.

Eastern Europe

The collapse of the Soviet Union and freeing of satellite states in Eastern Europe led to a revival of Christianity. President Vladimir Putin has attempted to enlist the Russian Orthodox Church in his nationalist revival. In Poland, and elsewhere in Eastern Europe, Roman Catholicism is resurgent.

Latin America

In Central and South America, new religions often blend African themes with Christianity. New evangelical and Pentecostal missions, primarily from North America, are increasingly strong. Such Protestantism appeals widely, with its experiential vibrancy and conservative ethics.

Catholicism has been transformed by activist priests espousing Liberal Theology which combines left-wing views and the Biblical message – an activism that has often been opposed by the Vatican.

Africa

In Africa, especially West and South, the formation of many African Independent Churches – often blending indigenous themes with those of the Bible – has added a new dimension to Christianity that is beginning to eclipse the mainstream, especially in southern Africa.

South-East Asia

Catholicism has been successful in the Philippines and Protestantism in Korea, but in the rest of Asia the churches' progress is more modest. Christianity has re-emerged in China, Vietnam, and other countries following lengthy periods of Communist persecution, though it is particularly difficult to quantify as a result of its oppression.

Opposition

In a number of countries life has become more difficult for Christians. Islamic extremism has become the most significant source of persecution, particularly in the Arab Middle East and sub-Saharan Africa. Much of the Christian population fled Syria during the civil war that began in 2011. In Nigeria, Islamic militants have attacked Christian communities and abducted their children. In Iraq, the violent jihadist ISIS group has destroyed long-established Christian communities.

For a variety of different reasons, North Korea, Afghanistan, Pakistan, Vietnam, India, and China are all particularly difficult places to be Christian. Although some of these countries contain large Christian churches, they face opposition from governments and from Hindu and Buddhist leaders who feel threatened by Christian growth.

Worldwide Christianity Today

WORLDWIDE CHRISTIANITY TODAY

ROMAN CATHOLIC

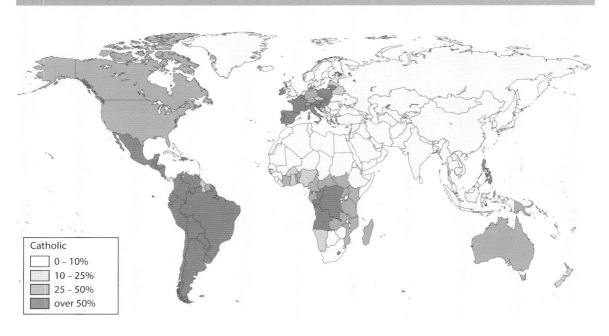

Catholic
- 0 – 10%
- 10 – 25%
- 25 – 50%
- over 50%

EASTERN ORTHODOX

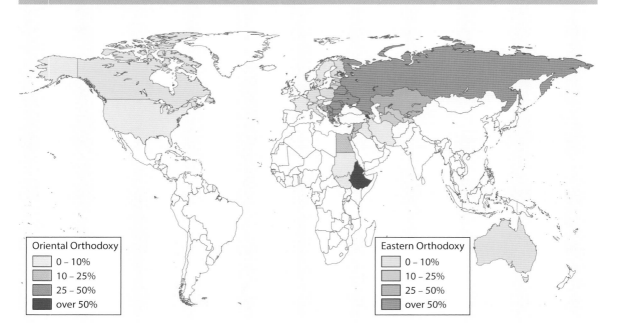

Oriental Orthodoxy
- 0 – 10%
- 10 – 25%
- 25 – 50%
- over 50%

Eastern Orthodoxy
- 0 – 10%
- 10 – 25%
- 25 – 50%
- over 50%

map 59

PROTESTANT

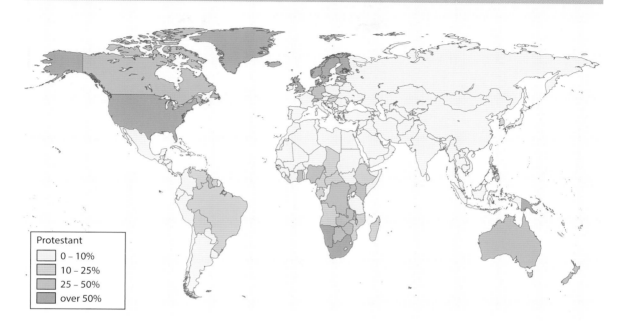

Protestant
- 0 – 10%
- 10 – 25%
- 25 – 50%
- over 50%

PERSECUTION OF CHRISTIANS

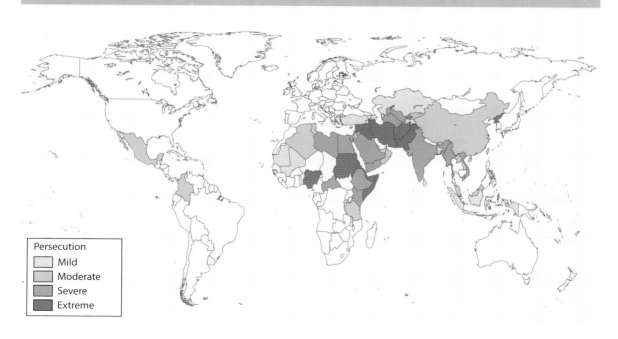

Persecution
- Mild
- Moderate
- Severe
- Extreme

A Chronology of Christian History

c. 4 BC	Jesus is born
AD 29, 30, or 33	Jesus is crucified
c. 35	Paul is converted
45–64	Paul's missionary journeys to Cyprus, Asia Minor, Macedonia, Athens and Corinth. Tried before Herod Agrippa II, appeals to Caesar in Rome.
60–100	Four Gospels written – Mark probably first
64	Great Fire of Rome; Nero persecutes Christians. Peter probably executed
c.67	Paul executed in Rome
66–70	Jews revolt against Rome
70	Romans destroy Jerusalem and Herod's Temple
81–96	Emperor Domitian: renews persecution at end of reign
84	Christians ejected from Jewish synagogue
111–13	Letters between Emperor Trajan and Pliny the Younger, governor of Bithynia, about how to treat Christians
c. 140–55	Hermas writes *The Shepherd*
c. 140	Christians start writing 'apologies' to rebut falsehoods and persuade heathens
144	Marcion excommunicated for heresy: rejecting Old Testament and Jewish origins of Christianity
140–200	Gradual agreement on canon – which books comprise New Testament.
155	Polycarp martyred; earliest evidence of 'cult of martyrs'
c.155	First *Apology* of Justin Martyr
c. 170	Montanist prophets active in Asia Minor: believed New Jerusalem coming shortly to earth
c. 178–200	Irenaeus Bishop of Lyons
c. 180	First version of Apostles' Creed (not so called till c. 390)
c. 200	Latin starts being used in some church services rather than Greek
250	Emperor Decius (r. 249–51) persecutes Christians Origen dies in Syria after torture Novatian founds separate church: believed apostate Christians should not be allowed back in the church
258	Cyprian (Bishop of Carthage since 248) martyred
c. 280	Gregory the Illuminator converts King Tiridates of Armenia Communities of hermits and monks grow in Egypt and Syria
284–305	Emperor Diocletian starts last great state persecution Many martyrs and apostates
c. 305	Antony of Egypt organizes colony of hermits in Egypt
311	Donatist schism begins in N. Africa They refuse new Bishop of Carthage because he was made bishop by a bishop who had sacrificed during the persecution
312	Constantine adopts Christian symbol at battle of Milvian Bridge
313	At Milan Emperor Constantine and E. Emperor Licinius agree toleration of Christians
c. 315	Eusebius becomes Bishop of Caesarea He writes first history of church
c. 320	First church of St Peter's, Rome
324	Constantine sole ruler
325	Council of Nicaea (called later 1st Ecumenical Council) condemns theology of Arius First draft of Nicene Creed
325–81	Arian controversy
328–30	Constantine makes Byzantium new capital as 'Constantinople' (or 'New Rome')
328–73	Bishop Athanasius of Alexandria defends Nicene Creed
c. 330	Macarius founds desert monastery at Wadi-el-Natrun
341–83	Ulfilas Bishop of the Goths: first to convert Germans on large scale Translates Bible into Gothic
346	Abbot Pachomius, author of famous monastic rule, dies
361–3	Julian last non-Christian emperor
364–79	Basil Bishop of Caesarea in Asia Minor; chief mentor for Eastern monks
c. 371	fl. Gregory of Nazianzus (d. 389) and Gregory of Nyssa (d. 395), Eastern theologians
371	Ambrose Bishop of Milan (d. 397)
378	Valens dies at Battle of Adrianople against Goths; leads to military decline of Empire
379–95	Emperor Theodosius I, first pious and orthodox emperor After his death, the 2 parts of the Empire grow apart politically
381	1st Council of Constantinople: settles Nicene Creed and Arian controversy
382	Pope Damasus lists canonical books of Old and New Testaments
386	John Chrysostom preaching at Antioch Jerome settles in Bethlehem: translates most of Bible into Latin, 1st version of Vulgate
390	Ambrose excommunicates Emperor Theodosius I for massacre at Thessalonica

395–430	Augustine Bishop of Hippo: writings against Donatists and Pelagians and his *City of God* dominate Western thinking till Aquinas
395–430	First monks in West at Nola and near Marseilles
398–404	John Chrysostom Patriarch (bishop) of Constantinople
406–7	Germans break through Roman frontier on Rhine
410	Roman army withdraws from Britain
	Goths under Alaric sack Rome
416	British monk Pelagius' teachings condemned at Council of Carthage
416–25	Visigoths take Spain
429–30	Vandals take North Africa
430–61	Leo I first pope with wide authority outside Italy
431	Council of Ephesus reaffirms the faith of Nicaea: *Theotokos* ('Godbearer') accepted as title of Virgin Mary
	Council deposes Nestorius, Patriarch of Constantinople; Nestorian churches spread E from Syria to China
438	Theodosian Code, first Christian codification of law, under Theodosius II
451	Council of Chalcedon affirms Christ is one person 'in two natures'
	Rejected by Christians in Egypt and Syria and elsewhere: 'Oriental' Orthodox Churches – Armenians, Copts, Ethiopians, and in Syria, Kurdistan, and Malabar – separate from Constantinople
455	Vandals take Rome: Pope Leo the Great (r. 440–61) negotiates with them
457	Barsumas, Metropolitan of Nisibis, Persia, founds Nestorian school there
c. 460	Death of Patrick 'Apostle of Ireland'
469–c. 480	Sidonius Apollinaris Bishop of Clermont
476	Romulus Augustulus, last Roman Emperor of W., deposed
488–553	Ostrogothic kingdom in Italy
492–96	Pope Gelasius drafts theory that two powers govern the world: the state for bodies and the Church for souls – the latter more important
496	Clovis, King of the Franks, baptized
c. 520	Dionysius Exiguus creates system of dating by B.C. and A.D.
c. 525	Boethius, author of *Consolation of Philosophy*, executed
527–65	Emperor Justinian I re-conquers N. Africa from the Vandals and Italy from Goths
529	Code of Justinian revises Theodosian Code: basis of law codes of Christian Europe
532–8	Justinian rebuilds Church of Hagia Sophia, Constantinople
c. 540	Benedict of Nursia draws up monastic rule at Monte Cassino
c. 542–78	Jacob Baradaeus founds Monophysite (Jacobite) churches E of Edessa
553	2nd Council of Constantinople
c.563	Columba leaves Ireland with 12 disciples: makes Iona his centre (d. 597)
590–604	Pope Gregory I, 'the Great'; statesman and first monk to become pope
c. 590	Columbanus leaves Ireland: introduces usages of Celtic Church in Gaul
597	Gregory sends Augustine to convert England and become 1st archbishop of the English

622	The *Hegira*: year 0 of Muslim calendar
632	Death of Muhammad
635	Aidan Bishop of Lindisfarne (d. 651)
638–56	Arabs conquer Palestine (and Jerusalem), Iraq, Syria, and Egypt
664	Synod of Whitby: Roman date for Easter prevails over Celtic
681	3rd Council of Constantinople: re-emphasizes Chalcedonian Christology
711–16	Arabs conquer Iberian peninsula
716	Boniface (Wynfrith) makes 1st missionary journey to Frisia
726–843	Iconoclast controversy in East
731	Bede finishes *Ecclesiastical History of the English People* (d. 735)
732	Charles Martel stops Arab advance in battle near Poitiers
754	Boniface martyred in Frisia
771–814	Charlemagne King of the Franks
775	See of Nestorian Patriarch moves from Seleucia-Ctesiphon to Baghdad
781	Alcuin adviser to Charlemagne: 'Carolingian renaissance'
	Sigan-Fu Tablet in China mentions Nestorian missionary there 146 years earlier
787	2nd Council of Nicaea upholds veneration of icons
793	Northmen raid Lindisfarne – and Iona two years later
800	Charlemagne crowned Holy Roman Emperor by Pope Leo III
c. 800	Book of Kells (Ireland)
823	Arabs conquer Crete: begin conquest of Sicily 827
829–65	Anskar of Bremen attempts to convert Denmark and Sweden
843	'Triumph of Orthodoxy': icons restored to E. churches
858–67	Nicholas I sole powerful pope for 2 centuries
858	Photius, 'most learned person in Europe', Patriarch of Constantinople
863–7	'Photian Schism': communion broken between Pope Nicholas I and Patriarch Photius of Constantinople
863	Cyril and Methodius, Orthodox 'Apostles of the Slavs' in Moravia
	Translate Bible and service books into Slavonic
871–99	Alfred the Great, King of Wessex, defeats Danes, promotes Christian learning
877	Death of Scotus Erigena: Irish philosopher, head of school at Laon
910	Monastery of Cluny founded; becomes centre of reform
961	Athanasius the Athonite founds Great Lavra on Mount Athos (d. 1003)
962	Otto the Great restores Holy Roman Empire
	Bases public order on rule by bishops
988	Conversion of Russia
	Vladimir, Prince of Kiev, baptized by Byzantine missionaries
995	Norway converts to Christianity, partly by force
996–1021	Caliph el-Hakim persecutes Coptic Church in Egypt
997–1038	King Stephen makes Hungary Christian
1000	Icelandic Thing (Parliament) legalizes Christianity
1009	Church of the Holy Sepulchre, Jerusalem, destroyed

1012	Romuald founds eremitic monastery of Camaldoli, Tuscany
1031	Caliphate of Cordoba falls
1049–54	Leo IX pope: begins papal reform
c. 1051	Monastery of the Caves founded at Kiev
1054	Mutual anathemas exchanged between papacy and Patriarch Michael Cerularius
C.11–1492	Christians conquer Iberian peninsula
1059–92	Normans conquer S. Italy and Muslim Sicily
1071	Seljuk Turks defeat Byzantines at Battle of Manzikert
1073–85	Pope Gregory VII (Hildebrand) strives to reform Church, rid it of lay control, and make priests celibate
1077	Emperor Henry IV made to do penance to pope at Canossa, N. Italy
1084	Bruno founds Carthusian Order
1088	Building of great church at Cluny begins
1093–1109	Anselm Archbishop of Canterbury
1095	Urban II preaches 1st Crusade at Council of Clermont
1098	Anselm's *Cur Deus Homo*: theology of the atonement
	Abbey of Cîteaux founded: Cistercian Order quickly spreads
1099	Crusaders take Jerusalem
c. 1116	Peter Abelard teaches at Paris
1120	Premonstratensian Order founded
	Templars founded to defend holy places in Palestine
	Order of St John of Jerusalem (Hospitallers) founded
1123	1st Lateran Council
1124	Conversion of Pomerania and S. Baltic coast begins
1139	2nd Lateran Council
1146	Bernard of Clairvaux (d. 1153) preaches 2nd Crusade at Vézelay
1154–59	Pope Hadrian IV: only English pope
1156	Carmelite order founded at Mt Carmel, Palestine
c. 1157	Peter Lombard's *Sentences* completed, Paris
1170	Archbishop Thomas Becket murdered at Canterbury
1174	Thomas Becket canonized
1176	Peter Valdes converted: forms 'the poor men of Lyons' – Waldensians
1177	3rd Lateran Council
1187	Saladin takes Jerusalem
1189–92	3rd Crusade
1198–1216	Pope Innocent III: politically most powerful pope
c. 1200	Teaching communities evolve into universities of Bologna, Paris, Oxford, Cambridge etc
1204	4th Crusade diverts to Constantinople: Latin troops sack city
1209	Francis of Assisi gives his friars first Rule
1209–29	Albigensian Crusade against heretics in S. France
1212	Children's Crusade

1215	4th Lateran Council: annual confession ordered, doctrine of Eucharist redefined
1215–50	Frederick II, Holy Roman Emperor and King of Sicily; strongest opponent of medieval popes
1216	Dominican friars established
1217–21	5th Crusade at Damietta
1220	Dominic gives final form to his Order of Friars Preachers (Dominicans)
1223	Franciscan Rule approved by Pope Honorius III
1224–44	Mongols invade Russia and Eastern Europe
1226	Death of Francis of Assisi
1232	Gregory IX establishes papal inquisition
1237–40	Mongol Tatars overrun Kievan Rus'
1239	Gregory IX excommunicates Frederick II
1244	Jerusalem finally lost to Muslims
1248–54	Louis IX of France on crusade in Egypt and Palestine
c. 1250	All Spain re-conquered for Christianity except Granada
1256	Augustinian Eremites (Austin Friars) founded
1261	Byzantine Emperor Michael VIII Palaeologus recovers Constantinople
1274	Death of Thomas Aquinas: his *Summa* marked apex of medieval theology
1291	Last Crusader outpost in Palestine, Acre, falls
1295	Mongol dynasty converts to Islam
1302	Pope Boniface VIII's bull *Unam Sanctam* claims universal jurisdiction of pope and superiority of spiritual power over secular
1305	Pope Clement V elected: start of French exile of papacy
1308	Death of Duns Scotus
1309–77	Popes at Avignon: 'Babylonian Captivity'
1311–12	Council of Vienne rules for strict party in dispute over Franciscan poverty
1312	Destruction of Templars
1314	Latest date for Dante's *Divine Comedy*
1324	Marsilius of Padua, *Defensor pacis*: church should be ruled by general councils
1327–47	William of Ockham (b. c. 1285) criticizes philosophy of realism
1327	Death of Meister Eckhart, German Dominican mystic
1337	Hesychast controversy: teaching of Gregory Palamas on Divine Light upheld by councils at Constantinople, 1341, 1347, 1351
c. 1340	Sergii of Radonezh founds monastery of Holy Trinity, near Moscow
1348–9	Black Death
1357	Death of Gregory Palamas, defender of Hesychasm in E.
1361	Death of Johann Tauler, disciple of Meister Eckhart
1374	Geert de Groote converted: founds Brethren of the Common Life, Deventer, Netherlands
1375–82	John Wyclif attacks clerical wealth, monasticism, and authority of pope 1378–1415 Great Schism in papacy: 2, then 3, simultaneous popes
1382–95	Wyclif's Bible: Middle English vernacular translation

1387	Monastery of Windesheim founded by Radewyns, disciple of de Groote
1409–49	Conciliar Movement: series of councils to end Great Schism and reform church
1413	Jan Hus writes the *De Ecclesia*: for reform of church along Wyclif's lines
1414–18	Council of Constance states general councils superior to popes
	Jan Hus burnt. Beginnings of Hussite churches
1418	*Imitatio Christi*, ascribed to Thomas à Kempis
1431–49	Council of Basel
1433	Nicholas of Cusa produces programme for reform of church and Empire
c. 1440	Reform of Ethiopian Church by Emperor Zara Jacob
1453	Ottoman Turks take Constantinople: turn Hagia Sophia into mosque
1454/5	Gutenberg Bible published
1479	'Spanish Inquisition' established with papal approval
1492	Muslims expelled from Spain
	Christopher Columbus lands in West Indies
1493–4	Pope Alexander VI partitions new discoveries between Spain and Portugal 1498
1501	1st bishopric in Hispaniola, Haiti
1503	Conflict in Russia between monastic 'Possessors' and 'Non-Possessors'
1506	Pope Julius II lays foundation stone of St Peter's, Rome
1508–12	Michelangelo paints ceiling of Sistine Chapel, Rome
1509	Erasmus attacks corruption in church and criticizes monasticism
1510	Martin Luther visits Rome
c. 1512	Copernicus suggests earth moves round sun
1516	Erasmus' Greek New Testament published
1517	Luther issues 95 theses against indulgences at Wittenberg
1519	Zwingli begins reform in Zurich
1519–21	Spain conquers Mexico
1521	Pope excommunicates Luther; Charles V outlaws him at Diet of Worms
1522	Luther publishes German New Testament
1522–3	Ignatius Loyola writes *Spiritual Exercises*
1524	Franciscans arrive in Mexico
1524–6	Peasants' Revolt in Germany
1525	Early Anabaptists in Zurich
1525–30	Protestant Reformation spreads in central and S.W. Germany
1526	Tyndale's English New Testament published
1528	Reformation adopted in Bern
1529	Diet of Speyer: some members protest against attempt to stop reform – hence 'Protestants'
1530	Diet of Augsburg: Confession of Augsburg, classic Lutheran statement of faith
	Denmark adopts Lutheran creed
1531	1st bishop appointed in Nicaragua
1533–35	Anabaptists seize Münster; overthrown by force

1534	Henry VIII usurps pope's authority in England by Act of Supremacy
	Luther Bible published
	Loyola founds Jesuits in Paris
1536	John Calvin publishes *Institutes*, arrives in Geneva
1537	Pope Paul III declares American Indians entitled to liberty and property
	Denmark and Norway adopt Lutheran Protestantism
1539	Henry VIII's Great Bible printed
1540	Pope Paul III approves Loyola's foundation of Jesuits
1542	Francis Xavier arrives in Goa, India, then Japan
1545–47, 1551–52, 1562–63	Council of Trent reforms Catholic Church
1549	First Book of Common Prayer, England
1550–2	Iceland adopts Lutheran Protestantism
1551–94	Palestrina at Rome: from 1570 composer to papal chapel
1552	Las Casas publishes account of oppression of S. American Indians
	Second Book of Common Prayer, England
1553–58	Mary I reigns in England; tries to restore Catholic Church
1553	Anti-Trinitarian Spaniard Servetus burnt as heretic in Calvin's Geneva
1555	Peace of Augsburg: Protestant faith legal in Lutheran states and cities: '*cuius regio eius religio*'
	Bishops Latimer and Ridley burnt at Oxford
1556	Archbishop Cranmer burnt
1557	1st *Index Librorum Prohibitorum*
1559	1st National Synod of French Reformed Church (Huguenots)
	Queen Elizabeth achieves moderate Protestant settlement, England
	1st *reduction* (reservation for Jesuit-led Indian community), Paraguay
1560	John Knox establishes Reformed church in Scotland
1561	Belgic Reformed Confession adopted in Antwerp
1562	Heidelberg Catechism for Palatinate: Calvinist with Lutheran modifications
	Theresa of Avila reforms Carmelites with teaching of mystical prayer
	Spain seizes Philippines
1562–94	French Wars of Religion
1562–1604	Fausto Sozzini spreads Unitarian ('Socinian') doctrines
1564	'Counter Reformation' decrees of Council of Trent confirmed by Pope Pius IV
1566	Calvinist 'iconoclast' movement in Netherlands
	Philip II of Spain crushes resistance
1568–1648	Dutch Wars of Religion: Eighty Years' War
1570	Pius V's bull *Regnans in Excelsis* declares Elizabeth I a heretic
1572	St Bartholomew's Day Massacre, Paris, attempts to end Huguenot power
1574	Calvinist university of Leyden established, Holland
1577	Formula of Concord: definitive statement of Lutheran Confession

1579	Jesuits at Mogul court, India
	Union of Utrecht; 7 N. provinces defy Philip II of Spain; S. Netherlands make peace
	1st Archbishop of Manila
1582	Gregorian calendar adopted
1588	Spanish Armada defeated
	Molina (Spanish Jesuit) defends free will against predestination
1589	1st Russian patriarch of Moscow
1590	1st complete Hungarian Bible, translated by Gaspar Karoli
1593	Henry IV turns Catholic, ending Wars of Religion in France
	Sweden establishes Lutheran church: last Scandinavian country to turn Protestant
1596	Council of Brest-Litovsk: majority of Orthodox in Ukraine join Rome as 'Uniates'
1598	Edict of Nantes guarantees toleration for Huguenots in Catholic France
1599	Synod of Udayamperur: Malabar Christians conform to Rome
1600	Giordano Bruno burnt in Rome
1601–10	Jesuit Matteo Ricci in Beijing
1605	Italian Jesuit missionary Robert de Nobili arrives in India
1611	Berulle founds French Oratory
	King James Bible (Authorized Version) published
1614	Christian worship prohibited in Japan
1618–19	Synod of Dort condemns Arminian doctrines
1618–48	Thirty Years' War in Germany: in early years attempts to reverse Protestant advances
1620	*Mayflower* sails from Holland and England to America with Puritans
1622	Bull of Pope Gregory XV, *Inscrutabili*, creates *Congregation de Propaganda Fide*
1624	Death of Jakob Boehme, mystic
1626	1st Christian church in Tibet (Jesuit)
1629	Patriarch Cyril Loukaris issues a Protestantizing Confession of Faith
1633	Galileo Galilei tried by Inquisition for advocating Copernican theory
	Sisters of Charity founded by Vincent de Paul and Louise de Marillac
1637	Shimabara Rebellion of persecuted Christians in Japan
1646	John Eliot starts mission to Native Americans
1647	George Fox begins to preach: organizes Quakers – 'Society of Friends'
1648	Peace of Westphalia ends Thirty Years' War
	Calvinists as well as Catholics and Lutherans legal in Germany
1649	Iroquois destroy Hurons and their Jesuit mission
1652–97	Jesuit Antonio Vieira works on behalf of Indians of Brazil
1654	Pascal converted in night of 'fire'
1655	Duke of Savoy persecutes the Vaudois (Waldenses)
1656–7	Pascal's *Provincial Letters* ridicule Jesuits and defend Jansenists
1659	Laval-Montmorency Catholic vicar apostolic at Quebec
1660	Restoration of Charles II and of Anglican Church in England

1662	English Book of Common Prayer revised
	'Half-way Covenant' in churches of Massachusetts Bay
1666	Nikon, Patriarch of Moscow, tries to reform church: lasting schism of 'Old Believers'
1667	Milton's *Paradise Lost*
1675	Philipp Jakob Spener begins 'Pietist' movement in German Lutheranism
1678	John Bunyan, *Pilgrim's Progress*
1682	Quaker William Penn founds Pennsylvania on basis of religious toleration
1683	2nd siege of Vienna; W. limit of Ottoman advance
1685	Louis XIV revokes the Edict of Nantes
	Huguenots flee to Britain, Germany, and America
1687	Lima earthquake — Jesuits there institute Three Hours Service of Good Friday
	Jesuit Eusebio Kino pushes into Arizona and California
	Pope Innocent XI condemns Quietism of Miguel de Molinos
1688	Roman Catholic James II driven from English throne
1689	Toleration Act grants freedom of worship to dissenters in England
	John Locke: *Letters Concerning Toleration*
1692	Imperial decree in China permits Christian worship
1698	Charter of East India Co. provides for chaplains to India
1699	Pope condemns Fénelon's quietism
1701	Society for the Propagation of the Gospel in Foreign Parts founded, London
1704	Papal legate arrives in E. to deal with Jesuit compromises with Chinese and Indian customs
1709–10	Louis XIV destroys the Jansenist centre of Port-Royal, Paris
1719	Death of Ziegenbalg, Pietist missionary, in India
1721	Peter the Great abolishes the Moscow patriarchate; puts church under 'Holy Synod'
1722	Count Zinzendorf founds the Pietist Herrnhut colony, Saxony
1723–26	Reign of Yung Cheng in China: Christians persecuted
1723–50	J. S. Bach at Leipzig: composes the great religious works
1724	Church of Utrecht (Jansenist connection) separates from Rome
1726	Great Awakening begins, N. America
1727	Jonathan Edwards converted: leading Calvinist theologian in N. America (d. 1758)
1728	William Law, *A Serious Call to a Devout and Holy Life*
1736	Joseph Butler, *The Analogy of Religion*
1738	John Wesley converted
1740	Election of Benedict XIV, great pope of C18 (d. 1758)
	George Whitefield preaches in America (also 1754, 1764, 1770)
1742	1st performance of Handel's *Messiah*
1746	Pietist missionary Christian Friedrich Schwartz to India

1759	British take Quebec; free exercise of religion guaranteed to Roman Catholics of Canada
	Jesuits expelled from Portugal
1773	1st Methodist Conference in N. America
	Pope Clement XIV suppresses Jesuits
1781	Emperor Joseph II's Patent of Toleration
1776	U.S. Declaration of Independence
1787	Protestant marriages legalized in France
	Constitution of the United States: separation of church and state; civil rights for members of any religion
1789–94	French Revolution: national assembly nationalizes church property, bans monastic vows
1792–3	'Terror' attempts to de-Christianize France
1792	Baptist Missionary Society founded, London
1795	London Missionary Society founded
1799	Church Missionary Society founded, London
	Schleiermacher publishes his addresses, appeals to religious feeling
1800	Camp meetings W. of Appalachians signal 'Second Great Awakening': revivalist Protestantism
1801	Bonaparte's Concordat with Rome revives French Catholic Church, restricted by state
	1st major persecution of Roman Catholics in Korea
	U.S. Congregationalists and Presbyterians organize 'Plan of Union' (dissolved 1837)
1804	British and Foreign Bible Society founded: seeks to translate Bible into every significant language
1805	Missionary Henry Martyn arrives in India as chaplain to East India Co.
1807	Britain prohibits slave trade after Wilberforce's campaign
	1st Protestant missionary arrives in China: still illegal to propagate Christianity
1808	Vatican establishes Baltimore as 1st metropolitan see in U.S.A.
1810–24	Future republics of Spanish America struggle for independence: Vatican backs Spain
1810	American Board of Commissioners for Foreign Missions (A.B.C.F.M.) formed
1813	East India Co.'s Charter amended to facilitate missionaries entering India
1814	Slave-trade made illegal in Netherlands
	Pope Pius VII revives Jesuits
	Bishop of Calcutta consecrated, 1st Anglican bishop in Asia
	Samuel Marsden's mission to Maoris of New Zealand
1815	Unitarianism splits from U.S. Congregationalism
1817	Lutherans and Calvinists unite in Prussia and other German states
	Missionary Robert Moffat arrives in South Africa; works there 50 years
1819	1st Provincial Council of U.S. Catholic bishops, Baltimore
1821	Greek revolt against Ottoman rule; Gregory, patriarch of Constantinople, executed
1822	Brazil gains independence from Portugal

1826–30s	Widespread suppression of religious orders in Latin America
1826	Widow-burning banned in British India
1829	Roman Catholic Emancipation in Britain
1830	*Protestant* starts Nativist crusade against Catholics
	Book of Mormon
1830–45	Churches in Australia and New Zealand organized
1832	Autonomy of Serbian Orthodox Church
1833	Start of Oxford Movement in Church of England
	Disestablishment of final U.S. church: Congregationalism in Massachusetts
	Slavery abolished in British territories
1836	1st Roman Catholic and Anglican bishops in Australia
1839	Bull of Gregory XVI condemns slavery
1840	German missionary J. L. Krapf expelled from Abyssinia
	Scots missionary David Livingstone arrives in Africa: continues explorations till 1873
1842	George Augustus Selwyn, 1st Anglican bishop of New Zealand
1843	Kierkegaard publishes his *Either-Or*, existential view of Christianity
	J. H. Newman's sermon on 'The Parting of Friends'
	Scottish Disruption: split in Scots Presbyterians over relations with church establishment
1844	Nativists riot against Catholic churches in Philadelphia
	J. L. Krapf sets up C.M.S. mission in Mombasa
	Adventist groups in U.S.A. and England expect the Second Coming: carry on with modified expectations – 1861 as 'Seventh-day Adventists'
1845	Baptists and Methodists in U.S. South split off from N. counterparts
	Newman converts to Roman Catholic Church
1846–78	Pope Pius IX (longest reigning pope).
	Opposed to world of his time: condemns it in *Syllabus of Errors* (1864)
1847	Catholic vicariate of Abyssinia created
	Brigham Young moves Church of Jesus Christ of the Latter-Day Saints (Mormons) to Salt Lake City, Utah
1848	F. D. Maurice and Charles Kingsley found Christian Socialist Movement, London
	Pope flees Rome revolution
	Slavery forbidden in all French territories
1850	Establishment of Roman Catholic hierarchy in England and Wales
1851	State support of religion ends in S. Australia
1852	Establishment of Holy Synod in Greece: autocephaly of Greek Orthodox Church
1854	Papal bull by Pius IX: immaculate conception of Virgin Mary an article of faith
1857	Universities' Mission to Central Africa founded

1858	Visions of Bernadette at Lourdes
	Isaac Hecker founds Paulists, 1st U.S. Catholic order of men
	Treaties of Tientsin imposed on China by Britain, France, Russia, and USA: legalizing of opium importation and free entry of Christian missionaries to interior
1859	Charles Darwin, *On the Origin of Species*
1864	Pope Pius IX's encyclical *Quanta Cura*, with attached 'Syllabus of Errors'
1865	Samuel Crowther 1st black Anglican bishop of Nigeria
	Foundation of the China Inland Mission
1866	St Joseph's College founded, Mill Hill, London
1867	1st Lambeth Conference of Bishops of the Anglican Communion
1868	Archbishop Lavigerie of Algiers founds White Fathers for African mission
1868–70	Italian nationalists seize Rome, annexe papal possessions
1869–70	1st Vatican Council: declares pope infallible
1871	Old Catholic Church formed in Germany, Switzerland, and Netherlands
	Disestablishment of Anglican Church in Ireland
1872–79	*Kulturkampf* in Prussia: Bismarck tries to restrict freedom of Catholic Church
1873	End of open persecution of Christians in Japan
1875	World Alliance of Reformed and Presbyterian Churches formed, Geneva 1878–92
1879	Australian Methodist missions to Solomon Islands begin
	Autocephaly of Serbian Orthodox Church
1881	Westcott and Hort's Greek New Testament
1884	Tembu national church founded
	Arrival of the 1st resident Protestant missionary in Korea
1885	Formation of Romanian Orthodox Church
1886	Archbishop James Gibbons of Baltimore made cardinal: major U.S. Catholic leader
	Catholics and Anglicans martyred in Buganda
	Roman Catholic hierarchy established in India
1889	Brazil established as republic: separation of church and state
1890	Anglicans, Methodists, and the L.M.S. agree spheres of mission work in Australian New Guinea
c. 1890	Prophet Harris, W. African revivalist
1891	Pope Leo XIII's encyclical *Rerum Novarum* on social problems
1894–96	Armenian Christians massacred in Turkey
1894–1906	Dreyfus case in France: disputes over anti-Semitism provoke separation of church and state in 1905
1895	Beginnings of World Student Christian Federation (or S.C.M.)
1896	Anglican Orders condemned as null and void by Rome
1898	Cuba, Puerto Rico, and Philippines gain independence from Spain; fall under U.S. hegemony
	1st Protestant missionaries enter Philippines
1899	1st Bush Brotherhood, Australia

1900	Boxer Uprising in China: many missionaries and Chinese Christians massacred
1900–7	Modernist controversy over the right of Catholics to study Bible with historical criticism. Encyclical *Pascendi* condemns Modernism
1902	Iglesia Filipina Independiente secedes from Roman Catholic Church
1905	Nihon Kumiai Kirisuto Kyokai (Japan Congregational Church) becomes independent of Western missionary control
1906–7	Separation of church and state in France: state takes church property
1907	Walter Rauschenbusch's *Christianity and the Social Crisis* proclaims 'social gospel'
1908	Federal Council of Churches founded for U.S. Protestants
	Churches in S. India unite in South India United Church
1910	Edinburgh Missionary Conference leads to modern reunion movement
1912	Australian Inland Mission (and flying doctor organization) founded
1913	J. Chilembwe, nationalist prophet in Nyasaland
	Theologian Albert Schweitzer to Africa as medical missionary
1914	'Assemblies of God' affiliation of Pentecostal Churches in N. America
1914–18	World War I
1915	2nd Ku Klux Klan formed: anti-Catholic, anti-Jewish, anti-Black
	Armenian Christians massacred in Turkey
1916	Charles de Foucauld, ex-soldier and hermit, murdered in Sahara
1917	Bolshevik Revolution, Russia
1918	All Russian church property nationalized
	Many Orthodox bishops and priests killed in Civil War
1919	World's Christian Fundamentals Association formed in U.S.A.
	Karl Barth's commentary on Romans published
1920	Serbian patriarchate re-established
1921	Church of Jesus Christ through the prophet Simon Kimbangu founded, Congo
1923	Christians expelled from much of Turkey
1924	Autonomy of Finnish Orthodox Church
	Autonomy of Polish Orthodox Church
1925	Patriarchal status for Romanian Orthodox Church
1927	Faith and Order Movement founded, Lausanne
	Metropolitan Sergii Stragorodskii accepts recognition of Russian Orthodox Church by Soviet authorities
1928	Conference of the International Missionary Council, Tambaram, S. India
1929	William Temple, Archbishop of York; of Canterbury, 1942–4
	Lateran Treaty, Rome: Mussolini creates Vatican City, independent state for pope
	Mother Teresa begins work in Calcutta
1932	United Methodist Church unites with Wesleyan and Primitive Methodist Churches
1933	Theologian Paul Tillich flees Germany to U.S.A. (d. 1965)
1934	Synod of Barmen: German churchmen opposed to Hitler found Confessing Church.

1937	Autocephaly of Albanian Orthodox Church
	Pope denounces Hitler in encyclical *Mit brennender Sorge*
1938	Frank Buchman, founder of Oxford Group, launches Moral Rearmament
	Kristallnacht: Nazis destroy Jewish shops and synagogues
1939–45	World War II
1940	Taizé (ecumenical religious order) founded by Roger Schutz
1943	Concordat with Stalin allows Russian Church to revive and have patriarch again
	Bishop of Chichester George Bell condemns bombing of German cities
1945	End of Japanese government attempt to control religion
	In Communist-controlled N. Korea new restrictions on religion
	Federation of Protestant churches of E. and W. Germany: 'Evangelical Church in Germany'
1946	Abolition of the Eastern-rite (Uniate) Catholic Church in the U.S.S.R.
1947	Church of South India founded (union of Anglicans, Methodists, and South India United Church)
1948	World Council of Churches founded, Amsterdam
	New communist governments in E. Europe obstruct and persecute church
1949	U.S. Baptist Billy Graham begins evangelistic tours
	Communist victory ends Christian proselytism in China
1950	Pope Pius XII makes Virgin Mary's bodily assumption into heaven article of faith
	National Council of Churches formed in U.S.: unites many Protestant and Orthodox churches
1951	Three-Self Patriotic Movement begins among Protestant Christians in China; similar movement among Roman Catholics: most foreign missionaries leave China
1953	Recognition of Bulgarian Orthodox Church by patriarchate of Constantinople
1958–64	Khrushchev starts new attack on Russian Orthodox Church
1958	1st Chinese Roman Catholic bishops: opposed by Vatican
1958–65	Roncalli becomes Pope John XXIII; opens up Roman Catholic Church
1959	Castro establishes 1st Communist dictatorship in Latin America, in Cuba; limited religious freedoms
c. 1960	Death of Isaiah Shembe, founder of the Nazareth Movement in South Africa
1960	John F. Kennedy elected 1st Catholic president of U.S.A.
1961	Russian Orthodox Church and most Orthodox churches of E. Europe join World Council of Churches
1962–65	2nd Vatican Council: Catholicism 'opens' to modern world; allows services in vernacular, seeks friendship with other denominations
1963	Death of writer C. S. Lewis
1964–85	Clergy criticize military regimes in Brazil for neglecting social justice and abusing human rights

1966	Archbishop Ramsey of Canterbury visits Pope Paul VI in Rome
	Pentecostal and charismatic movements in Protestantism and Catholicism in Americas and Europe
	Cultural Revolution begins in China: Red Guards close Christian churches
1968	Papal encyclical *Humanae Vitae* repeats ban on artificial birth control, stirs Catholic dissent
	Baptist pastor and civil rights campaigner Martin Luther King assassinated
	Pope Paul VI inaugurates bishops' conference, Medellín, Colombia: new openness to social reform
1970	World Alliance of Reformed Churches (Congregational and Presbyterian Churches)
	Formation of Church of North India and Church of Pakistan
1972	Collapse of proposals for Anglican-Methodist constitutional union in U.K.
1976	'Born-again' Jimmy Carter elected U.S. President
1978	Polish Pope John Paul II elected, first non-Italian since 1523
1979	Churches in China reopen for public worship
	John Paul II condemns excesses of liberation theology
	Nobel Peace Prize to Mother Teresa for work with destitute in Calcutta
1980	Spokesman for social justice Archbishop Romero of San Salvador assassinated
1986	Roman Catholic Church and other Christians help end Marcos regime in Philippines
	Desmond Tutu elected Anglican Archbishop of Cape Town
1988	Millennium of Russian Christianity
	3 Lutheran bodies merge as Evangelical Lutheran Church in America
1989	1st woman bishop ordained in U.S. Episcopal Church
	Ukrainian Eastern-rite (Uniate) Catholic Church authorized in U.S.S.R.
1989–90	Communist regimes in E. Europe and Russia fall; state persecution of church ends
1992	Church of England decides to ordain women
	New Catechism of the Catholic Church published
1993	International Lutheran Council founded
1999	Joint Declaration on Doctrine of Justification between Lutheran World Federation and Catholic Church
2001	1700th anniversary of Christianity as state religion of Armenia
2005	Election of Pope Benedict XVI
2007	After 80 years' schism, Russian Orthodox Church reunified
2009	Father Damien of Molokai canonized by Roman Catholic Church
2013	Argentinian Pope Francis becomes 1st non-European pope of modern era
2015	First woman bishop in Church of England

Further reading

Overviews

Diarmaid MacCulloch, *A History of Christianity: The First Three Thousand Years*, London, 2009

Adrian Hastings, *A World History of Christianity.* Grand Rapids, Michigan, 2000.

Stephen Neill, *A History of Christian Missions* (The Penguin History of the Church 6), London, 1991

Tim Dowley ed., *Introduction to the History of Christianity*, 2nd Edition, Minneapolis, 2013

Beginnings

Graham N. Stanton, *The Gospels and Jesus*, 2nd ed., Oxford, 2002.

E. P. Sanders, *The Historical Figure of Jesus*, London, 1993.

Ivor J. Davidson, *The Birth of the Church: From Jesus to Constantine AD 30–312*, Oxford, 2004.

W. H. C. Frend, *The Rise of Christianity*, London, 1984

J. Stevenson ed., rev. W. H. C. Frend, *A New Eusebius, Documents Illustrating the History of the Church to AD 337*, London, 1987.

Frances Young, *The Making of the Creeds*, London, 1991.

The Medieval Church

Ivor J. Davidson, *A Public Faith: From Constantine to the Medieval World AD 312–600*, Oxford, 2005.

J. Stevenson ed., rev. W. H. C. Frend, *Creeds, Councils and Controversies: Documents Illustrating the History of the Church AD 337–461*, London, 1989

Philip Jenkins, *The Lost History of Christianity: The Thousand-year Golden Age of the Church in the Middle East, Africa and Asia*, New York, 2008.

Peter Brown, *Augustine of Hippo: A Biography*, London, 1969.

Richard Fletcher, *The Cross and the Crescent: Christianity and Islam from Muhammad to the Reformation*, London, 2003.

Peter Brown, *The Rise of Western Christendom: Triumph and Diversity AD 200–1000*, Oxford, 1997.

Christopher Tyerman, *God's War: A New History of the Crusades*, London 2006.

Tibor Szamuely, *The Russian Tradition*, London, 1974.

The Reformations

Diarmaid MacCulloch, *Reformation: Europe's House Divided 1490–1700*, London, 2003.

Martin Marty, *Martin Luther*, New York, 2004.

Bernard Cottret, *Calvin: A Biography*, Grand Rapids and Edinburgh, 2000.

Robert Birley, *The Refashioning of Catholicism, 1450–1700*, Houndmills, 1999.

C. R. Boxer, *The Church Militant and Iberian Expansion 1440-1770*, Baltimore, 1967.

Towards the Modern World

Meic Pearse, *The Age of Reason: From the Wars of Religion to the French Revolution 1570–1789*, Oxford, 2006.

W. R. Ward, *The Protestant Evangelical Awakening*, Cambridge, 1992.

Owen Chadwick, *The Popes and the European Revolution*, Oxford, 1981.

Mark A. Noll, *A History of Christianity in the United States and Canada*, Grand Rapids, Michigan, 1992

David Bebbington, *Evangelicalism in Modern Britain: A History from the 1730s to the 1980s*, London 1989 and later eds.

Owen Chadwick, *The Secularization of the European Mind in the Nineteenth Century*, Cambridge, 1975.

Brian Stanley, *The Bible and the Flag: Protestant Missions and British Imperialism in the Nineteenth and Twentieth Centuries*, Leicester, 1990.

The Modern Age

Philip Jenkins, *The Next Christendom: The Coming of Global Christianity*, New York, 2011

Jeremy Morris, *The Church in the Modern Age*, London, 2007.

Ian Breward, *A History of the Churches in Australasia*, Oxford, 2001.

Grant Wacker, *Heaven Below: Early Pentecostals and American Culture*, Cambridge, MA, 2001.

Gazetteer

Note: Locators show map numbers, not page numbers

Ayacucho
  Catholic missions 35
Azores
  Catholic missions 35
Azotus
  Early Christian communities
    2
  Christianity by AD 300 4
  Pilgrimage routes 24 inset

Baalbek
  Early Christian communities
    2
Babylon
  Christianity by AD 100 3
  Spread of Islam 12
Baclayon
  Philippines 36
Baghdad
  Nestorian and Monophysite
    Churches 8
  Spread of Islam 12
  Missions to the Mongols 26
Bagusa
  The West in 1500 30
Balkh
  Nestorian and Monophysite
    Churches 8
  Missions to the Mongols 26
Baltimore
  Catholic missions 35
  North America in 1750 41
  Catholicism in the U.S.A. 49
Bamberg
  Early missions in the
    Christian West 14
  Jews oppressed 23
  European universities 25
  Catholic Reformation 33
Bangor
  Church in the West in the
    sixth century 9
  Early missions in the
    Christian West 14
  Charlemagne's empire 15
  British Church c. 800 16
Bangor Iscoed
  Spread of monasticism 10
Barcelona
  Charlemagne's empire 15
  Crusades 22
  Jews oppressed 23
  Pilgrimage routes 24
  European universities 25
  Reformation Europe 32
  Christian Europe in 1700 38
Bardsey
  Spread of monasticism 10
Bardstown
  Catholicism in the U.S.A. 49
Barga
  Spread of Islam 12
Bari
  Byzantium under threat 13
  Crusades 22
  Pilgrimage routes 24
Barka
  Spread of Islam 12
Barking
  British Church c. 800 16
Basel
  Jews oppressed 23
  European universities 25
  Friars 26
  Catholic Reformation 33
  Europe after 1648 34

Christian Europe in 1700 38
Basra
  Nestorian and Monophysite
    Churches 8
  Spread of Islam 12
Batang
  1920 missions 48
Bath
  Great Awakening 42
Bathurst
  Africa 1800–1914 46
Battle Creek
  New religious movements 50
Bat'umi
  Russia today 58
Baudiuen
  Jews oppressed 23
Beaufort
  Great Awakening 42
Beauvais
  Friars 26
Bebenhausen
  Cistercian monasticism 21
Bec
  European universities 25
Beijing
  Nestorian and Monophysite
    Churches 8
  Missions to the Mongols 26
  Catholic missions 35
  1920 missions 48
Beirut
  Early Christian communities
    2
  American missions 45
Beizhili
  1920 missions 48
Belakut
  Cistercian monasticism 21
Belém
  Catholic missions 35, 39
Belgian Congo
  Protestant mission stations
    1925 55
Belgorod
  Eastern Orthodox Church
    c. 1000 17
  Kievan Rus' 18
Belgrade
  Byzantium under threat 13
  Great Schism 19
Belo Horizonte
  Latin America 1900- 54
Beloozero
  Eastern Orthodox Church
    c. 1000 17
  Muscovy 29
Belozersk
  Eastern Orthodox Church
    c. 1000 17
Belyatovo
  Medieval heresy 28
Benevento
  Charlemagne's empire 15
  The West in 1500 30
Benghazi
  Africa 1800–1914 46
Benguela
  Africa to 1800 44
Berenice
  Jewish communities 3
  Christianity by AD 300 4
Bergen
  Pietism 40
Berlin
  Jews oppressed 23

Pietism 40
Bermondsey
  Cluniac monasticism 20
Bern
  Friars 26
  Reformation Europe 32
  Catholic Reformation 33
  Christian Europe in 1700 38
Beroea
  Christianity by AD 100 3
  Christianity by AD 300 4
  Justinian's empire 11
Besançon
  European universities 25
  Medieval heresy 28
  The West in 1500 30
Beth Shan
  Early Christian communities
    2
Bethel
  Early Christian communities
    2
Bethlehem
  Early Christian communities
    2
  Christianity by AD 300 4
  Constantine the Great 5
  Spread of monasticism 10
  Pilgrimage routes 24
Bethphage
  Pilgrimage routes 24 inset
Bethsaida
  Pilgrimage routes 24 inset
Bethsaida-Julias
  Early Christian communities
    2
Betogabris
  Early Christian communities
    2
Bettbrunn
  Pilgrimage routes 24
Bialystok
  Jews oppressed 23
Birka
  Early missions in the
    Christian West 14
Birmingham
  Ecumenical meetings 56
Bius les Barronnies
  Jews oppressed 23
Blantyre
  Africa 1800–1914 46
Bobbio
  Spread of monasticism 10
  Early missions in the
    Christian West 14
  Charlemagne's empire 15
Bodmin
  British Church c. 800 16
Bogenburg
  Pilgrimage routes 24
Bogotá
  Catholic missions 35, 39
  Latin America 1900- 54
Bolivia
  Latin America 1900- 54
  Protestant mission stations
    1925 55
Bologna
  European universities 25
  Friars 26
  Medieval heresy 28
Bordeaux
  Charlemagne's empire 15
  European universities 25
  The West in 1500 30

Charles V 31
  Catholic Reformation 33
Borneo
  American missions 45
  Missions to Asia 47
  Protestant mission stations
    1925 55
Borovsk
  Muscovy 29
Borsmonoster
  Cistercian monasticism 21
Bosporos
  Eastern Orthodox Church
    c. 1000 17
Boston
  North America in 1750 41
  Second Awakening 43
  Catholicism in the U.S.A. 49
  New religious movements 50
Bostra
  Early Christian communities
    2
  Monophysite Church 7
  Justinian's empire 11
Boulogne
  Pilgrimage routes 24
Bourges
  Early missions in the
    Christian West 14
  Jews oppressed 23
  European universities 25
  The West in 1500 30
  Charles V 31
  Catholic Reformation 33
Braga
  Church in the West in the
    sixth century 9
  The West in 1500 30
Brasilia
  Latin America 1900- 54
Brazil
  Latin America 1900- 54
  Protestant mission stations
    1925 55
Brazzaville
  Africa 1800–1914 46
Brechin
  British Church c. 800 16
Bremen
  Early missions in the
    Christian West 14
  Charlemagne's empire 15
  Friars 26
  The West in 1500 30
  Charles V 31
Breslau
  Jews oppressed 23
Brest-Litovsk
  Jews oppressed 23
Brindisi
  Spread of Islam 12
  Byzantium under threat 13
  Crusades 22
  The West in 1500 30
Brioude
  Pilgrimage routes 24
Brisbane
  Australasia 53
Bristol
  Medieval heresy 28
British Guiana
  Protestant mission stations
    1925 55
Brogne
  Cluniac monasticism 20

Bruges
  Pilgrimage routes 24
Brünn
  Catholic Reformation 33
Brunswick (Germany)
  Pietism 40
Brunswick (USA)
  American missions 45
Brussels
  Jews oppressed 23
  The West in 1500 30
Buda
  European universities 25
Buenos Aires
  Catholic missions 35, 39
  Latin America 1900- 54
Buffalo
  Second Awakening 43
Bukhara
  Spread of Islam 12
Bukowo
  Cistercian monasticism 21
Bundaberg
  Australasia 53
Burdigala
  Christianity by AD 300 4
  Arianism 6
Burgos
  Jews oppressed 23
  The West in 1500 30
  Charles V 31
Burma
  Missions to Asia 47
Bury St Edmunds
  Jews oppressed 23
Busan
  Ecumenical meetings 56
Busta Gallorum
  Justinian's empire 11
Byblos
  Early Christian communities
    2
Byzantium
  Jewish communities 3
  Christianity by AD 300 4
  see also Constantinople

Cabasa
  Monophysite church 7
Cabinda
  Catholic missions 35
Cacheo
  Catholic missions 35
Caesarea
  Christianity by AD 300 4
  Arianism 6
  Monophysite Church 7
  Spread of monasticism 10
  Justinian's empire 11
  Byzantium under threat 13
  Pilgrimage routes 24 inset
Caesarea Maritima
  Early Christian communities
    2
Caesarea Mazaca
  Christianity by AD 100 3
Caesarea Philippi
  Early Christian communities
    2
Cagliari
  Charlemagne's empire 15
  The West in 1500 30
  Catholic Reformation 33
Cahors
  European universities 25

Cuenca
  Jews oppressed 23
  Catholic missions 35
  Latin America 1900- 54
Cuiabá
  Catholic missions 39
  Latin America 1900- 54
Cumberland Gap
  Second Awakening 43
Cuzco
  Catholic missions 35, 39
  Latin America 1900- 54
Cyrene
  Christianity by AD 100 3
  Christianity by AD 300 4
  Constantine the Great 5
Cyrrhus
  Pilgrimage routes 24
Czernowitz
  Russia today 58

Dallas
  Catholicism in the U.S.A. 49
Daman
  Missions to Asia 47
Damascus
  Early Christian communities
    2
  Christianity by AD 100 3
  Christianity by AD 300 4
  Arianism 6
  Monophysite church 7
  Nestorian and Monophysite
    Churches 8
  Justinian's empire 11
  Spread of Islam 12
  Byzantium under threat 13
  Crusades 22
  Pilgrimage routes 24 inset
  Missions to the Mongols 26
Danzig
  Charles V 31
  Europe after 1648 34
  Christian Europe in 1700 38
Dara
  Monophysite church 7
Darnis
  Monophysite church 7
Darwin
  Australasia 53
Deer
  British Church c. 800 16
Delaware Valley
  Great Awakening 42
Denkendorf
  Pietism 40
Derbe
  Christianity by AD 100 3
  Christianity by AD 300 4
Derbent
  Apostles and tradition 1
Derby
  Medieval heresy 28
Derry
  Charlemagne's empire 15
  British Church c. 800 16
Detroit
  Catholicism in the U.S.A. 49
Deventer
  Jews oppressed 23
  Medieval heresy 28
Diamantina
  Latin America 1900- 54
Dieppe
  Pilgrimage routes 24

Dijon
  Cluniac monasticism 20
Dillingen
  Catholic Reformation 33
Dinas Powys
  British Church c. 800 16
Diocaesarea
  Justinian's empire 11
Dionysias
  Early Christian communities
    2
Djibouti
  Africa 1800–1914 46
Doberan
  Cistercian monasticism 21
Dôle
  European universities 25
Dominican Republic
  Latin America 1900- 54
Dora
  Jewish communities 2
Dorchester
  British Church c. 800 16
Dorpat
  Kievan Rus' 18
Dorylaeum
  Crusades 22
Douai
  Catholic Reformation 33
Dover (Delaware)
  North America in 1750 41
  Great Awakening 42
Dover (England)
  Medieval heresy 28
Downpatrick
  British Church c. 800 16
  Pilgrimage routes 24
Dresden
  Reformation Europe 32
  Catholic Reformation 33
  Christian Europe in 1700 38
Dublin
  The West in 1500 30
Dubrovnik
  Friars 26
Dubuque
  Catholicism in the U.S.A. 49
Dumio
  Church in The West in the
    sixth century 9
Dunblane
  British Church c. 800 16
Dunedin
  Australasia 53
Dunkeld
  British Church c. 800 16
Dunn
  Pentecostalism 51
Dunwich
  Early missions in the
    Christian West 14
  British Church c. 800 16
Dura Europos
  Christianity by AD 300 4
Durango
  Catholic missions 35
Durban
  Africa 1800–1914 46
Durocortorum
  Christianity by AD 300 4
Dutch East Indies
  Missions to Asia 47
Dyrrachium
  Justinian's empire 11
  Eastern Orthodox Church
    c. 1000 17

Ebenezer
  New religious movements 50
Ebersburg
  Cluniac monasticism 20
Echternach
  Spread of monasticism 10
  Early missions in the
    Christian West 14
Ecuador
  Latin America 1900- 54
  Protestant mission stations
    1925 55
Edessa
  Christianity by AD 100 3
  Christianity by AD 300 4
  Constantine the Great 5
  Arianism 6
  Monophysite church 7
  Nestorian and Monophysite
    Churches 8
  Justinian's empire 11
  Spread of Islam 12
  Byzantium under threat 13
  Crusades 22
  Missions to the Mongols 26
Edinburgh
  Friars 26
  Catholic Reformation 33
  Ecumenical meetings 56
Edrei
  Early Christian communities
    2
Eger
  Jews oppressed 23
Egypt
  Africa 1800–1914 46
  Protestant mission stations
    1925 55
Eichstätt
  Early missions in the
    Christian West 14
  Pilgrimage routes 24
Einsiedeln
  Cluniac monasticism 20
El Paso
  Catholicism in the U.S.A. 49
El Salvador
  Latin America 1900- 54
Elista
  Russia today 58
Elizabeth
  Great Awakening 42
Elmham
  British Church c. 800 16
Elmina
  Africa to 1800 44
Elne
  Church in The West in the
    sixth century 9
Elvira
  Christianity by AD 300 4
Ely
  British Church c. 800 16
Embrun
  The West in 1500 30
Emesa
  Christianity by AD 300 4
  Monophysite church 7
Emly
  British Church c. 800 16
Emmaus
  Early Christian communities
    2
  Pilgrimage routes 24 inset

En-gedi
  Jewish communities 2
Ensisheim
  Jews oppressed 23
Ephesus
  Christianity by AD 300 4
  Arianism 6
  Monophysite church 7
  Nestorian and Monophysite
    Churches 8
  Justinian's empire 11
  Spread of Islam 12
  Byzantium under threat 13
  Charlemagne's empire 15
  Eastern Orthodox Church
    c. 1000 17
  Crusades 22
  Pilgrimage routes 24
  The West in 1500 30
Erfurt
  Jews oppressed 23
Eritrea
  Africa 1800–1914 46
Esbus
  Early Christian communities
    2
Esrom
  Cistercian monasticism 21
Esztergom
  Pilgrimage routes 24
Ethiopia
  Apostles and tradition 1
  Africa to 1800 44
  Africa 1800–1914 46
Euchaita
  Pilgrimage routes 24

Faenza
  Medieval heresy 28
Farfa
  Charlemagne's empire 15
  Cluniac monasticism 20
Fayette
  New religious movements 50
Fécamp
  Cluniac monasticism 20
Fernando Po
  Africa to 1800 44
Ferns
  British Church c. 800 16
Ferrara
  European universities 25
  Medieval heresy 28
Feuchtwangen
  Cluniac monasticism 20
Fez
  Jews oppressed 23
Fleury
  Cluniac monasticism 20
  European universities 25
Florence
  European universities 25
  Friars 26
  Medieval heresy 28
  The West in 1500 30
  Charles V 31
  Catholic Reformation 33
Florida
  Catholicism in the U.S.A. 49
  African-American churches
    52
Fontenay
  Cistercian monasticism 21
Fontfroide
  Cistercian monasticism 21

Foochow
  Missions to the Mongols 26
Forcalquier
  Jews oppressed 23
Fortaleza
  Latin America 1900- 54
Fossanova
  Cistercian monasticism 21
Fountains
  Cistercian monasticism 21
Frankfurt
  Charlemagne's empire 15
  Jews oppressed 23
  Pietism 40
Fredericksburg
  North America in 1750 41
Freetown
  Africa to 1800 44
  Africa 1800–1914 46
Freiburg
  European universities 25
Freising
  Early missions in the
    Christian West 14
Fruttuaria
  Cluniac monasticism 20
Fujian
  1920 missions 48
Fukuoka
  1920 missions 48
Fulda
  Spread of monasticism 10
  Early missions in the
    Christian West 14
  Charlemagne's empire 15
  Cluniac monasticism 20
  Jews oppressed 23
  Pilgrimage routes 24
  European universities 25
  Catholic Reformation 33
Funai
  Catholic missions 35
Funchal
  Catholic missions 35
Furness
  Cistercian monasticism 21
Fuzhou
  Missions to Asia 47

Gadara
  Early Christian communities
    2
  Pilgrimage routes 24 inset
Galich
  Eastern Orthodox Church
    c. 1000 17
  Kievan Rus' 18
  Muscovy 29
Galveston
  Catholicism in the U.S.A. 49
Gambia
  Africa 1800–1914 46
Gangra
  Justinian's empire 11
Gansu
  1920 missions 48
Gasper River
  Second Awakening 43
Gaza
  Jewish communities 2
  Christianity by AD 100 3
  Spread of monasticism 10
  Pilgrimage routes 24 inset
Genessaret
  Pilgrimage routes 24 inset

Jenne
  Africa to 1800 44
Jericho
  Early Christian communities
    2
  Pilgrimage routes 24 inset
Jerusalem
  Apostles and tradition 1
  Early Christian communities
    2
  Christianity by AD 100 3
  Christianity by AD 300 4
  Constantine the Great 5
  Arianism 6
  Nestorian and Monophysite
    Churches 8
  Spread of monasticism 10
  Justinian's empire 11
  Byzantium under threat 13
  Eastern Orthodox Church
    c. 1000 17
  Great schism 19
  Crusades 22
  Pilgrimage routes 24
  Missions to the Mongols 26
  Ecumenical meetings 56
Jiangsu
  1920 missions 48
Johannesburg
  Africa 1800–1914 46
Jonvelle
  Medieval heresy 28
Joppa
  Early Christian communities
    2
  Christianity by AD 100 3
  Christianity by AD 300 4
Julias
  Pilgrimage routes 24 inset
Jurev
  Kievan Rus' 18
Justiniana Prima
  Justinian's empire 11

Kabul
  Spread of Islam 12
Kadamattan
  Nestorian and Monophysite
    Churches 8
Kagoshima
  1920 missions 48
Kairouan
  Spread of Islam 12
Kalgan
  Nestorian and Monophysite
    Churches 8
Kalinin
  Russia today 58
Kalisz
  Jews oppressed 23
Kalocsa
  The West in 1500 30
Kaluga
  Russia today 58
Kampala
  Africa 1800–1914 46
Kandahar
  Spread of Islam 12
Kano
  Africa to 1800 44
Kansas
  Denominations in 2000 57
Kansas City
  New religious movements 50

Karakorum
  Nestorian and Monophysite
    Churches 8
  Missions to the Mongols 26
Kashgar
  Nestorian and Monophysite
    Churches 8
  Missions to the Mongols 26
Kashmir
  Missions to Asia 47
Kazan
  Muscovy 29
Kells
  Charlemagne's empire 15
Kentucky
  Second Awakening 43
  Denominations in 2000 57
Kerman
  Missions to the Mongols 26
Khartoum
  Africa 1800–1914 46
Khiva
  Spread of Islam 12
Khotan
  Nestorian and Monophysite
    Churches 8
Kiev
  Eastern Orthodox Church
    c. 1000 17
  Great schism 19
  Jews oppressed 23
  Missions to the Mongols 26
  Muscovy 29
  Charles V 31
  Russia today 58
Kildare
  British Church c. 800 16
Kilfenora
  British Church c. 800 16
Kimberley
  Africa 1800–1914 46
Kinston
  African-American Churches
    52
Kirov
  Russia today 58
Kirtland
  New religious movements 50
Kischenev
  Russia today 58
Kishinev
  Jews oppressed 23
Kobe
  1920 missions 48
Koblenz
  Jews oppressed 23
Konya
  Missions to the Mongols 26
Korea
  1920 missions 48
  Protestant mission stations
    1925 55
Korntal
  Pietism 40
Kostroma
  Muscovy 29
  Russia today 58
Krakov (Krakow)
  Early missions in the
    Christian West 14
  Eastern Orthodox Church
    c. 1000 17
  Kievan Rus' 18
  Jews oppressed 23
  Pilgrimage routes 24
  European universities 25

Charles V 31
  Reformation Europe 32
  Catholic Reformation 33
  Europe after 1648 34
  Christian Europe in 1700 38
Krasnodar
  Russia today 58
Kufa
  Spread of Islam 12
Kumasi
  Africa 1800–1914 46
Kursk
  Eastern Orthodox Church
    c. 1000 17
  Russia today 58
Kuruman
  Africa 1800–1914 46
K'ut'aisi
  Russia today 58
Kutná Hora
  Medieval heresy 28
Kuttenberg
  Catholic Reformation 33
Kyushu
  1920 missions 48

La Chaise Dieu
  European universities 25
La Charité
  Cluniac monasticism 20
La Ferté
  Cistercian monasticism 21
La Flèche
  Catholic Reformation 33
La Paz
  Catholic missions 35, 39
  Latin America 1900- 54
La Vega
  Catholic missions 35
Lad
  Cistercian monasticism 21
Ladoga
  Eastern Orthodox Church
    c. 1000 17
  Muscovy 29
Lagos
  Africa to 1800 44
  Africa 1800–1914 46
Lahore
  Missions to Asia 47
Lake Mohonk
  Ecumenical meetings 56
Lalibela
  Spread of monasticism 10
Lambarene
  Africa 1800–1914 46
Lamu
  Africa to 1800 44
Landévennec
  Charlemagne's empire 15
Laodicea
  Christianity by AD 100 3
  Christianity by AD 300 4
  Eastern Orthodox Church
    c. 1000 17
Laon
  Church in The West in the
    sixth century 9
  European universities 25
Laong
  Philippines 36
Larissa
  Justinian's empire 11
Las Huelgas
  Cistercian monasticism 21

Las Palmas
  Catholic missions 35
Latmos
  Spread of monasticism 10
Lauriacum
  Christianity by AD 300 4
Le Puy
  Pilgrimage routes 24
Leau Novellas
  Pilgrimage routes 24
Lebaba
  Early Christian communities
    2
Legio
  Early Christian communities
    2
Legnano
  Medieval heresy 28
Leicester
  British Church c. 800 16
Leiden
  Catholic Reformation 33
Leipzig
  European universities 25
Lemberg
  Jews oppressed 23
Léopoldville
  Africa 1800–1914 46
Leptis Magna
  Christianity by AD 300 4
  Justinian's empire 11
Lérida
  Jews oppressed 23
  European universities 25
  Friars 26
  Medieval heresy 28
Lérins
  Spread of monasticism 10
Lewes
  Cluniac monasticism 20
Lhasa
  Missions to the Mongols 26
Liaoyang
  Nestorian and Monophysite
    Churches 8
Liberia
  Africa 1800–1914 46
  Protestant mission stations
    1925 55
Lichfield
  British Church c. 800 16
Liège
  Cluniac monasticism 20
  Medieval heresy 28
  Catholic Reformation 33
Ligugé
  Spread of monasticism 10
Lima
  Catholic missions 35, 39
  Latin America 1900- 54
Limasol
  Crusades 22
Limoges
  Friars 26
Linares
  Catholic missions 35
Lincoln
  British Church c. 800 16
  Medieval heresy 28
Lindisfarne
  Spread of monasticism 10
  Early missions in the
    Christian West 14
  Charlemagne's empire 15
  British Church c. 800 16

Linköping
  Pietism 40
Lisbon
  Charlemagne's empire 15
  European universities 25
  The West in 1500 30
  Charles V 31
  Catholic Reformation 33
  Africa to 1800 44
Lismore
  British Church c. 800 16
Livorno
  Jews oppressed 23
Llanilltud Fawr
  British Church c. 800 16
Llantwit
  Spread of monasticism 10
Loanda
  Catholic missions 35
Lodz
  Jews oppressed 23
Løgum
  Cistercian monasticism 21
Londinium (see London)
  Constantine the Great 5
London
  Early missions in the
    Christian West 14
  Crusades 22
  Pilgrimage routes 24
  Medieval heresy 28
  Catholic Reformation 33
  Pietism 40
  Jews oppressed 232
  Protestant mission stations
    1925 556
Longpont
  Cistercian monasticism 21
Loreto
  Pilgrimage routes 24
Lorsch
  Cluniac monasticism 20
Los Angeles
  New religious movements 50
  Pentecostalism 51
  African-American Churches
    52
Lough Corib
  Early missions in the
    Christian West 14
Lough Derg
  Pilgrimage routes 24
Louisiana
  Catholicism in the U.S.A. 49
  African-American Churches
    52
Lourdes
  Philippines 36
Louvain
  Jews oppressed 23
  European universities 25
Luanda
  Africa to 1800 44
Lübeck
  Pilgrimage routes 24
  Friars 26
Lubiaz
  Cistercian monasticism 21
Lublin
  Jews oppressed 23
  Friars 26
Lucca
  Pilgrimage routes 24
Lucerne
  Jews oppressed 23

Muscovy 29
Mursa
  Jewish communities 3
  Christianity by AD 300 4
Muscat
  Spread of Islam 12
Mylapore
  Catholic missions 35
Myra
  Christianity by AD 100 3
  Christianity by AD 300 4
  Spread of monasticism 10
  Justinian's empire 11

Nag Hammadi
  Christianity by AD 300 4
Nagasaki
  1920 missions 48
Nagoya
  1920 missions 48
Nain
  Pilgrimage routes 24 inset
Nairobi
  Africa 1800–1914 46
  Ecumenical meetings 56
Najran
  Spread of Islam 12
Nanjing
  1920 missions 48
Nanking
  Missions to Asia 47
Nantes
  Charlemagne's empire 15
  Jews oppressed 23
  European universities 25
Napier
  Australasia 53
Naples
  Byzantium under threat 13
  Charlemagne's empire 15
  Great schism 19
  Jews oppressed 23
  Pilgrimage routes 24
  Friars 26
  The West in 1500 30
  Catholic Reformation 33
Narbonne
  Early missions in the
    Christian West 14
  Charlemagne's empire 15
  Medieval heresy 28
Narnaul
  Russia today 58
Nashville
  Catholicism in the U.S.A. 49
Natal
  Latin America 1900- 54
Navekath
  Nestorian and Monophysite
    Churches 8
Nazareth
  Early Christian communities
    2
  Pilgrimage routes 24 inset
Nazianzus
  Christianity by AD 300 4
  Arianism 6
Neapolis
  Early Christian communities
    2
  Christianity by AD 300 4
Nebraska
  Denominations in 2000 57
Nehavend
  Spread of Islam 12

Nendrum
  British Church c. 800 16
Neocaesarea
  Christianity by AD 300 4
  Spread of monasticism 10
  Justinian's empire 11
  Eastern Orthodox Church
    c. 1000 17
Neshaminy
  Great Awakening 42
Neuhaus
  Catholic Reformation 33
Neustadt
  Medieval heresy 28
Nevada
  Denominations in 2000 57
Nevers
  Church in The West in the
    sixth century 9
New Bern
  North America in 1750 41
  Great Awakening 42
New Delhi
  Ecumenical meetings 56
New Guinea
  Missions to Asia 47
  Protestant mission stations
    1925 55
New Harmony
  New religious movements 50
New Haven
  Protestant settlers 37
  North America in 1750 41
  Second Awakening 43
New Jersey
  Denominations in 2000 57
New Mexico
  Denominations in 2000 57
New Orleans
  Catholic missions 35
  Catholicism in the U.S.A. 49
  Pentecostalism 51
New South Wales
  Australasia 53
New York
  Protestant settlers 37
  North America in 1750 41
  Catholicism in the U.S.A. 49
  New religious movements 50
  African-American Churches
    52
  Ecumenical meetings 56
  Denominations in 2000 57
New Zealand
  Australasia 53
  Protestant mission stations
    1925 55
Newport
  Protestant settlers 37
Newton
  Second Awakening 43
Nicaea
  Christianity by AD 300 4
  Constantine the Great 5
  Arianism 6
  Justinian's empire 11
  Spread of Islam 12
  Byzantium under threat 13
  Eastern Orthodox Church
    c. 1000 17
  Crusades 22
Nice
  Spread of Islam 12
Nicomedia
  Christianity by AD 300 4
  Constantine the Great 5

Arianism 6
  Justinian's empire 11
  Crusades 22
Nicopolis
  Christianity by AD 100 3
  Christianity by AD 300 4
  Justinian's empire 11
  Jews oppressed 23
Niebla
  Church in The West in the
    sixth century 9
Nigeria
  Africa 1800–1914 46
  Protestant mission stations
    1925 55
Nineveh
  Nestorian and Monophysite
    Churches 8
Ningbo
  Missions to Asia 47
Nish
  Crusades 22
  Medieval heresy 28
Nishapur
  Nestorian and Monophysite
    Churches 8
  Spread of Islam 12
Nishni
  Eastern Orthodox Church
    c. 1000 17
Nisibis
  Nestorian and Monophysite
    Churches 8
Nitria
  Spread of monasticism 10
Nizhny Novgorod
  Kievan Rus' 18
  Muscovy 29
Nola
  Spread of monasticism 10
Nördlingen
  Jews oppressed 23
Norfolk
  North America in 1750 41
  Great Awakening 42
North Carolina
  African-American Churches
    52
  Denominations in 2000 57
North Dakota
  Denominations in 2000 57
Northampton
  Great Awakening 42
Norwich
  Jews oppressed 23
  Friars 26
  Medieval heresy 28
Novgorod
  Eastern Orthodox Church
    c. 1000 17
  Great schism 19
  Muscovy 29
  Russia today 58
Novgorod the Great
  Eastern Orthodox Church
    c. 1000 17
Nuremberg
  Jews oppressed 23
  Reformation Europe 32
  Catholic Reformation 33
  Europe after 1648 34
  Christian Europe in 1700 38
Nursia
  Spread of monasticism 10
Nutten Island
  Protestant settlers 37

Nyssa
  Christianity by AD 300 4
  Arianism 6

Oaxaca
  Catholic missions 35
Obazine
  Cistercian monasticism 21
Odilienberg
  Pilgrimage routes 24
Ohio
  Protestant mission stations
    1925 557
Oklahoma
  Denominations in 2000 57
Olinda
  Catholic missions 39
  Latin America 1900- 54
Oliwa
  Cistercian monasticism 21
Olmutz
  Eastern Orthodox Church
    c. 1000 17
Olon-Sume-in Tor
  Nestorian and Monophysite
    Churches 8
Olympus
  Spread of monasticism 10
Omsk
  Russia today 58
Oneida
  New religious movements 50
Oran
  Jews oppressed 23
Orange
  Jews oppressed 23
  European universities 25
Oregon
  Denominations in 2000 57
Orel
  Russia today 58
Oristano
  The West in 1500 30
Orleans
  Charlemagne's empire 15
  Cistercian monasticism 21
  European universities 25
Ormuz
  Missions to the Mongols 26
Oropa
  Pilgrimage routes 24
Orvieto
  Medieval heresy 28
Osaka
  1920 missions 48
Oslo
  see also Christiana
Otranto
  The West in 1500 30
Otrar
  Missions to the Mongols 26
Outer Mongolia
  1920 missions 48
Oxford
  European universities 25
  Friars 26
  Medieval heresy 28
  Pietism 40
  Ecumenical meetings 56
Oxyrhynchus
  Christianity by AD 300 4
  Monophysite church 7

Paderborn
  Charlemagne's empire 15

Padua
  Pilgrimage routes 24
  European universities 25
  Friars 26
Palencia
  European universities 25
Palermo
  Spread of Islam 12
  Great schism 19
  Friars 26
  The West in 1500 30
  Catholic Reformation 33
Palestine
  Early Christian communities
    2
  American missions 45
Palma
  Jews oppressed 23
  European universities 25
Palmyra
  Christianity by AD 300 4
  Justinian's empire 11
Pamplona
  Latin America 1900- 54
Panama
  European universities 25
  Catholic missions 39
  Latin America 1900- 54
Paneas
  Pilgrimage routes 24 inset
Paoay
  Philippines 36
Paphos
  Christianity by AD 100 3
Paraguay
  Latin America 1900- 54
Paraná
  Latin America 1900- 54
Paris
  Charlemagne's empire 15
  Cluniac monasticism 20
  Crusades 22
  Jews oppressed 23
  Pilgrimage routes 24
  European universities 25
  Friars 26
  Missions to the Mongols 26
  Medieval heresy 28
  Charles V 31
  Reformation Europe 32
  Catholic Reformation 33
Parma
  Medieval heresy 28
  Catholic Reformation 33
Passau
  Early missions in the
    Christian West 14
  Charlemagne's empire 15
  Jews oppressed 23
Patmos
  Apostles and tradition 1
  Christianity by AD 100 3
  Pilgrimage routes 24
Patrae
  Apostles and tradition 1
Patras
  Pilgrimage routes 24
Pavia
  Charlemagne's empire 15
  European universities 25
  Medieval heresy 28
Pécs
  European universities 25
  Friars 26

Pella
    Early Christian communities
        2
    Christianity by AD 300 4
Pelusium
    Jewish communities 3
    Monophysite church 7
Pennsylvania
    Great Awakening 42
    Denominations in 2000 57
Pensa
    Russia today 58
Pereyaslavi
    Eastern Orthodox Church
        c. 1000 17
    Kievan Rus' 18
Pereyaslavl-Zaleski
    Muscovy 29
Perga
    Christianity by AD 300 4
Pergamum
    Christianity by AD 100 3
    Christianity by AD 300 4
Perge
    Christianity by AD 100 3
    Monophysite church 7
Perpignan
    European universities 25
Persepolis
    Spread of Islam 12
Persia
    Apostles and tradition 1
    Nestorian and Monophysite
        Churches 8
    American missions 45
Perth
    Australasia 53
Peru
    Latin America 1900- 54
Perugia
    European universities 25
    Friars 26
Pervilis
    Missions to the Mongols 26
Peshawar
    Missions to Asia 47
Peterborough
    British Church c. 800 16
    European universities 25
Petra
    Arianism 6
    Justinian's empire 11
Pforta
    Cistercian monasticism 21
Philadelphia
    Early Christian communities
        2
    Christianity by AD 100 3
    Christianity by AD 300 4
    Protestant settlers 37
    North America in 1750 41
    Great Awakening 42
    American missions 45
    New religious movements 50
    African-American Churches
        52
Philippi
    Christianity by AD 100 3
    Christianity by AD 300 4
Philippines
    Missions to Asia 47
    Protestant mission stations
        1925 55
Philippopolis
    Justinian's empire 11

Eastern Orthodox Church
    c. 1000 17
    Medieval heresy 28
Piacenza
    European universities 25
Pinsk
    Eastern Orthodox Church
        c. 1000 17
    Kievan Rus' 18
    Jews oppressed 23
Pisa
    Crusades 22
    European universities 25
    Medieval heresy 28
Pispir
    Spread of monasticism 10
Pittsburgh
    New religious movements 50
Plymouth
    North America in 1750 41
Poblet
    Cistercian monasticism 21
Poetovio
    Christianity by AD 300 4
Poitiers
    Spread of monasticism 10
    Crusades 22
    Pilgrimage routes 24
    European universities 25
Polotsk
    Kievan Rus' 18
    Muscovy 29
Poltava
    Russia today 58
Pompeii
    Christianity by AD 100 3
Pondicherry
    Missions to Asia 47
Pontigny
    Cistercian monasticism 21
Popoyan
    Catholic missions 35
Portsmouth
    North America in 1750 41
Portuguese Guinea
    Africa 1800–1914 46
Posen
    Jews oppressed 23
P'ot'i
    Russia today 58
Prague
    Early missions in the
        Christian West 14
    Eastern Orthodox Church
        c. 1000 17
    Crusades 22
    Jews oppressed 23
    Pilgrimage routes 24
    European universities 25
    Friars 26
    Medieval heresy 28
    The West in 1500 30
    Charles V 31
    Reformation Europe 32
    Catholic Reformation 33
    Christian Europe in 1700 38
Pressburg
    European universities 25
Pretoria
    Africa 1800–1914 46
Pribram
    Pilgrimage routes 24
Providence
    Protestant settlers 37
    North America in 1750 41

Prusa
    Jewish communities 3
Pskov
    Kievan Rus' 18
    Muscovy 29
    Russia today 58
Ptolemais
    Early Christian communities
        2
    Monophysite church 7
    Justinian's empire 11
    Pilgrimage routes 24 inset
Puebla
    Catholic missions 35
Puerto Rico
    Latin America 1900- 54
Punta Arenas
    Latin America 1900- 54
Pupping
    Medieval heresy 28
Puteoli
    Christianity by AD 300 4

Quanzhou
    Nestorian and Monophysite
        Churches 8
Quebec
    Catholic missions 35
Quelimane
    Africa to 1800 44
Quilon
    Nestorian and Monophysite
        Churches 8
Quito
    Catholic missions 35, 39
    Latin America 1900- 54

Radom
    Jews oppressed 23
Ragusa
    Charlemagne's empire 15
    The West in 1500 30
Raleigh
    African-American Churches
        52
Rankweil
    Pilgrimage routes 24
Raritan Valley
    Great Awakening 42
Ratiaria
    Justinian's empire 11
Ratisbon
    Crusades 22
Ravenna
    Christianity by AD 100 3
    Constantine the Great 5
    Arianism 6
    Church in The West in the
        sixth century 9
    Justinian's empire 11
    Byzantium under threat 13
    Early missions in the
        Christian West 14
    Charlemagne's empire 15
    European universities 25
    The West in 1500 30
Ravensburg
    Jews oppressed 23
Recife
    Catholic missions 35
    Latin America 1900- 54
Red River
    Second Awakening 43
Regensburg
    Early missions in the
        Christian West 14

Cluniac monasticism 20
Crusades 22
Jews oppressed 23
European universities 25
Medieval heresy 28
Reichenau
    Early missions in the
        Christian West 14
Remis
    Arianism 6
Renkum
    Pilgrimage routes 24
Rennes
    Charlemagne's empire 15
Rewardashir
    Nestorian and Monophysite
        Churches 8
Rey
    Spread of Islam 12
Rhages
    Nestorian and Monophysite
        Churches 8
    Spread of Islam 12
Rhegium
    Christianity by AD 300 4
Rheims
    Church in The West in the
        sixth century 9
    Early missions in the
        Christian West 14
    European universities 25
    The West in 1500 30
    Catholic Reformation 33
Rhode Island
    Protestant settlers 37
Rhodes
    Justinian's empire 11
    Eastern Orthodox Church
        c. 1000 17
Riazan
    Muscovy 29
Ribe
    Early missions in the
        Christian West 14
Riberao Prêto
    Latin America 1900- 54
Richmond
    North America in 1750 41
    Great Awakening 42
    Catholicism in the U.S.A. 49
Rievaulx
    Cistercian monasticism 21
    European universities 25
Riga
    Eastern Orthodox Church
        c. 1000 17
    The West in 1500 30
    Christian Europe in 1700 38
    Pietism 40
    Russia today 58
Rimini
    Medieval heresy 28
Rimmon
    Early Christian communities
        2
Rio de Janeiro
    Catholic missions 35, 39
Rio Muni
    Africa 1800–1914 46
Ripon
    Early missions in the
        Christian West 14
    British Church c. 800 16
Rocamadour
    Pilgrimage routes 24

Roche
    Cistercian monasticism 21
Rochester
    Early missions in the
        Christian West 14
    British Church c. 800 16
Rochester (New York)
    Second Awakening 43
Rome
    Apostles and tradition 1
    Christianity by AD 100 3
    Christianity by AD 300 4
    Constantine the Great 5
    Arianism 6
    Church in The West in the
        sixth century 9
    Spread of monasticism 10
    Justinian's empire 11
    Spread of Islam 12
    Byzantium under threat 13
    Early missions in the
        Christian West 14
    Charlemagne's empire 15
    Eastern Orthodox Church
        c. 1000 17
    Great schism 19
    Cluniac monasticism 20
    Crusades 22
    Jews oppressed 23
    Pilgrimage routes 24
    European universities 25
    Friars 26
    Missions to the Mongols 26
    Medieval heresy 28
    The West in 1500 30
    Charles V 31
    Catholic Reformation 33
    Catholic missions 35
    Ecumenical meetings 56
Rosario
    Latin America 1900- 54
Rosenthal
    Pilgrimage routes 24
Roskilde
    Early missions in the
        Christian West 14
    Friars 26
Rossano
    The West in 1500 30
Rostock
    European universities 25
Rostov
    Eastern Orthodox Church
        c. 1000 17
    Kievan Rus' 18
    Russia today 58
Rothenburg
    Jews oppressed 23
Rouen
    Early missions in the
        Christian West 14
    Cluniac monasticism 20
    Jews oppressed 23
    European universities 25
    The West in 1500 30
    Charles V 31
    Catholic Reformation 33
Rouffach
    Jews oppressed 23
Royaumont
    Cistercian monasticism 21
Russia
    Russia today 58
Ryazan
    Eastern Orthodox Church
        c. 1000 17

Index

Locators are page numbers, not map numbers